REA

ALLEN COUNTY PUBLIC LIBRARY
FRIENDS
OF A W9-CET-753

Nursing Homes
&
Assisted Living
Facilities

Your Practical Guide for
Making the RIGHT Decision

Linda H. Connell
Attorney at Law

SPHINX® PUBLISHING
AN IMPRINT OF SOURCEBOOKS, INC.®
NAPERVILLE, ILLINOIS
www.SphinxLegal.com

AUG 2 5 2004

Copyright © 2004 by Linda H. Connell
Cover and internal design © 2004 by Sourcebooks, Inc.
Cover images © 2004 by Photodisc

All rights reserved. No part of this book may be reproduced in any form or by any electronic or mechanical means including information storage and retrieval systems—except in the case of brief quotations embodied in critical articles or reviews—without permission in writing from its publisher, Sourcebooks, Inc.® Purchasers of the book are granted a license to use the forms contained herein for their own personal use. No claim of copyright is made in any government form reproduced herein.

First Edition: 2004

Published by: **Sphinx® Publishing, An Imprint of Sourcebooks, Inc.®**

Naperville Office
P. O. Box 4410
Naperville, Illinois 60567-4410
630-961-3900
Fax: 630-961-2168
www.sourcebooks.com
www.SphinxLegal.com

This publication is designed to provide accurate and authoritative information in regard to the subject matter covered. It is sold with the understanding that the publisher is not engaged in rendering legal, accounting, or other professional service. If legal advice or other expert assistance is required, the services of a competent professional person should be sought.

From a Declaration of Principles Jointly Adopted by a Committee of t he American Bar Association and a Committee of Publishers and Associations

This product is not a substitute for legal advice.

Disclaimer required by Texas statutes.

Library of Congress Cataloging-in-Publication Data
Connell, Linda H.
  Nursing homes & assisted living facilities : your practical guide for making the right decision / by Linda H. Connell.-- 1st ed.
      p. cm.
  Includes index.
  ISBN 1-57248-376-8 (pbk. : alk. paper)
  1. Older people--Institutional care--Decision making. 2. Older people--Care--Decision making. 3. Nursing home care--Decision making. 4. Nursing homes--Evaluation. 5. Old age homes--Evaluation. I. Title.

RA997.C6386 2004
362.61--dc22
                                                              2004012748

Printed and bound in the United States of America.
BG — 10 9 8 7 6 5 4 3 2 1

Contents

Active Adult Community
Independent Living/Retirement Community
Home Health Care
Assisted Living
Long-Term Skilled Care (Nursing) Facility
Continuing Care Retirement Communities
Adult Day Care
Respite Care
Hospice

Assessing the Need for a Lifestyle Change
The Resistant Resident
Family Issues
Advance Medical Directives
Medical Evaluation
Mental Health Evaluation
Geriatric Care Managers

Doctor Recommendations
Social Service Provider Recommendations
Senior Advocacy and Health Care Organizations
State Ombudsman

Acknowledgments

Many thanks go to Gail Haviland, Director of Activities and Volunteer Coordinator for Alden-Naperville Health Care and Rehabilitation Center and Phyllis Stamper, Director of Community Services for Alden Management Services, Inc., for their invaluable assistance in the writing of this book.

Introduction

Among the most difficult events an adult may have to endure is when a parent or other elderly loved one suffers an incapacitating injury or illness. A person who once was strong and independent, now can no longer care for him- or herself.

Any number of circumstances can lead to a senior suddenly having to undergo a momentous lifestyle change. Broken bones from a fall is a typical culprit. In other cases, the change may be more gradual, as with the onset of Alzheimer's disease or another illness. Sometimes, the cause is not catastrophic, but the senior just does not seem able to get around as well as he or she used to.

As unpleasant as it is to have to consider such occurrences, thousands of families every year have to deal with these issues for the first time. As a person approaches senior status, the related issues of lifestyle and long-term care may begin to loom. It is always a good idea for those with elderly family members to have some sort of plan in place before a significantly life-altering event occurs.

Probably the most difficult situation is when illness or injury strikes suddenly. A family may receive almost no notice that a family member is to be discharged from the hospital and may have to make an extremely difficult and important decision in a very short period of time, with precious little knowledge to assist them. That is the reason why having a senior-care plan ahead of time is so very important.

Nursing homes and assisted living facilities conjure up negative images in the minds of many people, who view such communities as dismal and depressing. Many people believe that these facilities are nothing more than a place for seniors to go and wait to die, but that notion simply is not accurate. Elderly individuals who need assistance with daily activities or skilled nursing care can actually lead fuller lives in these senior-oriented communities than they would at home, where they may be more limited in their activities and social interactions. Even their physical well-being may improve in care facilities, because their physical and emotional conditions, diet, socialization, and sleep patterns are being monitored on a regular basis. Moreover, it is a myth that individuals who are admitted to these facilities remain there for the rest of their lives. A number of assisted living and skilled care residents are eventually rehabilitated to the point in which they can live independently again.

With more and more Baby Boom-era individuals facing eldercare issues with their own parents as well as in their own and their spouses' lives, these perceptions are set to change. In 2001, according to the Centers for Disease Control (**www.cdc.gov**), more than 1.4 million Americans resided in almost 17,000 skilled nursing facilities. Another one million senior citizens live in various types of assisted living communities, where they receive help with some of the routine activities of daily living, but generally do not require much in the way of specialized health care. Those numbers are sure to increase as Baby Boomers reach the age of 65. That generation, with their demands for health care and lifestyle options that require as little compromise as possible, is driving a rapid change in the number and types of senior living arrangements. Other contributing factors are the ever-increasing body of knowledge with regard to particular medical conditions, such as Alzheimer's disease, as well as greater sensitivity to end-of-life issues.

These circumstances have given rise to specialized service providers. For example, skilled care facilities have been created that cater specifically to the needs of Alzheimer's disease patients and hospice care for the terminally ill. A number of skilled care and assisted living facilities offer adult day care to seniors who actually live at home with their grown children. Some facilities also offer respite care, which means they provide occasional care to home-living seniors in order to give the family members a break from their caregiving responsibilities. There are even facilities equipped to provide acute care to patients just out of surgery—in some cases, the patient comes directly to the facility from the operating room, receiving post-operative care entirely from the facility's health care staff.

Another result of the Baby Boom generation is that the overall quality of long-term care provided to seniors can be expected to improve in the future. This is because the aging of this very powerful demographic group will lead them to advocate for reform in the nursing home industry. When members of the Baby Boom population themselves begin residing in skilled care and assisted living communities, you can be sure they will expect to receive the best long-term care possible.

The good news is, there are positive influences currently at work in the long-term care industry; the bad news is, there are fiscal crises presently occurring in many state and local governments. Some municipalities and counties have had to reduce or end support services that their elderly residents have relied on, such as free or reduced-rate local transportation for seniors. Even more troublesome is the reality that states are cutting public aid spending that is essential to many long-term care residents. This in turn leads to cuts in staffing at eldercare facilities. Many experts on nursing home reform agree that the most pressing issue facing these facilities is inadequate nursing staff. An increase in the ratio of residents to staff usually corresponds to a decrease in the quality of care. Overworked nurses' aides struggle with greater workloads and residents receive less one-on-one care as the nursing staff is spread increasingly thin.

The variety of living arrangements and levels of care available to seniors today can be overwhelming. Choices range from completely independent living, to remaining in one's home with occasional outside hired help, to taking up residence in a retirement or health-care facility. Sometimes it is the senior who is able to consider the options, while in other cases the decision has to be made by family members.

In order to determine which lifestyle option is best, the first decision to make is the need for care. In other words, ask the following questions.

◆ How independent is the senior?
◆ What is the state of his or her physical and mental health?

If he or she is lucid and in good health, but cannot quite manage to perform the routine activities necessary for personal care, remaining at home without assistance simply may no longer be possible. This is not a determination that a family needs to make on its own. A comprehensive professional assessment of the senior can help ascertain whether a lifestyle change is warranted.

Once the family has the idea that some extra level of care is needed for the senior, the next issue is locating the best caregiver or facility. There are a number of questions that should be asked, and many factors to look at when determining which caregiver or facility is right for the senior. Of course, the main concern is that the resident receives the best possible care. It cannot be denied, however, that cost considerations eventually will have an acute effect on the lifestyle decision that is made. Some seniors have the ability to pay for long-term care out of private funds. Others may have some sort of long-term care insurance to cover some or all of these expenses. Many others, however, rely on public funds, typically in the form of Medicaid or Medicare assistance, to pay for their care.

After the decision is made to change the senior's current living arrangements and a suitable facility is located, the senior and the family must make the transition to the new lifestyle. There are many ways to help the adjustment period go smoothly and try to ensure that the living situation remains satisfactory to the senior and the family.

If at any time the resident or the family has a dispute with the facility's staff, the facility's policies, or with another resident, the facility should be responsive to the resident and family and should have a fair and consistent method of dealing with the complaint. If the family suspects that their loved one has suffered any kind of abuse while residing in the facility, whether caused by an employee or another resident, the abuse should be reported and addressed immediately. All facilities should have their own procedures for handling abuse complaints and every state has agencies specifically created for the prevention and correction of nursing home abuse.

Chapter 1

Senior Lifestyle Options

There are a number of options available when choosing the living arrangement and type of care needed for a senior. What follows are very general descriptions of the various types of communities available to seniors.

Each state has its own legal definition of and regulatory scheme for these communities. Some types of communities are not licensed by every state—some are not licensed at all. Federal regulations exist that govern long-term care facilities.

The United States Department of Health and Human Services has published regulations that apply to all skilled care facilities in this country. Each individual state must enforce the regulations in order to be eligible to receive various federal funds. As a result, each state has enacted its own set of regulations, which are at least as strict as, and in many cases more strict than, the federal regulations. (Federal regulations may be found in Title 42, Part 483 of the Code of Federal Regulations (42 C.F.R Part 483). Selected sections of the regulations are provided in Appendix F.)

Active Adult Community

An *active adult community* generally describes a planned, age-restricted development. Residents own and maintain their own homes and are responsible for providing for their own needs. Such communities usually require that at least one homeowner be over a certain age, such as 55, and may or may not provide amenities for residents such as sports facilities, community centers, or scheduled social events. The advantages to a senior living in such a development are the ability to maintain a completely independent lifestyle and the opportunity to socialize with others in the same age group. There is no contract and residents may usually move elsewhere without penalty.

The disadvantage to living in this type of community is that, should the resident decide to relocate for whatever reason, the market for the home will be limited to a smaller section of the general population—that is, other seniors.

Independent Living/Retirement Community

In some cases, a senior will decide that, although in good health, he or she would prefer to not have to worry about caring for a home and yard. He or she may not know many other seniors or simply may not wish to live alone. A lifestyle option known as either an *independent living community* or a *retirement community* may be most appropriate.

In this type of community, residents live in their own space, often either a room or apartment-style home. In some such communities, residents have meals together in a main dining room, while in others, residents provide their own meals. Housekeeping and laundry services may or may not be included. There may be an activity staff that runs regular social events for the residents. Skilled nursing care is not provided by these facilities, although a resident should be able to hire home health-care professionals as needed.

Home Health Care

As the name suggests, this lifestyle option allows a senior with health-care issues to live in his or her own home, thus allowing independence. *Home health care* refers to the hiring of health-care aides or professionals to attend to the senior's medical needs and daily living activities, without the senior having to relocate to a health-care facility. Such a lifestyle option would be best suited for the senior who has a fulfilling life at home, is satisfied with his or her opportunities to socialize, and has no major physical or mental health concerns that would require a skilled nursing facility.

The home health-care agency and its employees are subject to federal regulations only to the extent that the agency receives payment from the federal Medicare program. Otherwise, home health-care agencies are regulated, if at all, by the states in which they do business. Home health-care aides are generally subject to some regulations from the state, but that does not mean that a senior is required to have a care-giver who is subject to such regulations. Sometimes, the care-giver is a family member, friend, or other person who may not have any formal training.

Assisted Living

Many seniors are fortunate enough to be in fairly good physi-cal and mental health, able to perform some day-to-day activ-ities, and not in need of constant medical oversight. However, sometimes these people have the need for some assistance, for example, with getting bathed, dressed, or even with walking to another room to eat a meal. *Assisted living communities* may provide the best lifestyle for these seniors. Such facilities gener-ally do not provide skilled nursing care but do have staff to assist with grooming, housekeeping, and other daily activities. Some assisted living facilities are geared toward a specific group of seniors, for example, those suffering from Alzheimer's disease. These facilities provide specialized services to a partic-ular segment of the senior population.

The advantage to placing a loved one in an assisted living facility is that the philosophy of such a community generally is to promote the independence of the residents and their freedom of decision-making as much as possible. If the senior is functionally able to live in an assisted living facility, the transition from his or her own home to the new surroundings is likely to be easier than if he or she had been moved into a skilled care facility.

As a general rule, Medicare does not cover assisted living expenses. Some facilities do accept Medicaid patients, but many do not. Assisted living facilities generally are not subject to federal regulation, unless they accept Medicaid patients. Many states regulate assisted living facilities, but some do not.

There is not even one single name or definition for such facilities. Sometimes they are called residential care facilities, retirement homes, or semi-independent communities. Because of this, it is difficult to pinpoint an exact definition of such a facility. Even more difficult may be comparing two or more such facilities and the services that they offer. (A sample state statute applying to assisted living facilities is included in Appendix G.)

Long-Term Skilled Care (Nursing) Facility

A *skilled care facility* is the present-day term for what has traditionally been called a *nursing home*. It is a facility that not only provides living assistance for those who are not able to care for themselves, but also provides health care in the form of staff nurses, and often various types of therapy programs, such as physical and occupational. Physicians are usually required to be on call to respond to particular needs of skilled care facility residents. Health care is provided in these facilities around the clock.

Skilled care facilities are subject to a myriad of federal and state laws and regulations. Among the most important is the federal *Nursing Home Reform Act*. This Act provides a uniform minimum standard for all such facilities across the country. (Selected sections of the *Nursing Home Reform Act* are included in Appendix H.)

Continuing Care Retirement Communities

Continuing Care Retirement Community (CCRC) refers to a mixture of some of the living situations previously discussed. Usually, a resident will enter into a contract for continuing care and the facility will guarantee whatever level of care the resident needs, even as the need changes over the years. Such communities will often have an independent living facility, some type of assisted living facility, and skilled nursing care—all in the same building or complex. Many CCRCs also have specialized Alzheimer's disease units.

The senior may enter the community as an independent living resident, but may move over to the skilled care facility at a later time if the need arises. In some ways, CCRCs are the *best of all worlds*, because they allow a tailor-made solution for a senior who may have changing needs for care. If a move becomes necessary, it usually means relocating a few steps away in another building on the facility grounds. This makes adjusting to changing lifestyle needs much less stressful on the senior. On the other hand, CCRCs can be quite expensive and a very large up-front investment usually is required. Depending on the contract, a senior may end up paying for services that he or she never actually needs.

CCRCs are a newly expanding phenomenon based upon an ancient idea of providing a continuum of care for the changing stages of later life. Regulation of this type of community is evolving, but in general, it is left to the states. (A sample state statute regulating CCRCs can be found in Appendix G.)

The part of a CCRC that functions as a nursing home is subject to federal nursing home laws and any facility that receives Medicare or Medicaid funding is subject to those related laws. Because there is no uniform regulatory framework applicable to CCRCs, the best way to search for a community of high quality is to consult the Continuing Care Accreditation Commission (**www.ccaconline.org** or 202-783-7286), the only organization in the country that gives accreditation to CCRCs that meet certain standards of excellence.

Adult Day Care

Adult day care programs provide care and social activities to seniors on less than a 24-hour basis. Usually, seniors who live with their adult children who have to be at work during the day use this service. Adult day care allows seniors with elevated care needs to remain at home for the most part, when otherwise they would have to be placed in an assisted living or long-term care facility.

Seniors in adult day care settings receive meals and opportunities to socialize that they might miss if they were on their own all day. Often, adult day care is provided in an assisted living facility or nursing home, so that the senior can receive proper health care as well as take advantage of the activities that are scheduled for the facility's residents. In some cases, transportation may be provided so that the senior can go on recreational outings or to doctor's appointments and the like. Personal assistance with toileting, taking medications, and eating should be offered as well. Sometimes for an additional charge, the staff will also help the senior with grooming, bathing, and dressing.

Adult day care may be offered only during regular daytime business hours or may be available during evenings and weekends, depending on the center. Costs may be charged by the hour or by the day. Fees of $40 or $50 per day and up are to be expected. In-home day care may also be possible, but is likely to cost quite a bit more. At the present time, there appears to be a shortage of adult day care centers in this country—one study estimates that there are less than half as many as are needed to serve the current demand for services.

Respite Care

Respite care is similar to adult day care in that it is provided for less than twenty-four hours a day. Where adult day care usually is provided on a regular basis, for example, Monday through Friday, respite care is generally used less frequently. It is defined as care of a functionally impaired senior that is designed to provide the senior's regular caregiver some relief from the constant stress of his or her obligations. It is most likely to be utilized by an adult child of a cognitively or physically limited senior who lives with the adult child on a full-time basis. In other words, it gives the adult child a break. Families often utilize respite care so that they may take a vacation or travel out of town for a family emergency without having to worry about their loved one.

Respite care may be provided by an adult day care center, an assisted living facility, a skilled care facility, or by a visiting nurse or other professional who comes to the senior's residence. Again, in-home care will come at a higher cost. Rates typically start at around $10 an hour for care in a center, depending on the amount of assistance the senior needs.

Hospice

Hospice is not a lifestyle option *per se*, but it is important to have an understanding of hospice services when selecting a senior care facility. The American Academy of Family Physicians (**www.aafp.org**) defines hospice simply as *a program designed to care for the dying and their special needs*. Hospice programs primarily provide pain and symptom relief for patients, through medication and other means, and assist the patient with the emotional issues of dying. Care is not geared toward curing the terminally ill patient but to providing *palliative care* to alleviate suffering.

Hospice services typically are available to those who are diagnosed as having less than six months to live. A team of professionals trained in handling end-of-life issues provides care. The team should include physicians, nurses, social workers, and counselors (who might either be laypersons or clergy).

Hospice is driven by a philosophy of death with dignity and as free of pain as possible. Care is geared not just toward the terminally ill patient, but also to the family members dealing with their loss. Hospice programs often provide care in the patient's home—this includes a nursing home. Medicare will pay for most hospice care, as will Medicaid in the majority of states.

Chapter 2

Introducing the Subject of Long-Term Care

Active adult and retirement communities are geared toward seniors who are fully independent and capable of taking care of their own needs on a day-to-day basis. In these settings, the residents themselves are the ones who make their own lifestyle decisions. In a home health-care situation, the family may make the decisions on behalf of the patient, but care is provided in the patient's own home, largely avoiding the transition issues that moving into a facility may produce.

It is commonly the skilled care or assisted living facility environment that is distressing for many seniors and their families. Seniors usually are very resistant to the idea of giving up their independence. Families dread the thought of placing their loved ones in a long-term care facility, because of the negative images connected with life in an institutional setting.

It is not always easy to know if it is time for a family member to move into a long-term care situation. Seniors move more slowly than younger adults do, but that does not mean they cannot care for themselves. They may be more forgetful than they used to be, but memory loss may be treatable. Many conditions that seem to indicate long-term care is necessary, may be overcome with medical treatment or hired help. Some families have the means to care for an elderly loved one in their own home, others accept that such a commitment is beyond their ability. Some have the financial resources to bring in hired help for their loved one around the clock, but most everyone else does not.

Assessing the Need for a Lifestyle Change

If you begin noticing changes in your loved one's personality or any difficulties with activities that always have come naturally to him or her in the past, it may be time to broach the subject of a lifestyle change. This, of course, does not necessarily mean that your family member must be placed in a skilled care facility. Many physical or mental difficulties that seem insurmountable at first, can be treated quite successfully with therapy or medication. Even when a senior has a condition that is not likely to improve, the many lifestyle options available, such as home health care and adult day care, make it possible for the senior to remain fairly independent and in his or her own home.

There are some things to look for, especially if they occur on a regular basis, that may indicate that the senior is in need of increased care. Consider approaching him or her to discuss this need if any of the following become apparent:

◆ changes in behavior;

◆ changes in sleep patterns (sleeping too much or not sleeping at night);

◆ changes in eating (particularly if he or she is eating much less than usual);

◆ no longer showing interest in socializing with friends or family;

◆ loss of interest in hobbies;

◆ mood swings (deep sadness, anger, or unusual irritability);

◆ excessive or irrational fears;

◆ delusions;

◆ loss of balance or inability to complete simple physical tasks;

◆ disorientation;

◆ forgetfulness (not remembering names, not recognizing familiar faces, not knowing the date or year, missing appointments);

◆ trouble completing the basic activities of daily living (also called ADLs by long-term care personnel), such as bathing, dressing, eating, toilet use, and getting in and out of a chair or bed; or,

◆ difficulties with other routine life activities (laundry, housework, cooking, driving, or managing money).

The Resistant Resident

No matter how obvious it seems to you that your loved one needs to be placed in an assisted living or skilled care facility, it is likely that you will encounter hesitancy. It probably will be the senior him- or herself who provides the strongest resistance, but do not be surprised if other family members also resist. In some cases, one of the senior's children lives closer to the senior than the others and ends up taking on more responsibility for the senior's care than the others. The caregiver child may see the need for long-term care more clearly than the others, who may not be in as close of contact with the parent. The other children may be more hesitant to see the parent placed in a facility.

Ideally, the senior will already have had a chance to discuss his or her wishes long before it becomes necessary to act upon the family's concerns. Doing so will prevent it from being a complete shock for the senior when his or her family brings up the subject of a lifestyle change. If the suggestion is met with resistance and there is no way to convince the senior to consider such a move, enlisting the assistance of other people the senior trusts may make things go more smoothly.

The senior's physician may be most helpful in this regard, especially if the doctor occupies a position of trust with the senior. Moreover, the physician is likely to have had a good deal of experience in this area and may be able to provide insight that others are unable to do. Perhaps a trusted member of the clergy or a family friend can help as well. Even another member of the family, closer in age to the senior, such as a sibling or cousin, may be able to make some headway. The senior may be more willing to listen to someone he or she sees as being in authority or as a contemporary, than to one of his or her children. Of course, another relative may be reluctant to step into the middle of a situation such as this, especially an older relative who may be facing his or her own loss of independence issues.

Most importantly, be sensitive to the senior's fears. Before bringing up the subject, the family members should try putting themselves in the senior's place. Speak in the way you would like your children to speak to you if you were the one faced with a lifestyle change. The senior should know that any physical examination is for evaluative purposes and that it is not a foregone conclusion that he or she will be placed in a long-term care facility. Allow the senior to voice his or her concerns and reassure the senior that his or her wishes are of the utmost importance and will be respected to the greatest extent possible. Explain the assessment process the best way possible, and encourage the senior to keep track of any questions that are unanswered, so that he or she can ask a physician. Discuss the different lifestyle options available. However, be realistic about both his or her health and financial situation, as these most likely will determine the range of accommodations the senior will have to choose from.

The main reason for sensitivity to your family member is to ensure that his or her dignity remains as intact as possible. Your empathy for his or her position will help the senior deal with what he or she sees as a loss of freedom. This may be a time of great sadness and anxiety for your loved one. Because discussions of assisted living or nursing home placement usually follow on the heels of a life-altering injury or illness, the family member probably already is feeling a degree of depression or even anger over his or her condition. On top of that is the prospect of having to leave his or her home. Add to that some of the other accompanying issues of reaching advanced age, such as seeing close friends pass away. It is clear that your loved one needs to be treated with respect and compassion.

Helping Yourself

The other person who will benefit from treating your loved one in this manner is yourself. Relatives who must place a family member in an institutional setting often feel guilty, not only because of the placement, but also because of their own feelings and dealings with the family member before the placement. Sometimes, adult children of seniors find themselves increasingly frustrated with their elderly parents because of the heightened demands the parents place on their children. Seniors may move more slowly and be more resistant to change than they once were. As already mentioned, they may be unhappy much of the time and may seem to direct their unhappiness at their children. The situation may be especially acute when the seniors are actually living with their children. The children may find themselves wishing that they could put the senior in an assisted living or nursing facility and then feel ashamed for having those thoughts. Treating the parent with respect, patience, and dignity will make the ultimate decision and transition easier for both the parent and the child.

Family Issues

Unless there is only one child in the family and the senior is widowed, chances are there will be deeper issues involved in the decision to place the senior in long-term care. There may be as many different perspectives on the subject as there are other family members. Personality differences between family members may stretch back for years and will not disappear now that the family needs to make a difficult decision. The most important thing is that family members work to help make the best decision for the senior, regardless of the family *baggage* involved.

Be sure to involve all family members in the decision-making process. If possible, get together with all the adults in the immediate family, including the senior, to set out all the options. Including the whole family in the process may reduce the likelihood of hard feelings, because everyone will have the opportunity to voice an opinion. This in turn will benefit the senior, by putting a number of ideas on the table for everyone's consideration.

If possible, try to get all of those involved to agree on one person to be the representative of the senior's interests for purposes of dealing with long-term care facilities, making medical and legal decisions on behalf of the senior, and so on.

If the senior is competent, have him or her execute advance medical directives (discussed in the next section) to clear up any confusion over his or her wishes regarding future care.

If the senior is not competent, the relative who is chosen to be the representative should consider pursuing a *guardianship*. This is a judge's order appointing a *conservator* to take care of the incompetent family member's affairs. The conservator (guardian) has authority to manage the senior's finances and to execute documents on his or her behalf. Guardianship is a legal procedure that should be handled by an attorney experienced in such matters.

Advance Medical Directives

An *advance medical directive* is a document that assists a person in seeing that his or her wishes regarding health care are followed in the event that he or she becomes unable to communicate these wishes. There are several types of advance directives, but the two main types are the *health care proxy* and the *living will*.

These instruments may be called by various other names in different states. In addition, state law regulates the documents, so the requirements for a document to be valid may differ depending on where you live. For example, in Illinois, living wills do not need to be notarized in order to be valid, but in other states notarization is required. Check with your state's *agency on aging* for the proper forms and rules. (A list of agencies can be found in Appendix A.)

Health Care Proxy

A health care proxy, sometimes called a *power of attorney for health care*, allows a person to appoint an agent to make health-care decisions if the person is unable to make those decisions for him- or herself. The agent usually is a relative or someone else the person trusts. The health care proxy can be tailored so that the agent has only the authority that the person wishes the agent to have.

What follows is the Illinois Statutory Short Form Power of Attorney for Health Care. It is provided as a sample of what such a health care proxy might look like. Check your own state's requirements for this or a similar document.

ILLINOIS STATUTORY SHORT FORM POWER OF ATTORNEY
FOR HEALTH CARE

POWER OF ATTORNEY made this _____ day of _____(month) _____(year).

1.   I, _____, (insert name and address of principal) hereby appoint: _____(insert name and address of agent) as my attorney-in-fact (my "agent") to act for me and in my name (in any way I could act in person) to make any and all decisions for me concerning my personal care, medical treatment, hospitalization and health care and to require, withhold or withdraw any type of medical treatment or procedure, even though my death may ensue. My agent shall have the same access to my medical records that I have, including the right to disclose the contents to others. My agent shall also have full power to authorize an autopsy and direct the disposition of my remains. Effective upon my death, my agent has the full power to make an anatomical gift of the following (initial one):
____Any organ.
____Specific organs:_____

(The above grant of power is intended to be as broad as possible so that your agent will have authority to make any decision you could make to obtain or terminate any type of health care, including withdrawal of food and water and other life-sustaining measures, if your agent believes such action would be consistent with your intent and desires. If you wish to limit the scope of your agent's powers or prescribe special rules or limit the power to make an anatomical gift, authorize autopsy or dispose of remains, you may do so in the following paragraphs.)

2.   The powers granted above shall not include the following powers or shall be subject to the following rules or limitations (here you may include any specific limitations you deem appropriate, such as: your own definition of when life-sustaining measures should be withheld; a direction to continue food and fluids or life-sustaining treatment in all events; or instructions to refuse any specific types of treatment that are inconsistent with your religious beliefs or unacceptable to you for any other reason, such as blood transfusion, electro-convulsive therapy, amputation, psychosurgery, voluntary admission to a mental institution, etc.):
_____
_____
_____

(The subject of life-sustaining treatment is of particular importance. For your convenience in dealing with that subject, some general statements concerning the withholding or removal of life-sustaining treatment are set forth below. If you agree with one of these statements, you may initial that statement; but do not initial more than one):

I <u>do not</u> want my life to be prolonged nor do I want life-sustaining treatment to be provided or continued if my agent believes the burdens of the treatment outweigh the expected benefits. I want my agent to consider the relief of suffering, the expense involved and the quality as well as the possible extension of my life in making decisions concerning life-sustaining treatment. Initialed _____

I <u>want</u> my life to be prolonged and I want life-sustaining treatment to be provided or continued unless I am in a coma which my attending physician believes to be irreversible, in accordance with reasonable medical standards at the time of reference. If and when I have suffered irreversible coma, I want life-sustaining treatment to be withheld or discontinued. Initialed _____

I <u>want</u> my life to be prolonged to the greatest extent possible without regard to my condition, the chances I have for recovery or the cost of the procedures. Initialed _____

(This power of attorney may be amended or revoked by you in the manner provided in section 4-6 of the Illinois "Powers of Attorney for Health Care Law." Absent amendment or revocation, the authority granted in this power of attorney will become effective at the time this power is signed and will continue until your death, and beyond if anatomical gift, autopsy or disposition of remains is authorized, unless a limitation on the beginning date or duration is made by initialing and completing either or both of the following:)

3.   ( ) This power of attorney shall become effective on _____
(insert a future date or event during your lifetime, such as court determination of your disability, when you want this power to first take effect)

4.   ( ) This power of attorney shall terminate on _____
(insert a future date or event, such as court determination of your disability, when you want this power to terminate prior to your death)

(If you wish to name successor agents, insert the names and addresses of such successors in the following paragraph.)

5.   If any agent named by me shall die, become incompetent, resign, refuse to accept the office of agent or be unavailable, I name the following (each to act alone and successively, in the order named) as successors to such agent:

_____

_____

For purposes of this paragraph 5, a person shall be considered to be incompetent if and while the person is a minor or an adjudicated incompetent or disabled person or the person is unable to give prompt and intelligent consideration to health care matters, as certified by a licensed physician.

(If you wish to name your agent as guardian of your person, in the event a court decides that one should be appointed, you may, but <u>are not</u> required to, do so by retaining the following paragraph. The court will appoint your agent if the court finds that such appointment will serve your best interests and welfare. Strike out paragraph 6 if you <u>do not</u> want your agent to act as guardian.)

6.   If a guardian of my person is to be appointed, I nominate the agent acting under this power of attorney as such guardian, to serve without bond or security.

7.   I am fully informed as to all the contents of this form and understand the full import of this grant of powers to my agent.

Signed _____ (principal)

The principal has had an opportunity to read the above form and has signed the form or acknowledged his or her signature or mark on the form in my presence.

Witness: _____ Residing at: _____

(You may, but are not required to, request your agent and successor agents to provide specimen signatures below. If you include specimen signatures in this power of attorney, you must complete the certification opposite the signatures of the agents.)

Specimen signatures of agent   I certify that the signatures of my
(and successors)   agent (and successors) are correct.

_____   _____
(agent)   (principal)

_____   _____
(successor agent)   (principal)

_____   _____
(successor agent)   (principal)

(Source: 755 Illinois Compiled Statutes 45/4-10)

Living Will

A living will allows a person to instruct a physician to withhold life-prolonging procedures, should the person become incapacitated, incompetent, or be diagnosed with a terminal illness. A living will saves an incapacitated person's family from struggling with the agonizing decision of whether and when to call off death-delaying treatments.

The following is a sample form for a living will used in Maryland. (Remember, the form that a living will must take in your state may be different.)

DECLARATION

This declaration is made this _____ day of _____ (month, year). I, _____, being of sound mind, willfully and voluntarily make known my desires that my moment of death shall not be artificially postponed.

If at any time I should have an incurable and irreversible injury, disease, or illness judged to be a terminal condition by my attending physician who has personally examined me and has determined that my death is imminent except for death delaying procedures, I direct that such procedures which would only prolong the dying process be withheld or withdrawn, and that I be permitted to die naturally with only the administration of medication, sustenance, or the performance of any medical procedure deemed necessary by my attending physician to provide me with comfort care.

In the absence of my ability to give directions regarding the use of such death delaying procedures, it is my intention that this declaration shall be honored by my family and physician as the final expression of my legal right to refuse medical or surgical treatment and accept the consequences from such refusal.

Signed _____
City, County, and State of Residence _____

_____

_____

The declarant is personally known to me and I believe him or her to be of sound mind. I saw the declarant sign the declaration in my presence (or the declarant acknowledged in my presence that he or she had signed the declaration) and I signed the declaration as a witness in the presence of the declarant. I did not sign the declarant's signature above for or at the direction of the declarant. At the date of this instrument, I am not entitled to any portion of the estate of the declarant according to the laws of intestate succession or, to the best of my knowledge and belief, under any will of declarant or other instrument taking effect at declarant's death, or directly financially responsible for declarant's medical care.

Witness _____

Witness _____

(Source: Office of the Attorney General of the State of Maryland)

Sometimes, both documents are used together, because one appoints the agent, while the other specifically gives the instructions that the agent is to follow. Both documents are legally binding if they have been properly executed according to the law of the state in which they are to take effect. Many states' laws will honor an advance directive that has been prepared in another state, so long as it meets the requirements of that other state's laws. If the documents have been provided to the treating physician, they must be followed.

Miscellaneous Advance Directives
There are other advance directives that your loved one and family members may wish to consider executing.

◆ *Do Not Resuscitate* (DNR) orders—a directive instructing that no cardiopulmonary resuscitation be administered to a patient who is stricken with sudden cardiac or respiratory arrest. Subcategories of this type of directive are:
  • *Do Not Intubate* orders, which allow resuscitation measures but does not allow the insertion of a tracheal tube in the patient to aid ventilation and
  • *Do Not Defibrillate* orders, which prohibit the administering of cardiac defibrillation but do allow other resuscitation methods.

◆ *Organ Donor Card*—a directive instructing that usable organs of the patient be removed and donated to others in the event of the patient's death.

◆ *Restriction on Artificial Feeding*—a directive that nutrition is not to be given to the patient through tubes in the event the patient is incapacitated and unable to eat naturally.

◆ *Restriction on certain treatments*—instructions as to specific life-prolonging treatments the patient does not wish to receive.

◆ *Request for Autopsy*—a directive that the patient's body is to be examined by a medical expert upon the patient's death in order to determine a cause of death.

In general, if a physician refuses to honor an advance medical directive, he or she must notify the patient or the patient's agent, so that the patient may find another doctor who will follow the directive. If possible, discuss any advance directive with the physician at the time it is executed to be sure that the physician will comply with the document.

It is advisable for all adults to have advance directives in place, so that there will be no question as to a person's wishes should he or she ever become unable to make or communicate health-care wishes. Copies of any directives should be provided to the person's physician, next of kin, and in the case of assisted living or nursing home residents, to the administration so the directive can be included in the resident's medical file.

Medical Evaluation

Before delving into the many options available for senior care, you will want to ascertain what level of care is necessary. Sometimes this determination is not difficult, as in the unfortunate case of a family member suffering an incapacitating illness or injury. Other times, the family feels a conflict between the senior's wishes and what is actually in his or her best interest. The best way to begin an objective investigation into suitable lifestyle options is by consulting the senior's primary physician.

Finding a Doctor

If the senior has no physician, the family can help locate one. First, determine which local physicians are in-network under his or her insurance. In other words, find the doctors the senior's insurance will pay for, if the expense of physician's services is a concern. Friends or neighbors then may have a recommendation from that list.

A doctor may also be found by contacting the American Medical Association (AMA). It has an online physician locator,

AMA Physician Select (**http://dbapps.amaassn.org/aps/amahg.htm**), which may be searched by specialty, such as geriatrics. If all else fails, consult the Yellow Pages as a starting point. Once a list of names is formed, contact the offices to gather some preliminary information in order to narrow down the choices of doctors.

Ask how long the doctor has been practicing medicine; whether he or she has experience with geriatric patients; whether he or she is board certified; and, which hospitals he or she is affiliated with. Ask if references from other patients are available. If so, contact them and ask if they are satisfied with their care.

Once a doctor who may be suitable is found, pay a visit to the office to see if the senior and the doctor are compatible. The doctor should be respectful and should be willing to take the time to explain items of concern to both the senior and his or her family member. If there are questions relating to medical treatment, the doctor should answer them in as much detail as is necessary so everyone understands the treatment and should detail any risks associated with treatment as well. Once everyone, most importantly, the senior, feels comfortable with a certain physician, then discuss the necessity of a lifestyle change for your family member.

Working with the Physician

If this is a new physician, be sure to provide as complete a picture of the senior's medical history as possible. The doctor's office staff probably will ask him or her to fill out a detailed form, providing information about any current or previous illnesses, injuries, conditions, surgeries, allergies, and medications. Contact doctors and any therapists or specialists who have treated the senior in the past and request copies of his or her medical records. (If a family member, rather than the senior, is making the request, it will be necessary for the actual patient to complete a release allowing the family member to receive the records.) Bring to the doctor's office a list of all prescriptions that the senior is taking or has taken recently.

When taking the senior for a medical evaluation, it is important to respect his or her privacy. He or she will probably want to be alone for the examination. The doctor is subject to rules of confidentiality, and may not discuss the senior's condition with anyone, including family, unless he or she has been given consent. Of course, in an emergency situation or if the senior is unable to understand what is happening, rules of confidentiality do not apply. Again, however, it is advisable to have the senior execute an advance care directive or health care proxy before there is a question as to his or her competence to make health care decisions.

Mental Health Evaluation

The primary care physician may feel that a separate mental health assessment may be necessary in addition to a physical evaluation. The doctor should be able to provide a reference to a suitable mental health professional, but request several names so that there is a choice.

Another resource might be the hospital with which the doctor is affiliated. It may have such a professional on staff who may be qualified to perform the evaluation. The professional may be a psychiatrist, a psychologist, or a licensed social worker. Psychiatrists and psychologists both have doctorate degrees, but only psychiatrists are authorized to prescribe medications. Social workers have specialized degrees, but are not doctors. Each profession is licensed and regulated by the state. If a mental health professional needs to evaluate the senior, be sure to inquire whether the professional has training and experience in the area of geriatrics.

Families that find it necessary to seek out a mental health professional on their own can contact:

American Psychiatric Association
(for a psychiatrist)
703-907-7300
apa@psych.org
or

American Psychological Association Referral Service
(for a psychologist)
800-964-2000

Geriatric Care Managers

With the growth in the elderly population in this country in the last decade, families are turning increasingly to *geriatric care managers* to assist them in planning and locating long-term care for their loved ones. A geriatric care manager is a professional who, for a fee, will help a family through the process of assessing the family member, finding a suitable facility, making the transition to the new lifestyle, and monitoring the new living arrangements on an ongoing basis. This is a particularly attractive option for a family who must make long-term care decisions for a senior who is living far away, because the geriatric care manager can serve as the *eyes and ears* of the family.

Geriatric care managers may have a background in social work, nursing, or another profession related to elder care. However, in general there are no license requirements or statutory regulation of the field. Therefore, it is important to find a care manager who is qualified to create and implement a plan of care for your family member. A successful geriatric care manager is one who is familiar with the community in which he or she works. He or she knows what living options are available for seniors in the area, has a relationship with the administrations in those facilities, and has experience in evaluating the services offered and in navigating the financial issues involved.

A geriatric care manager may be helpful in convincing your loved one to consider a lifestyle change and may be able to soothe the fears of other family members who oppose the idea. Geriatric care managers usually have a great deal of experience with resistance, and specialize in providing support to both the senior and the family members.

The services provided by a geriatric care manager begin with a comprehensive assessment of the senior, usually provided in the senior's home. The care manager then will recommend what level of care the senior should receive and will research the available options for that type of care. A good care manager should also take into account the senior's resources and should assist in finding the most suitable arrangements within the senior's ability to pay. The care manager then formulates a comprehensive plan of care for the senior.

The senior and his or her family are not required to take the geriatric care manager's recommendation. However, once the family arrives at a decision as to the best lifestyle option for the senior, the geriatric care manager should help the senior, as well as the family, to transition to the new environment. The care manager should continue to observe the senior's living situation on behalf of a long-distance family. He or she may provide further assistance, for example, by helping the senior deal with government agencies or by securing additional services for the senior on an as-needed basis.

Hiring a Geriatric Care Manager

As with any search for a professional, it is important to ask questions when hiring a geriatric care manager. Find out his or her educational and professional background, length of time in business in the area, the number of clients assisted, and how he or she goes about forming a care plan. Determine whether the geriatric care manager will be the only care manager for the senior, or if he or she works with other managers who also will work on the case.

Ask how emergency situations are handled, for example, if the senior must be admitted to the hospital suddenly. If the care manager works alone, be sure there is a back-up person in case he or she is on vacation or otherwise unavailable. Ask for references from clients and follow up with them as to their level of satisfaction with the care manager. Discuss fees and get in writing what services are provided at what cost.

The assistance of a geriatric care manager does not come cheaply. Fees can run upwards of $75 per hour. Some care managers will charge a flat fee, others will charge extra for their travel and other expenses. These costs are not covered by Medicare or Medicaid, but may be covered by long-term care insurance. Some agencies may provide free or reduced-rate geriatric care management services. Also, seniors eligible for Veterans Health Administration (VHA) benefits may have access to a VHA-sponsored program of geriatric care assessment and management. Contact information for the National Association of Professional Geriatric Care Managers and for the Veteran's Health Administration can be found in Appendix E.

Tip: Even if you are unable to convince your loved one to discuss the prospect of lifestyle change with you, encourage him or her to gather copies of important documents in a folder so that they are in a single location, even if he or she will not turn them over to you. Copies of bank statements and other financial statements, insurance policies, real estate deeds, mortgage papers, birth and marriage certificates, and Social Security or Medicare cards are all documents that may be necessary to have for long-term care purposes.

Chapter 3

Locating the Appropriate Facility or Services

Once the decision is made that a family member needs some additional assistance and the level of care is determined, the next step is to begin searching for the right facility or service. Several options are available, from asking friends to using the Yellow Pages. Other resources that may be more focused on the needs of the seniors are the subject of this chapter.

Doctor Recommendations

Often, the best way to locate to locate a suitable facility is to ask the senior's own physician, who probably has seen a number of facilities in the area and may even be acquainted with the staff and administration to some extent. In addition, the senior hopefully has a relationship of trust with his or her doctor and will be reassured if the doctor recommends a particular facility.

In most states, a medical diagnosis is required in order to have a patient admitted to a skilled care facility—a psychiatric diagnosis is not enough. In addition, a doctor's order is required for admission to a skilled care facility in the case of Medicare or Medicaid patients. As a result, almost anyone who is seeking placement in a nursing home will have had contact with a physician who can be used as a starting point in searching for a suitable facility.

Social Service Provider Recommendations

Often, seniors who are still living independently have at some time had contact with social service organizations. Groups that provide meals or transportation to seniors or community centers that cater to the 55 and older group, for example, may have personnel who are familiar with area facilities and who might be able to provide a recommendation.

Another resource is the local Social Security office, which is where seniors go to enroll in Medicare or Medicaid. The caseworkers there, who prepare paperwork for eligibility determinations, may be able to provide assistance in finding local assisted living or skilled care facilities.

Senior Advocacy and Health Care Organizations

A number of organizations list nursing homes and assisted living facilities by region. They may be reached by telephone or via the Internet. For example, *Nursing Home Compare*, found on the federal government's official Medicare website **www.medicare.gov**, provides information on all Medicare-certified skilled care facilities in the country.

The *American Health Care Association* (**www.ahca.org**) can direct you to other search tools for long-term care facilities. The *Assisted Living Federation of America* (**www.alfa.org**) has a search tool that uses a number of criteria to locate assisted living facilities. (Appendix E lists a number of organizations that may be of use in locating a suitable facility.)

The United States Administration on Aging sponsors a service called the *Eldercare Locator*. It provides help to seniors seeking services in their area. The Eldercare Locator can be accessed online at **www.eldercare.gov** or by telephone at 800-677-1116. Contacting the Eldercare Locator will lead the senior to one or more resource agencies—either information and referral services or the local Agency on Aging—that may be of assistance in finding a suitable facility. (Appendix A lists other state senior agencies that can direct the user to the appropriate Agency on Aging.)

State Ombudsman

The federal *Older Americans Act* requires each state to have a long-term care ombudsman's office. This office provides information to seniors and investigates residents' complaints against facilities. In many states, the ombudsman's office can direct families to skilled care facilities located in the desired area. Links to each state's ombudsman program can be found at the National Long-Term Care Ombudsman Resource Center website at **www.ltcombudsman.org**. (The National Long-Term Care Ombudsman Resource Center's address and telephone number are included in Appendix E.)

Chapter 4

Evaluating the Facility

Finding potential facilities is no easy task. However, that is only one step in the process. After coming up with a list of choices, each one must be evaluated to determine if it is right for the senior and his or her situation.

Visiting a Facility

The best way to evaluate any facility is to see it and talk to the staff and administration. You should make an appointment for your first visit so that the administrator and department heads will have scheduled sufficient time to speak with you and answer all your questions. However, you should visit more than once, at different times of the day and evening, and even on the weekend. This will give you a better idea of how the facility functions during different shifts, with and without the full administrative staff present.

One or two surprise visits are a good idea. The administrator on duty should welcome your visit. Observe the residents as well as the staff. Talk to the residents if you can. Ask them how they keep busy, whether they like the food and the staff, how they like their rooms, and so on. Their answers will be informative, and by simply talking to them you will have the chance to observe their demeanor and their level of enthusiasm. This, in turn, will give you an idea of how the residents are functioning and how comfortable they are in their environment.

Talk to the staff as well. Do not simply focus on the nursing home staff—visit different areas of the facility, such as the kitchen and laundry, and speak to some of the employees there as well. Ask them for their views on the facility, the administration, and the residents (if they have time to answer questions). This will provide insight into the professional attitudes of the staff, and help get to know the caregivers if you end up using that facility. Establishing a rapport with the staff at the facility can help make the transition to assisted living or skilled care easier. Discussing the senior's condition, likes, and dislikes with the staff will foster a more personal relationship between the resident and the caregivers. These positive relationships between the resident, the family, and the staff will be beneficial even after the resident has adjusted to the new lifestyle.

Chapter 5 lists a number of things to look at and questions to ask when you are looking over a facility.

Nursing Home Compare

The *Centers for Medicare and Medicaid Services* (CMS), a division of the United States Department of Health and Human Services, operates a database called *Nursing Home Compare*, which can be accessed online via the CMS website at **www.medicare.com**. The information contained in Nursing Home Compare comes from assessments that the federal government requires facilities to complete on all Medicare- and Medicaid-funded nursing home residents and from the results of state inspections or surveys that federal law also mandates.

This search tool can be a useful source of information about all Medicare- and Medicaid-certified facilities in the country. Facilities can be searched by geographical location or by name. You can select one or more of the facilities listed as a result of your search and the database can provide you with information on each facility chosen. Nursing Home Compare lists many items, including the following.

◆ General information about each facility, such as:
  • whether it is Medicare-certified, Medicaid-certified, or both;
  • number of certified beds;
  • nursing staff hours per resident per day;
  • facility ownership—whether church-affiliated, for-profit corporation, and so on;
  • whether it is located in a hospital;
  • whether the facility is one of a chain; and,
  • whether the facility has a resident council, a family council, or both.

◆ Quality measures for each facility, for example:
  • percent of residents who have moderate to severe pain;
  • percent of residents who have pressure sores;
  • percent of residents who were physically restrained;
  • percent of residents who are depressed or anxious;
  • percent of residents who spend most of their time in bed or in a chair; and,
  • percent of residents whose ability to move about in and around their room has decreased.

◆ Results of most recent state inspections, in particular:
  • environmental deficiencies, such as employees' failure to properly wash hands or failure to correct dangerous conditions in the facility;
  • mistreatment deficiencies, such as improper use of restraints or theft of residents' property;
  • quality care deficiencies, such as failure to provide special services that are called for in a resident's care plan;

- resident rights deficiencies, such as failure to keep residents' records confidential;
- resident assessment deficiencies, such as failure to develop a care plan for a resident;
- administration deficiencies, such as failure to obtain proof that a nurses' aide has state-required training; and,
- nutrition and dietary deficiencies, such as failure to handle food properly.

Nursing Home Compare can be a helpful instrument in the search for a suitable nursing home. Not only can the information provided be used to narrow down the search, but two or more facilities can be directly compared to see which has the better track record with regard to state inspections.

As useful as Nursing Home Compare is, remember that it only gives information on facilities that accept Medicare and/or Medicaid patients. Even more importantly, however, keep in mind that the data found in Nursing Home Compare is provided by the facilities themselves and is not checked for accuracy. Nursing Home Compare is a good way to get a feel for how different facilities compare to one another, but it is only one tool to use in your search for and evaluation of facilities.

State Offices

In general, the information found in the Nursing Home Compare database comes from the inspections performed by each state's nursing home survey agency as well as the facilities themselves. However, contacting the state survey agency directly after checking Nursing Home Compare in order to get the most up-to-date information on any deficiencies that may have found in the database might be wise. Another reason for speaking with the state survey agency is to get details about any problems with a facility that are in the database. (Appendix A lists the state survey agencies for each state.)

The state ombudsman's office, which each state is required to set up to serve as an advocate for residents of long-term care facilities, may also be able to give additional information about facilities being considered. The ombudsman can certainly provide a wealth of consumer information to assist in searching and evaluating nursing homes and might even be able to give input in seeking an assisted living facility. Contact the ombudsman's office by calling the National Long-Term Care Ombudsman Resource Center at 202-332-2275.

Evaluating Assisted Living Facilities

Assisted living facilities can be more difficult to evaluate than nursing homes, because they may not be regulated in your state and because there is no standard definition of just what an assisted living facility entails. Some facilities may provide very little in the way of assistance with activities of daily living, while others may offer many services or many various packages of services. This makes it difficult to compare two or more different facilities. Homework and research are necessary to find the right assisted living facility.

Some information about facilities in your area may be found through the *Assisted Living Federation of America* (ALFA). ALFA provides listings of assisted living facilities in the United States and is affiliated with a number of state organizations that can be accessed through ALFA's website at **www.alfa.org**. ALFA's office may also be reached by telephone at 703-691-8100.

Remember, however, that ALFA is the organization that primarily represents the assisted living *industry*. This means it does not necessarily represent the interests of assisted living *residents*. Therefore, it is not enough to base a decision about a facility solely on information provided by ALFA or its affiliated organizations. It will still be necessary to visit any prospective facilities yourself.

> **NOTE: People who are dealing with a change of residence of a family member living in another state, might want to consider retaining the services of a geriatric care manager to help find the best accommodations for the senior.**

World Wide Web

There are other sources of information that may be helpful in the evaluation of an assisted living or skilled care facility. The Internet can provide all kinds of background on long-term care communities in any desired geographical area.

Many facilities have their own websites, but take any information given there with a grain of salt. Many such sites are vague on what services are provided and it is not likely that even a ballpark estimate of the cost can be obtained without speaking to someone at the facility or its corporate office. This is intentional—they want to make their sales pitch directly.

The Internet typically is no more than a means of advertisement for most long-term care providers. Usually, they want to give enough information to convince the user to contact them, hoping that they can get him or her to take a closer look at the facility. This is not a bad thing in and of itself. It is important to remember, however, that much of the information online is meant for marketing purposes. The best evaluation that can be made will be one that is based upon personal observations and the answers to questions asked of the facility's staff.

Chapter 5

Questions to Ask

Many of the things that people should be concerned with as they evaluate a nursing home are already well regulated by each state. Do not assume, however, that a facility follows the law simply because the law is on the books. Besides, even a facility that follows the letter of the law may not be the right place for the senior if he or she is not comfortable there and does not come to see the facility as home.

What follows is a checklist of questions to ask and things to inspect and consider when evaluating a long-term care facility. Some items will apply to both assisted living and skilled care facilities, others will be relevant only to one or the other. Also, not everything listed here will be significant to each family's particular search for a facility. While the list attempts to be comprehensive, there may be other questions not listed here that should be asked, depending upon the inspection of the facility. If anything seen or heard is confusing or is not acceptable in any way, do not hesitate to ask the facility administrator for an explanation or for more information.

Probably the most useful guide when evaluating the facility is each person's own set of standards—Is it clean enough? Is the food that is served edible?—and so on. If it is not good enough to meet a family member's standards, it is probably not adequate for the senior.

Geographical Location

POINTS TO CONSIDER
- Location of facility
- Closeness to family members
- Nearness to a full-service hospital
- Convenience to shopping, doctors' offices, and other service providers

A number of experts believe that the location of a facility is the single most important factor to consider in deciding where to place a loved one. Do not underestimate the significance of the distance between the facility and the homes of those who will be most likely to visit. A 45-minute drive may not seem so difficult at first, especially to those who live in urbanized areas and routinely spend a good deal of time in the car. However, over time, having to travel such a distance on a regular basis may make family members resentful about visiting and may result in fewer visits to the resident.

A particular set of problems comes with trying to place a loved one in a facility that is located in a state that is different from the rest of the family. One of the best ways to ensure that the senior has a satisfactory experience residing in an assisted living or a skilled care facility is to be active in his or her life and be present at the facility on a regular basis. Family participation in resident care conferences, family councils, and specially-planned social events for families is extremely important to overseeing the senior's care. It may also help to prevent some of the unfortunate situations that sometimes occur in institutional settings, such as neglect of a resident or theft of property. Unless there is an unavoidable reason why the senior cannot be moved closer to the rest of the family, consider locating a facility in your geographical area rather than the senior's.

Sometimes a senior's only immediate family is transient, for example, corporate employees and military personnel. In such a case, the family should consider the location where the senior will have the most stability. You should not move your family member to a facility near your home if you are expecting a job transfer to another state in the near future. Having to relocate from one facility to another can be quite traumatic for the elderly, so it should be avoided except under the most compelling circumstances.

The distance from the facility to local services and amenities should be taken into account as well, particularly if it falls on the family to transport the resident to doctor's appointments, on shopping trips, and so on.

> *TIP: You, as well as your loved one, may find it preferable to have visits that are shorter, but occur more often, rather than visiting less frequently, but staying for an entire afternoon. This is especially true if you are bringing children with you. For this reason, consider the distance of the facility from your home carefully when deciding where to place your family member.*

Preliminary Questions (before going to visit)

Once you have several facilities in mind, call each one and ask for answers to your points of concern. The answers to these questions may eliminate one or more of the choices right away, which will save the time and effort of having to inspect those facilities. Also, if there are no openings and a long waiting list ahead of the senior, it may be necessary to move on to another facility, especially if the senior is in the hospital about to be discharged.

POINTS TO CONSIDER
- Number of beds/rooms/apartments in the facility
- Number of openings available

If the senior is being released directly from the hospital after a Medicare-qualifying stay, Medicare may pick up some of the cost for a limited time period. Medicaid, a public aid program separately administered by each state, may cover many long-term care costs for qualifying low-income individuals.

However, only facilities that meet certain requirements for Medicare and Medicaid certification are eligible to receive payments under these programs.

A facility is not required to accept Medicare or Medicaid patients and some facilities that do accept them only set aside a certain number of beds for those patients. That is why you should call first if you have enrolled or are considering enrolling your family member in Medicare or Medicaid. (Medicare and Medicaid are discussed more thoroughly in Chapter 6.)

The number of beds is also important because you can get an idea of the size of the facility, which may indicate how much attention is given to each resident. Staff-to-resident ratios may be a better gauge (discussed on p.46). A large percentage of empty beds may be a red flag, requiring further investigation to determine why the facility has a low resident count.

TIP: To get the most accurate answers when posing preliminary questions about the facility, be sure to speak with the facility administrator or admissions director, rather than the person in charge of marketing.

POINTS TO CONSIDER

- The administrator's credentials (*i.e.,* educational and employment background)
- Experience of the other department heads (the staff dietician, the activity director, the director of housekeeping, and the director of nursing)
- Ability to meet with each of these staff members
- History of state inspections
- Nature (sanitation in kitchen, treatment of residents, etc.) of previous violations

Licensing and Records of Violations

In general, skilled nursing and, in some states, assisted living facilities, are subject to licensing and regulation by state agencies. Each state issues its own set of regulations for facilities located in that state. Some rules are mandated by the federal government and are uniform across all states. At the present time, all fifty states require skilled care facility administrators to be licensed. Although each state may have different requirements, such as minimum age and minimum level of education for licensure, all states require administrators to pass a national examination overseen by the *National Association of Boards of Examiners of Long-Term Care Administrators.*

Licensing information, along with records of violations that have been cited at the facility, are matters of public record in each state. Both the facility itself and the administrator must be licensed and in good standing. As discussed in Chapter 4, the state survey agency for the state in which the nursing facility is located is the best source of information regarding deficiencies in care that have been found at the facility. (State survey agency contact information can be found in Appendix A.)

TIP: Inquire into the ownership of the facility. Many facilities are owned by publicly traded companies whose performance and financial stability are easier to determine than facilities owned by an individual, family, or privately-held company. Also check to see if ownership has changed at any point in the last year or two. If it has, there will be less of a track record as to deficiencies in the care of residents.

Assessments and Care Planning

Federal law requires that residents be assessed within fourteen days of admission to a skilled care facility. It also requires that a comprehensive care plan for the resident be developed. The care plan must include objectives and

POINTS TO CONSIDER
- Frequency that residents are fully assessed
- Which professionals are involved in formulating the resident's plan of care
- Frequency that care conferences are held
- Length of the care conferences

timeframes for meeting the resident's medical, mental health, and social needs as identified by the assessment, and must describe the services that will be provided to the resident in order to meet these needs.

The resident must be assessed at least once a year after the original comprehensive assessment. There is also a requirement of an *assessment review*, called a *care conference*, every three months. A care conference is not as in-depth an examination as the yearly assessment and the review relies more heavily on input from the resident and his or her family. Generally, the team performing the assessment should include, at the least, nursing and activities staff, any staff therapists treating the resident, and the facility's dietician. The resident's physical health, emotional condition, activities, eating habits and diet, and other aspects of his or her life at the facility are reviewed with the resident. If the resident has consented or is incapable of giving consent, the family is invited to join in the care conference. Any concerns are discussed and the plan of care is revised as necessary. There should be several care conferences for each resident every year. These most likely will be in conjunction with the quarterly assessment review.

> *TIP: Nurses' aides of both genders work with nursing home residents, but it is not surprising that many residents are comfortable only with orderlies of their own gender. If a resident or family has a preference as to the gender of the nurses' aides that attend to the resident, be sure to bring that up at the initial assessment.*

Health Care Staff
(*for nursing home evaluation*)

Obviously, treatment of the residents by the medical staff is of the greatest importance. However, the number and stability of the staff and the ease of obtaining health care should not be overlooked. The federal *Nursing Home Reform Act* (found in Appendix H), requires that skilled care facilities have sufficient staff to provide licensed nursing care for all residents, twenty-four hours a day. In addition, an RN must be available at least eight hours a day, seven days a week.

Seniors tend to be resistant to change. In the case of a confused resident or one suffering from dementia, a high rate of staff turnover can be quite detrimental. A resident who has been resistant to medical treatment or advice in

POINTS TO CONSIDER
- Ratio of residents to registered nurses (RNs)
- Ratio of residents to certified nursing assistants (CNAs)
- Presence of an RN at the facility during all shifts
- Number of physicians on staff
- Number of physicians on-call at any one time
- Turnover rate for health-care professionals on staff
- Treatment of residents

the past and who finally responds to a particular member of the nursing staff may revert to a state of reluctance. Even in lucid residents, there is a trust issue that may be hard to resolve with many staff changes. This is not limited to the nursing staff. Activities workers, dieticians, and administrative personnel may become like a second family to the residents. Turnover can become a quality-of-life consideration for some residents.

Unfortunately, turnover is a fact of life in health-care facilities. Historically overworked and underpaid, nursing home employees in all areas of the facility often come and go at a brisk rate. If this is a main concern and you do not remain realistic about turnover, you may severely limit your available options. Rather, consider turnover rates as one factor in your evaluation.

Do, however, be wary of any policy requiring residents to see doctors not of their own choosing, unless there is a state or federal regulation at the root of the policy. In other words, some states may regulate the circumstances under which physicians see residents. For example, in Illinois, each nursing home resident must be seen by his or her physician at least once a month. That means that either the resident must be able to travel to the doctor's office every month or the doctor must be willing to make a monthly house call. Many doctors are not willing to do this, unless they have a large number of patients in one particular facility, in which case it might be worth the doctor's time.

Travel to the doctor's office may be offered as a service by the facility. More often than not, however, it is provided only if the resident is covered by Medicare or if the resident or his or her family arranges transportation privately. In some cases, the facility will provide free transportation to a nearby hospital or medical office complex that the facility is affiliated with in some way.

TIP: Be sure to inquire about the resident-to-nursing staff ratio, as well as the resident-to-staff ratio. Sometimes the facility will give you the more-attractive sounding resident-to-staff ratio, which includes kitchen, maintenance, and laundry room workers. Resident-to-nursing staff ratio indicates whether there are enough qualified employees to provide health care on a daily basis. (The resident-to-staff ratio is important, however, in determining whether there is sufficient staff to evacuate residents from the facility in case of an emergency.)

POINTS TO CONSIDER
- Availability of staff to remind residents to take necessary medications
- Routine assistance with bathing, dressing, and grooming
- Other activities of daily living (ADLs) residents are assisted with (*i.e.*, housekeeping, laundry, meal preparation)
- Any extra charges that accompany differing levels of required assistance

Aides (*for assisted living evaluation*)

While the questions regarding health-care staff for nursing home evaluations overlap with the concerns of staffing with assisted living facilities, in the case of assisted living facilities, the point is to determine exactly what level of assistance can be expected. If staff will not routinely help with toileting, for example, and the senior is incontinent, then the facility is not a good match. Assisted living facilities vary in the types and amounts of assistance they provide. Therefore, it must be very clear to both the staff and the family what is included, not only for the present time, but also in the future, when the resident may actually need greater assistance than he or she needs now.

TIP: If possible, opt for the facility that offers the greatest range of service, in case it is needed at a later time.

Contract Terms and Fees

As a general rule, it is in everyone's best interest to have a written contract spelling out the terms of your agreement with the facility regarding the senior's residency there. However, the family will want to be sure that the contract is thorough and will want to understand all of the fine print that may be included.

NOTE: Only the resident should sign the contract, unless the resident's representative is signing with the resident's power of attorney.

If a family member, rather than the resident, signs the contract, that

POINTS TO CONSIDER
- Services covered by the contract
- Fees and charges included in the rate
- Optional services that can be obtained for an additional fee
- Possible separate charges for utilities
- Limits on the amount fees may increase per year
- Procedure for appealing a discharge or transfer
- The facility's policy when a resident has to leave the facility temporarily (*i.e.*, for a hospital stay)
- Limits on how long a room is held
- Additional charges to keep the room open

family member may be held responsible for paying the bills for the senior. Nursing homes cannot require someone other than the resident to co-sign or otherwise assume liability for the resident's nursing care charges. They also cannot require a senior to pay as a private pay resident if the senior is eligible for Medicare or Medicaid.

Rate Terms

The most important item in the contract will be the rate terms. Typically, the contract will specify a monthly rate to be charged, along with provisions relating to when and how payment is to be made. Make sure that the contract spells out exactly what type of room is included in that rate, whether it is a private or semi-private room, how many beds will be in the room, and so on.

Additional Services

The contract should state whether any additional services are included in the rate, such as medical equipment, medications, therapy of any nature, or any extra amenities. If no special services are included in the base rate, a separate schedule of charges for these items should appear in the contract.

In the case of an assisted living facility contract, fee provisions should specify whether extra charges apply to increased assistance requirements. Some assisted living facilities charge by the hour or even the quarter-hour for staff assistance. Be sure that all extra charges for staff time are spelled out in writing in the contract.

Payment

The facility should allow payment to be made on a month-by-month or other periodic basis and should not require you to allow direct withdrawal of funds by the facility. Do not agree to deposit your family member's private funds with the facility. It is illegal for the facility to require a resident to do so.

However, if a resident wishes to keep cash on hand for personal use, he or she should allow the facility to hold it for safekeeping. A facility is required to have a procedure for holding and accounting for residents' personal funds and each resident's funds must be accounted for separately from those of all other residents. The facility must keep a written record of all transactions involving a resident's personal funds. That record must be made available for inspection by the resident or his or her representative.

Medicare/Medicaid

As mentioned previously, geographic location is the most important area of concern. After geographical location, the next most important point of concern (if your family member will not be a private-pay resident) is whether the facility is Medicare or Medicaid certified. Medicare and Medicaid are different federal programs that cover certain medical expenses for qualifying individuals. Medicare and Medicaid are discussed more thoroughly in Chapter 6. Only properly certified facilities are eligible to take Medicare and Medicaid patients.

Additional Fees

If the resident is admitted halfway through the month, the contract should state whether the charges are prorated. Similarly, if the resident leaves the facility part of the way through the month—either temporarily or permanently—the contract should indicate whether and how a refund will be given for the rest of the month.

Also, any security deposit or advance payment required by the facility should be in writing. Be aware of any provision in the contract that makes you or the resident liable for late charges, interest on unpaid balances, or attorneys fees and costs if your account is turned over to a collection agency. Provisions such as these are routine; however, they can have a serious effect on the amount the senior will have to pay if he or she ever runs into financial difficulty and has to make late payments.

Readmission

Another issue that may arise during the resident's stay in the facility is the *readmission*, or *bedhold policy*. This issue comes up whenever a resident leaves the facility for a hospital stay or for what is known as a therapeutic home stay, which refers to an extended (at least overnight) visit with family away from the facility. The facility should have a policy outlining the requirements and procedure for readmission. One common policy is a daily fee for holding a bed. Be sure that the family is informed of the charge to reserve the bed if the senior needs to leave the facility for a hospital stay.

Residents who have been discharged to the hospital or on therapeutic home leave should have priority in being readmitted to the facility. Some facilities have different policies for residents who have been discharged for other reasons. State law governs bedhold requirements for Medicaid recipients who have been discharged or who are on therapeutic home leave, but federal law requires that Medicaid recipients be allowed readmission to the first available bed in a semi-private room.

If the facility has separate requirements for admission of non-private-pay residents, for example, those receiving Medicare, Medicaid, or Veterans Affairs benefits, the requirements should be clearly spelled out in the contract, whether they result from facility policy or from local, state, or federal law.

Fee Increases

Fees should be expected to increase from time to time, but be sure that you understand and agree with the manner in which increases are handled. Sometimes, families are told that fee increases will be small and manageable. It is after the family member is settled into his or her new home, however, that the reality of the situation becomes clear—the rate hikes are greater than the family's resources. It may be that the base rate goes up or perhaps the facility determines that additional services need to be provided to the resident at an extra charge. Or, the facility may cut out a necessary service without providing a rebate, forcing the family to obtain and pay for the service elsewhere.

This is a particularly difficult position for residents of assisted living facilities to be in, because they generally are not able to count on Medicaid to help with the burden. (see Chapter 6.) The family then must decide whether to accept the rate increase, fight it, or find new accommodations for the resident—none of which are desirable options. When searching for a skilled nursing or assisted living facility, do not accept statements from facility personnel that fee increases will not outpace the family's ability to pay. Get it in writing. If possible, require the contract to state that no charges will be assessed other than those specifically enumerated in the contract. Even better, ask that the contract state a limit on the percentage that fees may increase per year.

Termination and Discharge
The contract also should include any policies regarding termination of the contract by either side and discharge of the resident. For the protection of the senior, be sure that time is provided to secure other living arrangements if the contract is terminated. Under federal law, the family should be allowed at least thirty days to secure other living arrangements, unless applicable law specifies a different time period. State law may be stricter than the minimum standards provided for under the federal act, so more notice might be required where you live.

According to the federal *Nursing Home Reform Act*, found in Appendix H, a nursing home may not transfer or discharge the resident unless:

◆ the transfer or discharge is necessary to meet the resident's welfare and the resident's welfare cannot be met in the facility;

◆ the transfer or discharge is appropriate because the resident's health has improved sufficiently, so the resident no longer needs the services provided by the facility;

◆ the safety of individuals in the facility is endangered;

◆ the health of individuals in the facility would otherwise be endangered;

◆ the resident has failed, after reasonable and appropriate notice, to pay for a stay at the facility; or,

◆ the facility ceases to operate.
  (42 USC Sec. 1395i-3).

Waivers

The contract probably will contain a clause requiring the resident to waive any and all claims against the facility of whatever nature, whether it be for a loss of personal property or for a personal injury incurred on the facility premises. It is best if the senior refuses to sign such a waiver, but the reality is that the facility can deny admission without it. On the other hand, a release of any and all liability for negligence on the part of the facility may be unenforceable. Attempt to have a waiver of all liability on the part of the facility left out of the contract.

Negotiating the Contract

Unless state or federal law requires that a particular provision be present in a contract, any aspect of the resident's admission agreement is subject to negotiation. That may even include the rates that are charged and the services that are provided. If the resident or the resident's representative and the administration agree to change the standard contract, both parties must acknowledge the change in writing, on the face of the contract.

Generally, this is accomplished by crossing out the clause that is to be omitted and/or by writing in the clause that is to be included and by having both parties initial the changes. Be sure that the person agreeing to the change is someone the facility's owner has authorized to make the agreement. If the facility is owned by a corporation, check with the corporate management as to who has authority to change the admission contract (usually it will be the administrator of the facility).

Appendix I includes a sample resident admission agreement. There are no provisions in the sample agreement regarding residents paying via Medicaid programs. This is because Medicaid-eligible residents have different requirements than residents paying in other ways. A waiver of liability is included in the form to see what one might look like. Keep in mind that the sample agreement is a generic form and that any agreement your family member may be asked to sign might look quite different. Examine the contract with a critical eye, especially if you see clauses limiting the facility's liability or requiring blanket consents for medical procedures (see the following section). Forms will vary from facility to facility, due to the makeup of the resident population (that is, depending on whether they are private pay or not) and due to the requirements of a particular state's law.

TIP: When evaluating a facility (if possible) or at some point prior to admitting your family member, ask for a copy of the contract and other admission documents in order to have it reviewed by an attorney familiar with contract law.

Placement Interview/Admission

Certainly in the case of nursing homes, and often with assisted living facilities as well, expect there to be some sort of pre-admission procedure to follow. Often, a nursing home or assisted living facility will have an application form for a prospective resident to fill out, either prior to accepting that person for admission or at the time of admission itself. The main reason for this is to gather important background information, such as the identity of the resident's representative (if there is one) and whether the resident has been admitted to any other facilities in the past. There also should be some sort of interview or inquiry into the specific needs of the prospective resident to determine whether the particular facility is properly equipped to meet the level of care that person requires.

POINTS TO CONSIDER
• Documents (other than the contract) the resident or the resident's representative should expect to sign upon admission
• Facility-provided orientation for the resident and the family as to the operations and policies of the facility
• Facility assistance for the resident in completing a Medicare or Medicaid application

At admission, the resident (or representative with power of attorney) will execute the admission contract and should be given some sort of orientation to the facility. This may involve a tour if the resident and his or her family have not already had a chance to see the facility for some reason. It also should include an in-depth explanation by the administration of the facility's policies, procedures, and operations.

Besides the admission contract, there probably will be a flurry of documents presented to the resident or the resident's representative at the time of admission. Read every document and do not allow anyone to rush you through the process. The person who signs the documents will be presumed to have understood them.

Policies

Most likely, the resident will have to sign a document showing that he or she has received a copy of the facility's policies and that the policies have been explained. Other documents that might be seen are various consents, including consent to photograph the resident for various purposes, and release forms, such as a release allowing the facility to provide personal information about the resident to outside medical providers, insurance companies, or state agencies. There also may be a number of forms required by various state or federal regulations, such as Medicaid-related forms or Social Security Administration documents.

Health-Care Consents

Another form you are almost certain to see is a consent for the health-care staff to perform routine examinations and procedures. In some cases, the facility may ask that a blanket consent be signed to cover any test or exam that may or may not become necessary, just in case. Such consent may be reviewed with the senior's physician so that the doctor can clarify exactly which procedures need to be done on a regular or routine basis. However, the consent should be limited to cases where a specific procedure is deemed to be necessary. For example, if your family member is diabetic and must have blood glucose testing performed several times daily, a blanket consent makes more sense than having to execute a consent every time the finger stick is done.

> NOTE: The resident should not sign such a consent that allows "any and all necessary procedures" or words to that effect.

Personal Property Inventory

The staff should also inventory the items of personal property that the resident brings with him or her upon admission. This should be done with or in the presence of the resident. The resident or the resident's representative will probably be asked to sign the inventory list to indicate that its contents are accurate.

> *TIP: If the facility has not asked for copies of your family member's important documents prior to the signing of the admission contract, contact the administrator and ask which documents will be necessary to provide, as well as whether a copy will suffice, rather than the original.*
>
> *Documents that might need to be provided include the senior's Social Security card, driver's license, birth and marriage certificates, bank statements and other documents pertaining to monetary or stock/bond accounts (perhaps going back as much as three years for Medicaid patients), life insurance policies, long-term care or health insurance policies, vehicle titles, real estate deeds, Medicare or Medicaid card, any application forms or notifications from Medicare or Medicaid officials, and any court documents relating to the appointment of a guardian for the senior.*
>
> *Have copies of advance directives available for placement in your family member's file, as well.*

Room Placements

As more and more people stay reasonably healthy for longer periods of time, facilities will be dealing increasingly with issues of sensitivity toward married, as well as unmarried resident couples. Families evaluating assisted living and nursing facilities for married couples should be sure that the staff respects couples' privacy and relationships. When the staff needs to discuss health care and other issues affecting the couple, the residents should be treated as a unit, as much as their physical and mental condition will allow.

POINTS TO CONSIDER
- Availability of private rooms
- Number of residents that share semi-private rooms
- Ability of a resident to relocate to another room if there is a problem with a roommate

Just as in society in general, intimate relationships sometimes occur in long-term care situations. Oftentimes the parties involved are not married. The key consideration in these situations is whether both people consent to the relationship. If both are competent, consenting adults, the facility should do nothing to discourage the relationship.

On the other hand, if one party is confused, incapacitated, or otherwise nonconsenting or incapable of consenting, the facility is legally obligated to protect that person from the one making advances. If the facility does not provide adequate protection, it may be liable for negligence and also may be cited with a deficiency by the state survey agency if the incident is reported.

NOTE: Unwanted sexual contact with a resident by another resident may rise to the level of abuse and should be reported. Nursing home abuse is discussed more thoroughly in Chapter 8.

In some cases, a married couple will request that they not be placed together, because they feel that they will get along better if they spend time apart and have their own space. This is not an altogether unusual request and the administration should work with the family to find the best room assignments for both spouses.

A good facility will have a written, nondiscriminatory policy regarding room assignments. It will give weight to certain factors, such as gender and medical condition, when assigning a room, but will not consider race, ethnicity, or religion.

In the case of assisted living facilities, there may be a choice of floor plans available to prospective residents. Many different kinds of residences may be considered assisted living. Accommodations may range from a single room in a hotel-type building, to a multi-room apartment, to a separate villa. It is especially important that the senior and the senior's family members see the living space first-hand so the senior's preferences and abilities can be discussed when choosing a floor plan.

TIP: Many facilities have a policy that it is the resident who complains (or whose family complains) about a roommate who is moved to a new room. Find out if this is the policy at the facility, and if it is, weigh it carefully in the event you consider asking for a new roommate for your family member.

POINTS TO CONSIDER
- Visiting hours
- If family members are welcome at any time
- If family or friends are allowed to take the resident out for the day
- If family or friends are allowed to take the resident out overnight or for an extended period of time

Visitors

Regular visiting hours for family members should be liberal, should extend from morning until evening, and should be available seven days a week. While there should be an end to regular visiting hours each day, so as not to disturb other residents during nighttime hours, family members should be allowed to enter the facility even during off-hours for extenuating circumstances. In the case of a late evening visit, there should be a policy requiring the visit to take place in such a location as to avoid intruding on the peace or privacy of other residents.

A resident should be allowed to leave the facility as his or her physician deems appropriate. Independent seniors should have the freedom to travel to nearby locations on their own, such as taking a walk to the neighborhood convenience store. Of course, if there is any issue of physical or mental ability, then the resident should be allowed to make such a trip only with proper supervision.

Family and friends also should be allowed to take the resident from the facility for day or overnight visits, so long as the resident's doctor or the facility's medical staff finds no danger to the resident's well-being in doing so. If the resident suffers from confusion or dementia, the family should provide the facility with a list of people who are authorized to take the resident from the premises and should insist that the facility allow no one else to remove the resident without permission from the resident's representative.

TIP: Make a visit to a prospective facility in the evening, toward the end of regular visiting hours, to check out nursing staff or aide levels. After placing your family member in a facility, continue to make periodic visits after hours to monitor the quality of care given by the night-shift staff.

Cleanliness

This one seems obvious, but it is more than just a matter of the floors shining and the linens being fresh. Bathroom fixtures, kitchen sinks, even telephones and doorknobs can be major harbors of bacteria. Laundry bins

POINTS TO CONSIDER
- Procedures followed for disinfecting the kitchen and bath areas
- Separation of clean and soiled laundry
- Handling of food in the kitchen
- Cleanliness of the dining area
- Cleanliness of common area furniture
- Frequency that residents' rooms and common areas are cleaned

used to carry soiled clothes or linens should never be used to hold clean laundry and vice versa. Dishes, silverware, and serving equipment should be sanitized in a disinfectant solution. Ask to see laundry and kitchen operations in action and ask questions about procedures. Ask more than one person in each department to see if you receive consistent answers.

If you notice an unpleasant odor, determine whether it is present throughout the facility or confined to one location. Accidents do happen and it may be that the problem is in the process of being cleaned up. Even a pleasant smell is suspect if it is too strong—it may be a sign that heavily-scented air fresheners are being used to mask bad odors. This is another reason why repeat visits are helpful.

TIP: Do not confuse décor with cleanliness. While pretty sofas and artwork on the walls are a plus, they are not as important as living in a hygienic environment.

POINTS TO CONSIDER
- Taste of the food
- Number of meals provided per day
- Number of days per week meals are provided
- Limits on how much food a resident may have at a particular meal
- Frequency that a particular item is served in a week or a month
- Snacks provided between meals
- Availability of menus to residents ahead of time
- Policies regarding keeping food in one's room

Meals

No matter what other limitations a person may encounter with age, dining should continue to be an enjoyable experience. Do not underestimate the importance of meal service when evaluating a facility. Ask to sample some of the food when visiting. Even after the senior has been placed, try to join him or her for a meal, on occasion, so you can be sure that food quality remains consistent. Ask to have a meal of your own, even if there is a charge for it.

Federal regulations provide that skilled care facilities must employ a qualified dietician. Meals should be varied and menus should be provided to residents or posted ahead of time so that the residents know what will be served. Dietary policies should be generous rather than restrictive. If there is no health-related reason for limiting a resident's type or amount of food, residents should be given choices as to what entrees and sides they are served and should be given the opportunity to snack between large sit-down meals.

A policy barring residents from keeping food in their rooms makes sense for pest control purposes. In such a case, however, the facility should have a means by which residents can keep snacks of their own choosing in a food storage area and can remove the snacks for immediate consumption in their own room or in a dining area.

TIP: When evaluating a facility, try to make at least one visit during mealtime and observe the atmosphere of the dining room. Even though the quality and taste of the food are the main considerations, the atmosphere is also important to a pleasurable dining experience. See if the room is excessively noisy and note whether the dining room staff rushes the meal or allows the residents to relax and enjoy their food.

Special Services

Facilities may differ greatly in the level of so-called ancillary, or special, services that are offered to residents. Assisted living facilities may be less likely to provide such services than will a skilled care facility. However, if a senior is looking for an assisted living residence and therapies are not offered, be sure that the services of a therapist can be retained on the family's own accord. Expect to pay separately for services on an as-needed basis, although it is possible that a facility will include the fee for the ancillary services in the monthly charge. If this is the case, beware that you are not paying for services that your family member does not actually need. Again, when reviewing the contract, be sure that all charges are itemized and in writing.

POINTS TO CONSIDER
• Ancillary services provided
• Availability of occupational therapy
• Availability of physical therapy
• Availability of speech therapy
• Frequency that therapists are available
• Availability of dental care
• Availability of foot care
• Availability of eye care
• Availability of hospice care

Hospice services are usually provided by an organization that is independent of the facility, but that has a contract with the facility. When deciding on a nursing home, find out the policy of the facility regarding nonaffiliated hospice organizations.

The main advantage to using the hospice provider that is under contract with the facility is that the resident benefits from favorable terms in the agreement. The responsibilities of the affiliated hospice provider should be specifically spelled out in the contract, so that there is no confusion over which duties are performed by hospice and which are to be performed by the facility itself.

Many states' regulations prohibit hospice from discharging a patient from hospice if he or she becomes unable to pay or if Medicare or Medicaid benefits run out. If this is not the case in your state, inquire whether the facility's contract with the hospice organization provides that hospice may not terminate care to a patient who no longer can pay.

TIP: Find out if the facility offers available therapies seven days a week. Many nursing homes only have therapists available Monday through Friday. Although most patients do not receive therapy every day, seven-day-a-week availability is a great convenience to residents, because they are able to make up sessions that may have been missed during the week on account of doctor's appointments, special social events at the facility, and so on.

Quality of Living Space

While service and care are tantamount issues for any facility evaluation, do not discredit other quality of living space issues. The amount of available storage space for a resident's clothes, toiletries, and other personal property can directly impact the comfort level of the resident.

Do not underestimate the importance to your family member of the room temperature in a facility. Although some people may find it amusing that some seniors complain that they are too cold or too hot, there is nothing humorous about being uncomfortable day in and day out. It is a real quality of life issue.

POINTS TO CONSIDER
- Temperature of the room
- Temperature of the water in the residents' sinks and showers
- Amount of storage space for clothing and personal effects
- Amount of storage space in the bath area for toiletries

Personal Property

Facilities should have written policies regarding residents' personal property. A good facility will provide the family with recommendations for what type and how many clothing items a resident should have. Typically, the facility will take an inventory of personal property at the time of admission and will ask the resi-

POINTS TO CONSIDER
- Facility's policy regarding the resident's personal property
- Any items that may be forbidden
- Facility's policy regarding the keeping of valuables

dent or the resident's representative to sign the inventory.

The facility will almost certainly decline responsibility for personal property of the resident. Residents may misplace their own belongings or a confused resident may take another resident's belongings by mistake. Unfortunately, in spite of background checks performed on staff, occasionally there may be instances of theft by employees. For these reasons, items of personal property that are monetarily valuable should not be left in the resident's room. Any personal property the resident keeps in his or her room, such as clothing, toiletry items, books, picture frames, and so on, should be labeled in as permanent a manner as possible.

Cash should not be kept in a resident's room. The facility is required by law to have a system to account for each resident's personal funds that are held by the facility for the resident's benefit. Moreover, federal regulations require facilities holding more than $50 of a resident's personal funds to deposit that money in an interest-bearing account for the benefit of the resident. There must be a written record of all transactions involving the resident's money and the resident must be allowed to examine the record.

In the case of a resident who is competent to manage his or her own money, the facility should not impede the resident's access to his or her own funds. However, in the case of a confused resident, the facility should have a procedure in place whereby the resident's representative must approve withdrawals of funds from the resident's account. Federal regulations dealing with the handling of nursing home resident's personal funds can be found in Appendix F.

Facilities should have a written policy regarding the labeling of clothing and other personal items. Some facilities will require that residents' names be written in permanent ink in an inconspicuous place on the clothing. This is to allow the resident his or her dignity, by avoiding having his or her name plastered across his or her back. Facilities also should have a procedure by which a resident or family can report missing property and by which the administration investigates all such reports.

TIP: Prior to placing your family member in an assisted living or a skilled care facility, take photographs of any items of durable personal property, such as clothing, television sets or other electronics, furniture, books, and costume jewelry. Fine jewelry should not be kept in the resident's room. Photographs will provide documentation not only of the property itself, but also of the condition of the property should anything become damaged.

Laundry and Housekeeping

Laundry is handled differently by different facilities, so be sure you understand what the options are for the resident's clothing. Some facilities have their own laundry rooms, while others send laundry out to a cleaner. In some cases, laundry service is an extra charge by the facility and in others, it is included in the basic monthly rate. Some facilities do not separate clothing items into loads according to color or fabric, but others will go so far as to iron residents' clothes after washing. If you are having the facility do your loved one's laun-

POINTS TO CONSIDER
- Frequency that laundry is done
- Assistance provided with housework in an assisted living situation
- Frequency that the rooms are cleaned in a skilled care facility
- Frequency that sheets and towels are changed

dry, be sure that all of his or her clothing is machine washable, so that nothing gets ruined.

Some families prefer to bypass the facility's laundry entirely and wash their loved one's clothes at home. If you choose to do this, be sure you are not being charged for laundry service. Even if you do your family member's wash yourself, his or her clothing still should be labeled inconspicuously with his or her name, in case the laundry staff picks up the clothing by mistake or it otherwise is misplaced.

TIP: If the family will be doing the resident's laundry at home, put a sign on the resident's closet notifying the staff, so that they do not take the resident's laundry to the facility's laundry room.

Disputes and Grievances

Sometimes a resident or his or her family may have a dispute with an employee, another resident, or a particular policy of the facility. It is important to know how the administration handles these circumstances. Policies relating to dispute resolution should be in writing and available for examination by prospective residents and their families.

Facilities typically have a *resident council*, which is a group of residents

POINTS TO CONSIDER
- Manner in which disputes are handled between residents
- Manner in which disputes are handled between residents and staff
- Manner in which disputes are handled between family and administration
- Procedure for filing a grievance
- Availability of a resident council
- Availability of a family council
- Availability of the administrator to meet with the resident or family to discuss concerns

who represent the interests of all the residents. They may also have a *family council,* made up of relatives of the residents. Of the two, it is more important to have a resident council, because it is important that the residents have their own voice in their own home. Resident councils also are important because residents may have different concerns than their family members and those concerns should take precedence.

Regular meetings are held between the council, department heads, and other administrative personnel to address the concerns of the residents. If possible, sit in on such a meeting when you are evaluating a facility in order to get an idea of how the staff and administration respond to matters that residents bring to their attention.

When voicing a grievance, be sure that you are addressing the best person to respond to the situation. Shouting at the weekend receptionist may make you feel better, but it probably will not get you the results you desire. Unless the situation is endangering the life or health of the resident, start by voicing the concern directly to the responsible employee. If that does not solve the problem, take the next step, and speak to the director of the employee's department. Then go to the administrator if necessary. If you are dealing with a corporate-owned facility, the next move is to bring the problem to the attention of the corporate management. The concept of a corporate ethics committee to deal with a variety of long-term care issues, including residents' concerns, has become more typical in recent years.

A potential problem occurs when the facility increases fees. If the increase is large, unexpected, or if it does not seem to be in line with the services that are being provided, the resident and his or her family have a dilemma. Do they accept the increase in charges, try to dispute it, or do they move the senior to a new facility?

If you find yourself in this situation, you should contact the long-term care ombudsman for the area in which the nursing home resides. The ombudsman's office has experience dealing with circumstances such as these and may be able to help you resolve the dispute with the facility. You can locate the ombudsman's office in your state online at **www.ltcombudsman.org**, or by calling the National Long-Term Care Ombudsman Resource Center at 202-332-2275.

> *TIP: If possible, get to know family members of other residents. Introduce yourself to your loved one's roommate's family, attend facility-sponsored family events and the like, and strike up some conversations. This networking is a good way to find out if anyone else has had a similar complaint to yours and having acquaintances among other residents' families may provide you with extra eyes when you are not visiting the facility.*

Activities

Residency in an assisted living or skilled care facility should enhance life by providing opportunities to meet others and participate in daily social and educational activities. Look for a facility that offers activities seven days a week, including evenings. Some facilities cooperate with local colleges and park districts to offer a variety of classes held at the center.

Transportation should be available to allow residents to attend community events, churches, restaurants, and shopping malls. Voting in local and nation-

POINTS TO CONSIDER
- Social and leisure activities available for residents
- Methods used to notify residents of organized events
- Availability of books or other reading materials to residents in the facility

al elections should be made convenient. Residents' prior interests should be allowed to continue and their individual recreational needs should be assessed. Activities should be available for people with different levels of functional ability, so that those who require more assistance can participate as well as those who are fairly independent.

It is also important that the community is welcomed to the facility, so that residents can keep in touch with local veterans' groups, libraries, neighborhood schools and parishes, and other local organizations of interest.

> *TIP: Although the physical appearance of a facility is important, do not make the décor your primary consideration. The "heart" of a nursing home or assisted living facility is the opportunity for residents to socialize and remain active to the greatest extent possible. Give great weight to the number and variety of activities provided to the residents.*

Conveniences

The availability of telephones and televisions to residents is a quality of life concern, as both conveniences will make the resident feel more at home in the facility. If possible, provide the senior with his or her own television in his or her room, even if it is a small one.

POINTS TO CONSIDER
- Telephone access
- Hours set for television viewing, either in common areas or one's own room
- Resident's access to cable television, a VCR, or a DVD player

This is important not just for entertainment purposes, but so the senior can stay informed of current events. Many televisions are equipped with an outlet for an earpiece or set of headphones, so the television can be watched into the evening without disturbing a roommate.

TIP: If telephone service is an extra charge, consider pro-viding your family member with a prepaid telephone card so that he or she may make telephone calls without having to be billed by the facility. See if the facility will keep the card in a secure location, as it should do for residents' cash. Keep the card balance at a small amount in case it gets lost.

NOTE: In an assisted living facility, if the resident needs assistance in placing a telephone call, it may be considered a service for which there is an extra charge.

Amenities

As with the activities that are offered, extras provided by the facility will help make the senior feel more comfortable in the new surroundings. Some examples of amenities one might find include in-house religious services, a beautician, an ice cream parlor, or a convenience shop for sundries. The availability of these extras may depend on the location of the facility. Rural areas or lower income neighborhoods may not be as likely to have facilities containing extras, so it is important to compare several similar facilities, if possible, to determine what the stan-dard is for the area.

TIP: If you would like to see an amenity offered in your family member's facility after the senior has moved in, talk to the activity director to see if it may be offered. If there is an obstacle to providing the amenity, take the initiative and see if you can bring it to the facility. For example, a local drugstore or discount chain may be willing to make a donation of or give a reduced price for sundry items the facility does not provide, such as sam-ple-sized lotions, combs, or special snack items.

Behavioral Concerns

The issue of restraints addressed by federal law and by the laws of most states. The federal *Nursing Home Reform Act*, found in Appendix H, provides that residents may not be physically or chemically restrained for purposes of discipline or convenience. Such restraints may be imposed only if required to treat the resident's medical symptoms. This provision sometimes is liberally interpreted by long-term care facilities, however, and residents who are confused and may pose a danger to themselves or others sometimes are administered sedatives as a form of chemical restraint.

POINTS TO CONSIDER
- Policy regarding placing restraints on a resident
- Manner in which the facility handles cases in which the resident may be a danger to him- or herself or others

Some senior advocacy organizations encourage families to insist upon restraint-free care for their loved ones. There are two sides to this issue. On one hand, physical and chemical restraints can have adverse side effects on the patient, including depression and withdrawal from social interaction, and physical ailments such as circulation problems and medication interactions. On the other hand, a resident may need protection from falls and other injuries that may occur as a result of confusion or unsteadiness. An example is a resident who needs assistance getting out of bed, but who forgets to call the nurse for help when waking up in the middle of the night and tries to get up on his or her own.

A resident who is competent, may not be kept in a facility against his or her will. However, those who leave against the advice of a physician, with the intent not to return, risk losing benefits not only under Medicare or Medicaid, but also possibly under health-or long-term care insurance. Typically, a facility will contact the family in the event a resident tries to discharge him- or herself from the facility and may even call in a mental health-care professional to do an evaluation, if possible. The facility should have a policy of working with the family to encourage the resident to remain at the facility for the resident's own welfare.

Federal law also authorizes skilled care facilities to discharge and transfer residents who pose a danger to the health or safety of themselves or others. Some facilities are hesitant to do this, however, because they are concerned about the possibility that the state survey agency will be called to cite the facility for a violation and because facilities generally prefer to have as many beds filled as possible.

TIP: The National Citizen's Coalition for Nursing Home Reform is a leading advocacy group that provides consumer information about issues concerning long-term care facilities. The organization has a number of suggestions for families seeking restraint-free care for their loved ones. Their fact sheets, Restraint Use and Individualized Assessment with Behavioral Symptoms, are available online at www.nccnhr.org or by calling 202-332-2275.

Safety

Most states have extensive regulatory safety codes that apply to buildings such as assisted living facilities and nursing homes. This does not necessarily mean that a facility is abiding by those codes. In other words, do not trust that any facility that you are considering has taken safety precautions. Check it out for yourself.

POINTS TO CONSIDER
- Carpeted or skid-resistant floor surfaces
- Number of emergency exits
- Emergency exits locked to those outside
- Handicap-accessible and private bathrooms and showers
- Grab bars and call buttons in bathrooms and showers
- Procedures the nursing staff follows regarding biohazards

As the list of safety questions indicates, there are a great number of possible safety hazards present in an institutional setting. Many of these exist simply because of the nature of the facility. Falls are a particular concern when dealing with the elderly and biohazards are present because of the health care function provided. While the risks are real, a good home will have strict policies in place that are carefully followed by the staff. When giving baths, for example, aides must be trained in proper techniques for lifting and moving residents who are not mobile.

Biohazardous materials (blood and other bodily fluids, used bandages, used sharps and injection needles, and so on) must be kept secure and out of reach of residents until properly disposed. Likewise, medications must be kept locked and access to medication cabinets should be limited to appropriate nursing personnel.

At a minimum, be sure that fire alarms are low enough to be reached by residents in wheelchairs. See that each resident's room has a call button, and preferably two—one that can be reached from the bed, and one that can be reached from the toilet. Grab bars should be present in all toilet and bath areas and there should be seating available if bathing takes place in a shower stall. The floor should either be carpeted or the surface of the floor should be made up of nonslip material. Every room should have its own sprinkler and fire extinguishers should be easy to access (these items usually are covered by state fire codes).

TIP: If your family member has a hearing deficiency, ask the administrator if it is possible to test the pitch of the smoke alarm to ensure that the sound is within your family member's range of hearing. Sometimes smoke alarms can be too high-pitched for elderly people to hear.

Security

Nursing homes and assisted living facilities must have procedures in place to prevent confused residents from wandering off the premises, particularly if the facility caters to residents with Alzheimer's disease. Similarly, facilities also must have a method of screening those coming in, to protect the residents from predators. Doors should be locked to those coming in from outside after visiting hours, but should not be locked to those inside, in case evacuation is necessary.

POINTS TO CONSIDER
- Whether comprehensive background checks are performed on applicants for staff positions
- Video surveillance equipment used on the grounds

Some facilities place confused residents in separate wings with key-padded doors. Anyone passing through the doors must know a code, otherwise an alarm will sound to alert the staff that an unauthorized person has opened the door. Facilities with more than one floor may place residents with dementia on the upper floors to make it more difficult for them to leave the premises without being noticed.

Another security issue is that of the staff. Long-term care facility employees often are underpaid and a critical nationwide shortage of licensed nursing employees means that staff is likely to be overworked as well. As a result, facilities may not necessarily have the best qualified or most highly motivated personnel caring for the residents. For this reason, it is imperative that thorough background checks are performed on all nursing staff. (Security issues connected with staffing are discussed more thoroughly in Chapter 8.)

TIP: Note how you and your loved one's other family members are screened the first few times you enter a prospective facility, before you become familiar to the staff. Are you able to come and go as you please? Does anyone greet you? Is there a sign-in sheet to track who is in the building? If no one questions your presence in the facility, chances are they are not questioning anyone else, either.

Prevention of Abuse

In some cases, there may be a fine line between a consensual relationship between two residents and a predatory situation. Be sure the facility's policies are understood for protecting residents, who may experience confusion or suffer from dementia from nonconsensual contact, sexual or otherwise, at the hands of other residents. Such contact at the hands of employees must be strictly forbidden by the administration. (Prevention of nursing home abuse is discussed more thoroughly in Chapter 8.)

POINTS TO CONSIDER
- Training the staff has received to protect residents from physical or sexual abuse
- Whether facility has been subjected to discipline from the state or litigation by a resident or family resulting from allegations of physical or sexual abuse

TIP: Although there is no foolproof way to prevent nursing home abuse or neglect, one method of minimizing the likelihood of it happening is to maintain a presence in the facility. Do this by making frequent visits at varied times, by participating in care conferences and facility-run family events, and by getting to know staff and other families. Make sure the staff knows you as well as your family member by name.

Emergency Situations

The geographical location of the facility will determine which emergency situations need to be addressed by the administra-

POINTS TO CONSIDER

- Practice drills for weather situations
- Plan for contacting residents' families in the event of a public emergency

tion—a hurricane evacuation procedure is not necessary in the Midwest, but a tornado emergency plan will be mandatory. Some emergency situations must be prepared for no matter what the location—fires, gas or other chemical leaks, and at this point in human history, biological or other terrorist situations all must be considered a possibility.

Ask the administrator for the written policies for emergency situations and inquire as to the amount of preparation and training the staff has undergone for such events. If possible, find out when the next training session or drill will be held and visit at that time.

TIP: Contact the fire department or fire protection district that serves the facility you are considering and request records of calls made on the facility in the past several years. Such records should be accessible under the state's Freedom of Information Act (FOIA). Usually, there is an administrative charge for copying documents requested under FOIA, but it may be worthwhile to review the types of calls, if any, that the fire department has had to respond to at the facility.

CHECKLISTS

Pre-Admission and Admission

❏ Is the facility accepting residents? _____

   ❏ If not, is there a waiting list? _____

❏ Is the facility Medicare- and Medicaid-certified?_____

❏ Does it accept Medicare or Medicaid patients? _____

❏ Does the facility hold a current state license? _____

❏ Is the administrator licensed? _____

❏ Has the facility been cited for deficiencies in its most recent survey?

_____

   ❏ Have the deficiencies been corrected? _____

❏ Can the administrator provide references for the facility? _____

❏ Is there a contract? _____

   ❏ Can a copy be examined before a decision is made? _____

   ❏ Can the contract be amended at a later date if necessary? _____

❏ Is a security deposit or application fee required? _____

   ❏ Can fees be increased? _____

   ❏ How much notice is given before an increase? _____

❏ How is billing and payment handled? _____

_____

❏ What happens to a resident who becomes unable to pay, either because private funds have run out, insurance has lapsed, or public aid/Medicare eligibility has been lost? _____

_____

❏ Is the resident's room kept open for him or her during a temporary leave?_____

❏ What is the admission procedure for the facility? _____

❏ Does the facility require a prospective resident to fill out a formal application?_____

❏ Is there a placement interview prior to admission? _____

Treatment of Residents

❑ Is the resident's plan of care followed? _____
  ❑ Does the resident and the family have sufficient input into the plan of care?_____
❑ Do the same nursing staff members treat a resident on most days or does the resident see many different nurses and aides? _____
_____

❑ Is the nursing staff comprised of payrolled employees or is it mainly temporary or agency hires? _____
❑ Can a resident see his or her own physician or is the resident limited to staff- or facility-approved doctors?_____
❑ If the resident's physician does not make house calls, will the facility provide transportation to the doctor's office? _____
❑ Will the facility obtain the services of a specialist for the resident if necessary? _____
  ❑ Who determines if the resident needs to see a specialist? _____
❑ Does the facility provide dental care? _____
❑ Do staff members appear to know the residents on a personal basis?
_____

❑ Are residents dressed in hospital gowns or are they wearing normal clothing?_____
❑ Do staff members respond to residents' call lights in a timely fashion?
_____

❑ Do they respond to residents who are verbally asking for help? ____
❑ Are residents allowed to administer their own medications? _____
❑ Will staff assist with feeding if the resident needs help eating? _____
❑ Is assistance provided with management of personal business, such as shopping, keeping doctor's appointments, and paying bills? ____
_____

❑ Will staff assist with toileting, if necessary?_____
❑ Is there is a special service unit? _____
  ❑ Who determines whether the resident should be placed in the special service unit? _____
  ❑ Who determines whether the resident should be removed from special service unit? _____

❏ Can a resident be discharged or transferred? _____
   ❏ On what grounds can a resident be discharged or transferred?

   _____

   ❏ How much notice would be given before a discharge or transfer?

   _____

❏ Will the facility take an inventory of the personal property the resident brings into the facility upon admission?_____

❏ In the case of an assisted living facility, are there different floor
plans to choose from?_____

❏ Can a married couple share a room? _____
   ❏ Are there any policies in place regarding the privacy rights of
   married couples residing at the facility? _____

❏ If therapists are not affiliated with the facility, can the resident
secure therapeutic services on his or her own? _____

❏ Are there special service living units, such as an Alzheimer's disease
wing? _____

❏ Does the facility require medications to come from an affiliated
pharmacy or can the resident choose his or her own pharmacy?

   _____

❏ If hospice care is provided, does the agreement between the facility
and the hospice provider prohibit the provider from discharging the
patient from hospice if the patient becomes unable to pay for hospice services?_____

❏ May a resident check him- or herself out if he or she is adamant
about leaving? _____

Life at the Facility

❑ How does the kitchen staff handle meals? _____

❑ Are meals served on dishes or disposable plates? _____

❑ Is the meal served at a suitable temperature? _____

❑ Are entrée or side dish options provided for each meal? _____

❑ Is fresh produce ever served or is food usually processed (canned or frozen)? _____

❑ May a resident request a substitution? _____

❑ Will dietary restrictions or preferences be catered to? _____

❑ Will meals be provided to the resident in his or her room if requested or only if it is required? _____

❑ Is the living space acceptable? _____

❑ Is the living space decorated or sparse? _____

❑ Is the living space roomy or cramped? _____

❑ Are the chairs and bed comfortable? _____

❑ Is the resident able to get in and out of the bed and the chairs? ____

❑ Do semi-private rooms have privacy curtains for each resident's living space? _____

❑ Does each resident's room have its own thermostat? _____

❑ How many residents share a bathroom or shower area? _____

❑ How often are showers available? _____

❑ May the resident bring any furniture for the room? _____

❑ Are toiletry items, such as toothpaste or razors, or other supplies, such as over-the-counter medications, included in the basic contract rate? _____

❑ Is laundry service included in the basic monthly charge? _____

❑ In an assisted living facility, who does laundry—the resident or staff? _____

❑ Is laundry done on-site or is it sent out? _____

❑ Can family members do the resident's laundry at home if they choose? _____

❑ Do at least some of the residents appear to be engaged in activities or are they mainly sitting around common areas or confined to their rooms? _____

❑ Are there organized events or are residents left on their own to find opportunities to socialize? _____

   ❑ Are activity schedules posted? _____

   ❑ Does the staff approach residents and encourage them to join a particular activity? _____

   ❑ Are activities offered on evenings and weekends? _____

   ❑ May residents decline to participate in an activity if they wish?

_____

   ❑ Are there group outings to outside locations, such as movies or shopping? _____

   ❑ How is transportation provided? _____

❑ If access to a telephone is shared, who is responsible for payment for phone service? _____

   ❑ Will the staff provide assistance to the resident in using the telephone, if necessary? _____

❑ May the resident have a television in his or her room? _____

   ❑ Is there a community room with a television? _____

Safety, Sanitary, and Security Concerns

❑ Does the facility appear clean? _____

❑ Are the bathrooms stocked with towels? _____

❑ Are bathroom fixtures clean? _____

❑ Are the showers free of mildew? _____

❑ Do kitchen workers have their hair pulled back? _____

❑ Are dishes clean when they come out of the dishwasher? _____

❑ Does the facility smell clean? _____

❑ Do kitchen and nursing staff wear gloves and do they change gloves as necessary to avoid contamination? _____

❑ Are safety issues addressed? _____

❑ Are all rooms and common areas equipped with sprinklers? _____

❑ Are hallways equipped with fire alarms and fire extinguishers? ____

❑ Are there visual alarms as well as auditory ones to serve residents who may be hearing-impaired? _____

❑ Does the facility have a written procedure in place in case of fire? _____

❑ Are staff members trained in those fire procedures? _____

❑ Are practice drills held? _____
   ❑ How often are practice drills held?_____
   ❑ Are the exits easy to find and well lit? _____

❑ Are there stairwells and if so, are they equipped with any devices to keep a resident from falling down them, such as a swinging bar that must be pulled back before one can get onto the steps? _____

❑ Are medications kept secure and are they dispensed only by staff who is legally authorized to give them? _____

❑ Is safety or medical equipment, such as shower chairs, walkers, and wheelchairs, available to those who may need it?_____

❑ Is smoking allowed in the facility? _____
   ❑ If so, is it restricted to certain areas of the facility? _____
   ❑ How are residents supervised if they are allowed to smoke on the premises? _____

❑ Can anyone walk into or out of the facility freely or is there security to monitor comings and goings?_____

❑ Is there a specialized unit with alarmed doors for residents suffering from dementia? _____

❏ Are emergency exits attached to an alarm so that the staff knows if someone is exiting from a place other than the front door? _____

❏ Are there emergency plans in place to deal with safety and weather situations, such as fires, tornadoes, gas leaks, power outages, and so on? _____

    ❏ Are these plans in writing and available for inspection? _____

Chapter 6

Considering Financial Options

It is normal to think that no long-term care facility is too good for your family member. You simply want the best for him or her. Perhaps, too, families carry some guilt over the decision to place a relative in an institutional setting. It may seem callous to have to talk about cost concerns when discussing lifestyle options for your loved one. The fact remains, however, that money usually plays a role in the long-term care choices people make.

The main methods of paying for long-term care are:

◆ private pay, which is the use of one's own savings or assets;

◆ benefits paid out under a long-term care insurance policy; and,

◆ Medicaid, a state and federally funded program for low-income Americans.

Another federal program, Medicare, also pays for some long-term care. To a lesser extent, other benefits programs may cover long-term care expenses, such as Veterans Health Administration (VHA) benefits earned through prior military service.

Medicare is administered by the federal Centers for Medicare and Medicaid Services (CMS). Medicaid is administered by the individual states. In 2001, according to the CMS (**www.cms.hhs.gov**), there were more than 1.1 million

Medicare- and Medicaid-certified beds in almost 15,000 facilities in the United States. The *American Health Care Association* (**www.ahca.org**) states that more than 66% of nursing home residents are Medicaid recipients and another 11% pay for their care with assistance from Medicare. The rest pay privately with savings, the proceeds of long-term care insurance, or some other benefits.

How to pay for long-term care ultimately depends on the senior's resources or lack thereof. If financially well off, the senior will not even be eligible for Medicaid and will have more choices as a private pay resident. With fewer assets or a lower income, it is more likely that the senior will rely on Medicaid to cover costs. A well-prepared person may have taken out a long-term care insurance policy, but again, that person is more likely to be on the high end of the income range, because long-term care insurance tends to be pricey.

Private Pay

According to AARP (**www.aarp.org**), with nursing home costs averaging in the neighborhood of $150 per day, not many seniors can afford to pay for skilled nursing care entirely out of their own pockets. Even assisted living facilities, with costs around half that of skilled care facilities, still run in the range of $28,000 per year.

Private-pay residents generally, have more freedom in their living and health care choices than do residents paying for their care with the assistance of Medicare, Medicaid, or other government benefit or insurance plans. Private residents are not as restricted by regulations, contractual provisions of insurance policies, and so forth. They may obtain whatever services they deem necessary and can afford. They can choose their own physicians and specialists and can secure certain types of accommodations that nonprivate-pay residents are usually unable to have, such as a private room.

For this reason, paying for long-term health care out of one's own funds may seem to be an attractive option.

However, spending years scrimping and saving in order to pay privately may be a let-down. Many find that all that hard work does not leave much to show for it, because the daily expense of long-term care will eat up those savings quickly. As a result, some people may end up in a less desirable position than if they had used the money to purchase a long-term care insurance policy or had simply allowed public aid funds to cover the costs.

Supplemental Income

Social Security is a program of retirement benefits paid out to those who have contributed to the program over the course of their working lives by paying Social Security taxes. Social Security also offers disability insurance for those who have worked a certain length of time at qualifying jobs and have paid into Social Security. *Supplemental Security Income* (SSI) is an assistance program for low-income individuals who are age 65 and older or are disabled. The SSI program is funded by general taxes—not Social Security taxes. A senior may receive Medicaid and Social Security benefits or SSI at the same time. To apply for benefits, the individual must visit a local Social Security office or call the Social Security Administration (SSA) at 800-772-1213 and make an appointment with an SSA representative.

Reverse Mortgages

An increasingly popular method of funding long-term care is through the use of a *reverse mortgage*. A homeowner whose mortgage is paid off or almost paid can draw on the equity in his or her home, in the form of a loan, to pay for skilled care, assisted living, long-term care insurance, or other long-term care costs. Unlike a traditional mortgage, with the homeowner making payments to the lender, in a reverse mortgage situation, the lender pays the homeowner. Payments may take the form of a line of credit, can be a monthly payment, or can be a lump sum amount. As with a traditional mortgage, interest and other costs, such as origination fees, accrue on a reverse mortgage. The senior eventually will have to pay back these costs. The loan becomes due when the home is sold, when the owner moves from the home permanently, or when the owner dies.

Funds that a senior receives from a reverse mortgage do not count as income for federal tax purposes. However, they do count as income for purposes of determining Medicaid eligibility. Also, unlike a traditional mortgage, payments that the senior makes to pay back the interest on a reverse mortgage are not deductible for tax purposes.

The downside to the reverse mortgage is the possibility that it will not be enough to cover the senior's long-term care costs as the years go on. The senior could live longer than the life of the loan or the total expense for long-term care could exceed the amount of the loan. If either is the case, the home may end up having to be sold to repay the loan. If there is equity remaining after the home is sold, it belongs to the senior. If no equity is left and the senior has few other assets, he or she may have to rely on Medicaid to cover continuing care expenses. Keep in mind, too, that the senior will remain liable for other homeowner expenses, such as real estate taxes, homeowner association dues, utilities, and homeowners' insurance, during the life of the loan.

Reverse mortgages are available from private lenders. The United States government also has a federally insured reverse mortgage program, called the *Home Equity Conversion Mortgage Program* (HECM). Only seniors aged 62 years and older are eligible for an HECM loan. HECM applicants also must participate in reverse mortgage counseling.

The advantage of HECM loans over private ones to the homeowner is that if the amount due on the loan is greater than the equity in the house, the homeowner will not be forced to sell the home until he or she moves, sells the home, or dies. Neither the senior nor his or her estate will be liable for the excess of the amount of the loan over the amount of equity, which is covered by federal insurance.

Tax Treatment of Long-Term Care Expenses

There are a number of tax implications when a senior relocates to a long-term care facility. The sale of one's home, giving away of one's property, and setting up of trusts for grandchildren all may have tax consequences that should be discussed with a competent tax attorney and are beyond the scope of this book. Long-term care expenses themselves may or may not be tax deductible, depending on the nature of the expense and the reason the taxpayer is in a long-term care facility. (See IRS Publication 502 for more information.)

The taxpayer may deduct the cost of medical care in a nursing home for him- or herself, his or her spouse, and his or her dependents. If the primary reason for the nursing home stay is for medical care, then the cost of meals and accommodations also can be deducted as a medical expense. If the main reason for the stay is for personal or custodial care, then meals and lodging are not deductible; however, the actual medical portion of the expenses still is deductible.

Custodial care is the type of care that does not lead to rehabilitation and includes routine assistance with activities of daily living such as bathing and dressing. In addition, the expense must be *unreimbursed*, which means it must be an out-of-pocket cost actually paid by the resident and must not already be covered by long-term care insurance or other benefits.

Insurance

Long-term care insurance policies exist that will cover the expense of skilled nursing care, but they can be expensive. The annual premium increases with the age of the insured. Such a policy will cost less when purchased by a 40-year-old than by someone age 70. However, the younger policyholder may end up paying much more over the life of the policy and may never end up making use of the proceeds. This is the same consideration as with any other type of insurance—you have it in case you need it, but if you are lucky, you never need the benefits.

Adult children faced with the prospect of placing an elderly loved one in long-term care will probably find that it is too late to obtain an insurance policy for him or her. Long-term care insurance companies generally are only interested in insuring younger, healthier individuals. Some companies will not insure anyone who has a pre-existing condition or who is past a certain age. If you do find a company that is willing to insure your family member, take a look at an insurance rating agency such as *A.M. Best*. Better insurance companies will be rated A or better. Oftentimes, only a lower-rated company will insure someone who is older or in poor health.

There are some important differences between long-term care insurance and other types of insurance that consumers need to know about. As with other kinds of insurance, obtain a number of quotes to find the best coverage for your money.

Premiums

According to the *American Health Care Association*, a typical annual premium for a long-term care insurance policy on a 50-year-old could run in the area of $800 and could be double that for a 65-year-old. This is a generalization. Premiums can fluctuate greatly depending on the age and health of the policyholder, the benefits desired, the length of the coverage period, and the quality of the insurance company.

Long-term care insurance premiums are set at the time the insured purchases the policy, and generally remain the same unless they are changed for all policyholders at the same time. In other words, the premium does not increase automatically just because the insured person gets older. However, if the insurance company decides that its payout of benefits for a certain class of insured—for example, all 80-year-olds—requires charging a higher premium for that class, it may increase the premiums for all 80-year-old insureds. For that reason, it may make sense to purchase a policy as a 50-year-old, when the premium is closer to the $800 example mentioned, than to wait until age 65, the price may be more than $1600 per year.

Another reason not to wait is that a long-term health care company usually requires prospective insureds to be in good health before the company will issue a policy. Those who wait too long to try to purchase a policy, may find that they do not qualify for insurance under most companies' rules because of ill health. In fact, some companies have an age limit, past which they will not issue a policy at all, regardless of the heath of the applicant.

Elimination Periods

Another difference between long-term care and other types of insurance is the concept of the *deductible*. With long-term care insurance, there is no requirement of a deductible, which is a certain out-of-pocket dollar amount that must be satisfied before insurance coverage begins. Instead, long-term care policies provide for an *elimination period*, which is a waiting period during which the insured must pay for his or her own long-term care expenses.

Examine elimination period provisions closely when shopping for long-term care insurance. Companies can define this time interval in many different ways. For example, some companies require a new elimination period if long-term care is ended and then restarted at a later date. Others may count each day of care cumulatively, even if they do not occur consecutively, until the elimination period is met. These various treatments of the elimination period can dramatically impact the benefits that are paid out, so be sure that you understand them before purchasing a policy.

Expenses Covered

Another area of wide disparity among long-term care insurance policies is the way expenses are covered. A typical policy offers coverage of care expenses in terms of a fixed amount per day—for example, $100 per day for nursing home care. Beyond that, there are any number of variations in coverage terms. Some policies pay only for nursing home and assisted living facility care, while others pay for home health care as well. If you are considering a long-term care policy, you probably should purchase the broadest coverage your budget reasonably will allow, so that your care options are not limited. At the very least, you should have coverage for care in either a nursing home or an assisted living facility.

As always, read the policy carefully before purchasing, especially any provisions regarding conditions that are excluded from coverage. You should be sure that long-term placement resulting from Alzheimer's disease is specifically covered, because some policies exclude Alzheimer's patients. Other common exclusions are drug and alcohol addiction and conditions resulting from suicide attempts.

Qualifying for Coverage

When comparing different long-term care insurance policies, pay attention to the conditions the policy requires before benefits will be paid out. Insurance policies will stipulate what must occur or the physical or psychosocial state that must exist before benefits kick in. You will want to look for the policy that allows the widest range of conditions in order for an insured to qualify for coverage.

There are several different measures that insurance companies use to determine qualification. One is cognitive impairment, which means that even though the insured is physically able to take care of him- or herself, there may be a psychological impediment that requires long-term care. Another criterion some companies use to determine when qualification for benefits begins is the need for assistance with activities of daily living (ADLs). Some insurance companies provide that an insured must need assistance with a certain number of ADLs before coverage will begin. Other companies may require different levels of impairment before their coverage takes effect. For example, one policy may provide that an insured is eligible for benefits if he or she needs someone to give him or her direction while eating, while another policy may say that the insured is not eligible unless someone actually has to feed him or her. Be sure that you compare the benefits qualification clauses of any insurance policies you consider purchasing.

Maximum Benefits

All insurance policies have a limit on the benefits that they will pay out, but how that maximum is determined differs by company. Some companies limit the number of years of coverage. In other words, the insured will be covered up to a maximum period of time, such as five years. Other companies have a dollar limit on coverage of expenses. Some policies have different maximums for different covered services. Again, careful inspection of the policy is warranted so that you know what you are getting for your money.

Extra Protections

Some insurance companies offer optional protections for an extra charge. One of these features is the *inflation adjustment*, which means that the daily coverage rate increases over the life of the policy to keep in step with the rise in the cost of living. This is an important protection to consider because nursing home costs almost certainly will rise over time. Someone who buys a policy that pays $100 per day at the time of purchase, may not actually need the benefit for a number of years. When the insured actually needs the coverage, years later, the daily cost for long-term care may be much higher than $100.

Another option to think about is a *nonforfeiture benefit*, which allows the insured to receive partial coverage in the event he or she stops paying the premium and the policy expires. With a nonforfeiture benefit, the insured receives some protection if his or her financial situation changes and he or she is unable to keep up with premium payments. The amount of coverage is typically fairly small, however, and the extra premium the insured will pay year after year for the protection may be substantial. A person looking to purchase long-term care insurance should try to determine his or her continued ability to pay the premiums over time when deciding whether to add a nonforfeiture benefit.

Tax Benefits

Certain long-term care insurance policies are considered *tax qualified* for federal tax purposes. This means two things for insureds. First, a portion of the premiums for these policies are deductible as medical expenses, if the total medical expenses are more than 7.5% of the adjusted gross income. If medical expenses do exceed that level, the amount of the premium that is deductible is limited according to the age of the insured.

For 2003, the limits on deductibility were:

Age	Amount of Premium that is Deductible
40 and younger	$250
41 – 50	$470
51 – 60	$940
61 – 70	$2,510
Older than 70	$3,130

Source: Internal Revenue Service Publication 502

These limits increase each year.

The second tax advantage to owning a qualified long-term care insurance policy is that most benefits paid out under the policy are not taxable as income. The exception is for excess benefits that are paid out on a *per diem* basis, that is, when the insured receives benefits in a certain amount per day of long-term care. For 2003, the allowable per diem amount that escaped tax liability was $220. That amount also increases each year.

So, for example, if a senior received an insurance benefit in 2003 of $250 per day for long-term care, the daily benefit amount paid out would exceed the tax-free limit. The excess amount, $30 in this example, would be treated as taxable income. If the insured's long-term care expenses were greater than the actual amount paid out, however, the excess amount would not be taxable.

TIP: Some states also give tax incentives to purchasers of long-term care insurance. Contact your state's Department of Revenue for more information.

Choosing an Insurance Company

When shopping for a long-term care insurance policy, there are a few things that everyone should find out from the insurance agents. First, make sure each agent sells insurance on behalf of several companies. Agents who sell exclusively for one company will not have as many policies to choose from. Second, any issuing company that is being considered should be rated A or better by an insurance rating agency. It may not be possible to find a highly rated company to issue a policy for someone who is past a certain age or not in the best of health. Finally, as a general rule, it is better to purchase long-term care insurance from a larger company that deals in many other types of insurance. A diversified company tends to be more financially stable than a company selling only one or two types of insurance.

Employees of the United States government may be eligible for federally-provided long-term care insurance. *The Federal Long-Term Care Insurance Program* (FLTCIP) provides insurance to both current and retired federal employees and also to certain qualified family members, such as parents, adult children, and mothers- and fathers-in-law. Applicants must be age 18 or older to apply. There is no maximum age limit on applying for the federal long-term care insurance, but the applicant does still need to pass a health screening in order to be enrolled.

FLTCIP has a number of different benefit options from which to choose. As with private long-term care insurance, the premiums depend upon factors such as the age of the insured at the time the policy is purchased. For more information, access the FLTCIP online at **www.ltcfeds.com** or contact the agency by telephone at 800-582-3337.

How Much Insurance to Buy

Only the person actually purchasing the insurance policy can answer the question—*How much is enough?* It is a very difficult decision for someone with limited resources. The purchaser has to take into account his or her current and projected future income and must see into the future to estimate how many years of coverage will be needed. This is almost an impossible task.

As a very general rule of thumb, the individual can start with the average yearly cost of long-term care and subtract from that the retirement income he or she believes can be safely counted on in later years, such as investment or pension income (counting on Social Security income probably is not a good idea for purposes of this formula). Once that number is determined, multiply the difference by the number of years of coverage desired.

For example, a senior who lives in a state where the average yearly cost of skilled care is $50,000 and who receives $30,000 per year in pension benefits would need another $20,000 per year to make up the difference if he or she had to be placed in a nursing home. To be prepared for five years of care, a policy that will give $100,000 of nursing home coverage will need to be purchased.

Again, this is a very imprecise formula for deciding how much long-term care insurance to buy. The purchaser's present and future ability to pay the premiums will have much to do with the amount of any policy purchased. The cost of options that are available, such as inflation adjustments and nonforfeiture benefits, may make it necessary to limit spending on other features, such as the maximum benefit duration of the policy.

The bottom line is that long-term care insurance can be a very good way to take care of long-term health-care costs down the road. However, if the premiums put a serious strain on a senior's budget, financial resources may be put to better use either by paying off debt on assets that are considered exempt when determining eligibility for Medicaid, such as mortgage or car payments, or by placing funds in a trust for a grandchild's education. (A consultation with an elder law attorney is a good way to determine the best course for long-term care financial planning.)

Medicare

Medicare is a *universal*, federally funded insurance program that covers Americans aged 65 and older, persons with permanent kidney failure, and certain disabled persons under the age of 65. Medicare *Part A* covers inpatient hospital care, some nursing home care, and hospice services. Some home health care is also covered. Medicare *Part B* is medical insurance that pays for physicians' services and outpatient-based treatments. *Part B* also covers various other services, such as physical therapy and certain cancer screenings. There are alternatives to the original Medicare plan, such as the *Medicare Plus Choice* plans, which include private plans under contract with Medicare that provide greater benefits, or Medicare managed care plans that operate much like an HMO.

Medicare generally does not pay for assisted living. It may pay for certain ancillary services provided to an assisted living resident under some circumstances, but the actual basic monthly bill will not be covered. Medicare *Part A* does pay for some skilled nursing care, but there are time limits for coverage.

A qualifying hospital stay is required prior to any nursing home admission in order for the care to be covered by Medicare and even then Medicare will fully pay for only the first twenty days of care following the hospital stay. After that, the patient is required to make a co-payment for care until the 100th day. ($109.50 in 2004.) In addition, some recipients under the original Medicare plan are required to pay a deductible. After day 100, Medicare will no longer cover care in a skilled care facility.

A *qualifying hospital stay* is one that lasts at least three days, before admission to a nursing home. The admission must occur within thirty days after discharge from the hospital. The nursing home admission must be for the purpose of recuperating from the injury or illness that caused the hospital stay.

Medicare *Part B* will pay a percentage of the expense for doctors and for necessary therapies during the skilled care stay. The patient, however, is required to pay an annual premium ($66.60 in 2004) and meet a deductible ($100.00 in 2004) before *Part B* coverage kicks in. The patient must also make a 20% co-payment for all services beyond the deductible.

Custodial care is not payable by Medicare. In the case of a low-income resident, Medicaid rather than Medicare will cover custodial care in a nursing home. Nursing homes must receive Medicare or Medicaid certification in order to receive Medicare or Medicaid funds for their eligible residents. Certification comes from the state and is granted according to that state's particular regulations.

Enrollment in Medicare is through the *Social Security Administration* (SSA). The SSA recommends that people seeking to enroll in Medicare apply about three months before their 65th birthday, which is when the initial enrollment period begins. Those who are already receiving Social Security benefits at that time will automatically be enrolled in Medicare, will receive a Medicare card, and do not need to do anything further. Those who are not yet age 65 but receive spousal Social Security benefits will not be eligible for Medicare until the age of 65.

To enroll, make an appointment at a local Social Security office several months before the applicant's 65th birthday or call 800-772-1213 to apply by telephone. The applicant has until three months after the month of his or her 65th birthday to enroll in Medicare *Part B*. Because *Part B* requires payment of a premium, applicants have the ability to opt out of *Part B*. If a Medicare *Part A* recipient wishes to add Medicare *Part B* at a later date, he may do so during the annual *open enrollment* period from January 1 to March 31.

Medigap

Medigap is a privately sold, supplemental insurance policy that covers deficiencies in traditional Medicare coverage. There are a number of different types of Medigap plans, all providing different benefits. The so-called *core* benefits, found in all plans, include partial coverage of the co-payment required for days 21 through 100 for skilled nursing care and of the yearly deductible for Medicare *Part B*. An example of possible coverage under certain Medigap plans is for routine annual checkups. These are not generally covered by Medicare, but may be covered by some Medigap policies.

In general, once you purchase a Medigap policy, and as long as you continue to pay the annual premium, the policy will be renewed automatically every year and your coverage cannot be terminated. Remember that this is a privately-obtained policy, separate from Medicare, and that the premium is in addition to the premium you pay for Medicare *Part B*. Only those who are enrolled in Medicare may purchase a Medigap policy.

Medicaid

Medicaid is a federally- and state-funded public aid program that is administered by each state to provide medical benefits to certain low-income people. United States citizens and legal residents of the U.S. may receive Medicaid if they are otherwise eligible. In general, eligibility is limited to children, adults age 65 and older, pregnant women, blind or disabled persons, and terminally ill persons seeking hospice care. The income level a person must fall below in order to qualify for Medicaid varies by state. States also may take into account exceptionally high medical bills in determining Medicaid eligibility.

Generally, Medicaid does not pay for assisted living. However, some states have obtained permission from the federal government to apply Medicaid funds to assisted living expenses for elderly residents of that state. For the most part, though, the covered costs are for services rather than accommodations. Many facilities do not try to obtain Medicaid certification because the return is not worth the effort. This is because an assisted living facility that becomes Medicaid-certified is subjected to a large number of federal and state regulations that it would not have to deal with otherwise. Therefore, keep in mind the limitations that go with relying on Medicaid—a senior who needs to receive public aid funds for long-term care costs usually has few options other than a skilled care facility.

> *TIP: Be skeptical of an assisted living facility if the administration claims that Medicaid will cover a resident's expenses once savings are depleted. Check with the local Medicaid office to try to determine if the claim is accurate.*

Eligibility

State law determines eligibility for Medicaid, but there are a number of federal statutes that also affect eligibility. As a general rule, a senior who receives SSI is automatically eligible for Medicaid. In order to qualify to receive Medicaid funding for long-term care, a senior must meet a state-established poverty requirement that takes into account assets as well as income. Some individuals are too wealthy for Medicaid to be a possibility. These people are more likely to fund their long-term care with personal savings or long-term care insurance policies. Other seniors have little or no wealth and Medicaid is their only hope for covering nursing care expenses.

It is those in the middle of this spectrum who have the most difficult decisions to make. A senior who is too affluent to be eligible for Medicaid, but does not have enough resources to pay for long-term care, may attempt to give away his or her savings and other assets to relatives in order to meet the poverty requirement in his or her state for Medicaid. This is called *asset transfer* or *self-impoverishment*.

Federal law seeks to prevent financially sound individuals from purposely becoming destitute, by providing for a period of Medicaid ineligibility in certain cases in which the individual has given away assets at less than their fair market value. This ineligibility period is based on the timing of a senior's transfer of assets and the date on which he or she has applied for Medicaid.

Look Back Date
The applicable federal statute prescribes a *look back period* of thirty-six months before the *look back* date, which is the date on which the senior both applies for Medicaid and is institutionalized. If the senior applies for Medicaid but is not institutionalized, the look back date is the date on which the senior applies for Medicaid or has transferred the assets, whichever is later.

The state will examine transfers of the senior's money or property made during this time. If the senior does not receive something in return that is equal to the value of the money or property, he or she will be ineligible for Medicaid for a certain amount of time, called a *penalty period* (discussed later). Transfers of the senior's property that are made by his or her spouse during the look back period also are taken into account. In the case of certain trusts, the look back period is sixty months.

Not all of the senior's property transactions are subject to the federal *look back* statute. An individual may still be eligible for Medicaid if:

◆ the transferred property is a home that has been conveyed to either the senior's spouse, the senior's child who is under 21 or is permanently disabled, a sibling of the senior who is a part-owner of the home and who lived in the home for at least a year before the senior moved to a long-term care facility, or a child of the senior who lived in the home and provided care to the senior for at least two years before the senior moved to a long-term care facility;

- the property was transferred to the senior's spouse or for the sole benefit of the spouse;
- the property was transferred by the senior's spouse to someone else, for the sole benefit of the spouse;
- the property was transferred to the senior's permanently disabled child (or to a trust for the child's benefit) or to a trust for the benefit of any disabled person under age 65;
- the reason the property was transferred was not to impoverish oneself to become eligible for Medicaid (an extremely hard claim to prove); or,
- denying Medicaid would cause extreme hardship to the senior.

Sometimes, a middle class senior will attempt to plan for eventual Medicaid eligibility by giving away a portion of his or her resources. The amount transferred would depend on the senior's total resources, income, and other factors. The senior then would use the remainder to pay for long-term care expenses during the resulting penalty period. Theoretically, by the time the penalty period is over, the remaining resources would have been depleted and the senior would be eligible for Medicaid. This situation is known as *half a loaf*. It is a risky financial plan for a senior, because it results in the senior becoming destitute within a span of three years, whether or not the senior actually needs long-term care at that time.

Another way some seniors try to plan for Medicaid is to create a trust that is funded with the senior's assets. If a trust is *revocable*, which means that the assets still may be available to the senior, the assets will be counted as resources for purposes of determining Medicaid eligibility. If the trust is *irrevocable*, meaning the senior may not reach the assets, then the trust may be considered a nonexempt transfer of assets that triggers a five-year period of ineligibility. Planning three to five years ahead of possible nursing home placement is difficult because of all the variables in each senior's financial situation and also because it is so difficult to predict whether Medicaid will be a necessity that far down the road.

Penalty Period

The period of Medicaid ineligibility, calculated in months, is determined by the following formula:

> the total value of property the senior or the senior's spouse transferred during the look back period divided by the average monthly cost for long-term care in the senior's geographical area.

For example, if the senior has given a $15,000 cash gift to a daughter two years before applying for Medicaid and the average cost of nursing home care in the senior's area is $3,000 per month, the penalty period during which the senior is not eligible for Medicaid is 15,000 divided by 3,000, or five months. Generally, the penalty period begins on the first day of the month in which the asset was transferred.

If a penalty period would be in place because of a large transfer made during what would be the look back period, the senior should *not* apply for Medicaid until the penalty period is over. If the value of the assets is great enough, the penalty period could exceed the 36-month look back period. If the person transferring money applies for Medicaid during the look back period, the larger penalty period will be used.

For example, if the senior gives $120,000 in cash to his daughter on December 25, 2003 and the average cost of long-term is $3,000, the penalty period will be forty months (120,000 divided by 3,000), ending March 31, 2007. However, the *look back* period is only thirty-six months long, starting on December 1, 2003, and ending November 30, 2006.

Therefore, the senior can apply for Medicaid in January of 2007 without having to be concerned about the $120,000 transfer, because it took place earlier than the thirty-six-month *look back* date for January 2007. If, however, the senior applies for Medicaid in October 2006, the large transfer will be included in the look back period, and the full forty-month penalty period will apply.

Excluded or Exempt Resources

Some income and assets are not counted when determining whether the senior is eligible for Medicaid. Exemptions and exclusions can come from either federal or state law. These include:

◆ the senior's home;

◆ household goods and personal effects;

◆ an automobile, up to a certain value;

◆ certain burial plans; and,

◆ certain insurance policies belonging to the senior or his or her spouse, to the extent of the policy's cash surrender value.

Federal law helps to protect a noninstitutionalized spouse from becoming impoverished, even though the institutionalized spouse has to deplete resources in order to be eligible for Medicaid. This is for public policy purposes—it is not good for society to have both spouses on welfare just so that one of them will be able to pay for long-term care.

For this reason, an at-home spouse is allowed to keep a certain amount of marital property, called a *resource allowance*, in his or her own name, according to federal law. Each state mandates its own resource allowance amount, within a range provided by federal law. This range changes from year to year. The Medicaid office in the senior's state can provide information regarding the resource allowance amount.

Spend Down

One technique some seniors employ when they are thinking about applying for Medicaid is called *spending down*. This is when a senior's assets are used for certain allowable transfers of property and thus become depleted for purposes of Medicaid eligibility without a resulting penalty period. Some states have very specific rules regarding *spending down* and expressly allow the senior to deplete resources, but require the transfers or assets to be for health-care costs.

In some states, the term *spend down* has a generic meaning. The expenditures are made for the purpose of using up nonexempt assets without transferring them in a manner that would trigger a penalty period for Medicaid eligibility. The transfers are not limited to health-care purposes. Examples include the senior using savings to pay off the mortgage, making improvements to his or her home, or purchasing a prepaid burial plan or exempt household goods. All of these expenditures are for assets that are not included as resources in determining eligibility for Medicaid.

If a senior gives property or savings away, it belongs to the recipient and he or she has no further say in what happens to it. The senior may give his or her savings to his or her children, but that does not mean that they will use the money for his or her care—legally, they are not under any obligation. If the senior retains control over his or her money or property, it can be counted in determining whether he is she is eligible for Medicaid. The senior can use up assets in order to qualify for Medicaid, but if he or she ends up not needing long-term care for the rest of his or her life, he or she may find him- or herself with no resources left once discharged from a nursing facility.

TIP: If you or a family member are considering transferring assets or spending down in order to achieve eligibility for Medicaid, it is strongly advised that you speak to an attorney with experience in elder and public aid law to help ensure that you are not left short of assets after a few years.

Applying

A senior can apply for Medicaid by contacting a local Medicaid office. The telephone number should be available in the blue government pages of the telephone book or may be obtained by contacting either the local Social Security office or the state Medicaid office. (Appendix D lists contact information for each state's Medicaid office.)

Each state has its own requirements and procedures for Medicare application. Regardless of the home state, however, a senior can expect to provide a fair number of documents when applying. Typically, the following are necessary in addition to whatever application form is required:

❑ birth certificate;

❑ driver's license, state identification card, or passport;

❑ Social Security card;

❑ bank statements going back for a certain amount of time (for example, three years);

❑ statements from financial accounts, such as mutual funds, money markets, IRA accounts, certificates of deposit, and so on;

❑ copies of life insurance policies;

❑ copies of any long-term care insurance policy;

❑ deeds to real property;

❑ real estate tax bills;

❑ current mortgage statements;

❑ marriage certificates;

❑ certified copy of divorce decree;

❑ death certificate for spouse, if applicable;

❑ titles to any vehicles;

❑ automobile loan statements;

❑ bill of sale for any personal property sold in the past three years;

❑ contract documents for prepaid burial plan; and,

❑ copies of health insurance or Medicare card.

In some states, an interview with a Medicaid intake worker is also required. This meeting usually serves to help the application process, because the intake worker can obtain any information that has been mistakenly left off of the application.

If you are trying to place your loved one in a long-term care facility, the administration at any Medicare- and Medicaid-certified facility you are considering should be willing to assist with the application process. It is in their interest to have your family member determined eligible as soon as possible, especially if they admit him or her while the determination is pending. This means that the senior will be admitted even though not approved for Medicare or Medicaid and will be expected to pay for the charges as if a private pay resident until determined eligible and receiving payments.

Community Organizations

Although personal savings, insurance proceeds, and public aid monies are the main methods for financing long-term care, there are hundreds of other resources out there that may be able to give some help. They may be state agency-sponsored programs, community service organizations, or religious ministries. Information on any such programs in the senior's area can be found either by searching the Internet or by consulting the agency on aging in his or her state. Some of these programs may actually make it possible for the senior to remain at home, by providing services that allow him or her to live independently. One example of such an organization is the Community Care Program of the Illinois Department on Aging, which serves to assist certain qualifying seniors with a number of daily life activities in their homes or in a community center setting. (Appendix A provides a listing of state agencies concerned with aging.)

Veterans Health Administration

The *Veterans Health Administration* (VHA) is an agency of the United States Department of Veterans Affairs (VA) that manages health-care facilities and benefits programs for U.S. military veterans. The VA defines veteran status as *active duty service in the military, naval, or air service and a discharge or release from active military service under other than dishonorable conditions*. Some veterans also have to have actively served for twenty-four continuous months. In 2003, almost 65,000 veterans received long-term care in VA-operated nursing facilities and other facilities under contract with the VA. The VHA also provides home health care, adult day care, hospice services, and other elder health-care services.

Eligibility for VA nursing home benefits depends mainly on what is known as a disability rating. This has to do with the level of impairment to the veteran's earning capacity as a result of his or her physical or mental condition. Total disability is equal to a 100% disability rating. The veteran must first be enrolled in the VA health-care system, which can be accomplished by contacting the VA at 877-222-8387 or by visiting a VA benefits office or health-care facility.

There is a copayment for VA-sponsored long-term care after the first twenty-one days of care within a twelve-month period. In 2003, the maximum copayment for veterans was $97 per day. However, the VA determines the copayment for each veteran individually, according to the financial information that is submitted by the veteran.

Hill-Burton Facilities

A little-known federal program is the Hill-Burton free or reduced-cost care program for low-income, uninsured individuals, administered by the U.S. Health Resources and Services Administration (HRSA). This program is the result of a trade-off between the federal government and certain not-for-profit medical facilities that have received federal funds in order to make improvements to the facilities. In return for the funds, the facilities agree to provide a certain amount of free or discounted care, also called *uncompensated services*, until the debt is repaid.

Only services that are not already covered by either private insurance or another government program such as Medicare or Medicaid may be covered under the Hill-Burton program, but it is the facility that decides which services will be provided free or at a reduced cost. Once the facility has satisfied its obligations under the Hill-Burton program, it no longer has to provide such services. In order to be eligible for care under this program, an individual must provide proof of income, which must be less than three times the current poverty level.

To apply for care under the Hill-Burton program, the individual first must check to see if a Hill-Burton obligated facility is located in his or her area. This can be done online at **www.hrsa.gov/osp/dfcr/obtain/hbstates.htm** or by contacting the HRSA Division of Facilities and Loans at 301-443-5317. After locating a facility, the individual should contact it directly to see if it still has uncompensated services available or if its obligation has been satisfied. If services remain available, the individual can apply for free or reduced-cost care at the facility's business office.

Obtaining care in a Hill-Burton obligated facility is not going to be an option for very many seniors. A recent check of the directory of obligated facilities indicated that only 373 health-care facilities (not limited to nursing homes, but including hospitals and health clinics) were listed for the entire United States. Some states did not have any obligated facilities at all. Even if one finds such a facility and is eligible for reduced cost care, there is no guarantee that the available services will meet the individual's needs or that the care will be continued as long as the individual needs it. Someone in a truly dire state of health combined with a low-income situation probably will be better off applying for Medicaid eligibility, because the coverage will be more reliable.

Chapter 7

Making the Transition

It should not be a surprise that the first days of life in a nursing home or assisted living facility are the most difficult for both the resident and for the resident's family. What might not be expected is that, in a large number of cases, the resident does eventually adjust to the new surroundings, and in time, actually comes to enjoy the new lifestyle. Part of the adjustment is a matter of simply becoming acclimated to the new environment, with its different sights, smells, and sounds. Much of it is the relationship the resident develops with his or her caregivers. The support received from family is also very important.

> *TIP: One report estimated a period of six months for a new resident to feel comfortable in a facility and to feel as if it truly were his or her home.*

A new resident goes through a number of procedural steps during the first days after admission. The actual admission procedure, including the signing of documents, is discussed in Chapter 5. After admission, however, the resident will be assessed and facility staff will formulate a plan for the resident's care. The staff also should make the effort to familiarize the resident with the layout and daily routine of the facility, a process that may take a number of days or weeks until the resident begins to feel comfortable.

Orientation

The resident may need repeated reminders of mealtimes, times of certain activities, locations of dining rooms and activity rooms, and certain rules for some time after admission, especially if the resident is confused. The staff should monitor the new resident's progress and should take special care to be sure that he or she does not miss meals, baths, and so on. Some residents will have trouble remembering how to find their rooms at first, but will eventually learn the way.

Some residents may have difficulty as long as they remain in the facility. In those cases, the staff should take steps to mark the resident's door to make the room easy to identify—for example, by attaching a sign to the door with the resident's name in large lettering or a picture of a recognizable object to help the resident differentiate his or her room from the others. All issues like this should be addressed in the resident's initial care conference and written care plan.

The staff should be expected to help not just the resident, but also the family, during the initial period after placement. The family will, understandably, be worried about every aspect of the resident's new lifestyle, such as whether he or she is able to sleep, whether he or she likes the meals, whether he or she is getting along with his or her new roommate, etc. The administration should reassure the family that the staff has a great deal of experience in helping new residents with this next part of their lives. Chances are that the staff has already had to deal with almost any issue that may come up with the new resident during the adjustment period.

Resident Assessment

One of the first things a nursing facility will do for a new resident is a comprehensive medical and psychological assessment, called a *resident assessment*. If a family member is admitted to a nursing home, the federal *Nursing Home Reform Act* requires that a full resident assessment be done within fourteen days after admission and yearly thereafter. In between assessments, quarterly reviews are made of the resident's condition. If there is a significant change, another assessment may be necessary. Assisted living facilities may or may not have an assessment requirement, depending on state law.

Resident assessments are performed using a *resident assessment instrument* (RAI). Medicare/Medicaid-certified facilities may use the RAI that has been developed by the federal government or may use another form that has been approved by the *Centers for Medicare and Medicaid Services*. The federally-established RAI currently in use is called the MDS 2.0, but it is amended from time to time. (A copy of the MDS 2.0 Full Assessment Form and Quarterly Review Form are included in Appendix I.)

The assessment will take a comprehensive look at many aspects of the resident's physical, emotional, and psychosocial condition, such as biographical information, patterns of daily living, behavior patterns, disease diagnoses, skin condition, vision and hearing problems, and mobility. Typically, all relevant departments of a skilled facility participate in the assessment, with each department signing off on the items relevant to its particular evaluation of the resident.

Written Care Plan

The *Nursing Home Reform Act* requires that facilities, with the assistance and input of the resident, and his or her family as well if the resident consents, develop a written plan of care that is tailored to the individual needs of the resident. The care plan is formulated during a care conference that is held with the resident and family, as well as representatives of the various departments of the facility, including the nursing staff, kitchen staff, social worker, activity department staff, therapists, and so on. The care plan focuses on the physical, emotional, and social needs of the resident. It is initially developed when the resident is admitted to the facility. It is reviewed on a regular basis and amended whenever a change in the resident's circumstances warrant.

The initial resident assessment is used to develop the care plan and all departments of the facility should be involved in the plan. The plan covers many aspects of the resident's life, not just the medical issues. The activity department should help formulate goals for the resident's involvement in social and educational opportunities available at the facility. The dietary department should be involved as well to ensure that the resident's nutritional needs are adequately met. Any therapists employed by the facility who may be called upon to treat the resident should assist in formulating the plan of care. Nursing care is usually the biggest part of the care plan.

Care plans should be goal-oriented wherever possible, so that the resident is always working toward an achievement and has no reason to stop looking forward in life. Typical items in a care plan might be to encourage the resident to join at least three resident group exercise sessions a week or to promote better nutrition by providing the resident with vitamin supplements. The possibilities are limitless. Almost any issue affecting the resident's quality of life in the facility may be addressed in the care plan. That is why it is so important for the family to participate in care conferences.

Family

The main role of the resident's family during this phase in a senior's life is to provide moral support during the period of adjustment. After becoming comfortable in his or her new home, the family's continued involvement in his or her life at the facility will add to the quality of the senior's life and will help ensure that the care received is consistent and of high-quality.

When helping your loved one make the move into an assisted living or skilled care facility, it is important to listen to his or her fears and to reassure your loved one that he or she will become comfortable in the new home soon. Although you have anxieties of your own regarding the move, remain positive in your conversations with your family member. Try to put yourself in his or her shoes and imagine how tough it must be to feel as though you are losing all of your independence. Even more difficult for those moving into long-term care is having to give up so many of their personal things and often, their home as well. Be empathetic to the very real feelings of loss, sadness, and perhaps even anger that your family member is going through.

A good way to help your loved one is to encourage him or her to pick out items of personal property to bring to the facility, if this is allowed. Let the senior choose which items of clothing he or she wants to keep, and suggest that he or she also bring things to furnish the room that have sentimental value, such as favorite pictures, decorative pillows and blankets, and even a favorite easy chair, if there is space in the new room. Giving the senior the ability to make decisions for him- or herself will help avoid feelings of powerlessness. Having treasured items from home will help in the adjustment to the new accommodations. Remember, however, to discourage the keeping of valuables in his or her room. If the senior insists on bringing items such as jewelry into the facility, be sure that the administrator can provide a safe in which to keep them.

TIP: If your family member saved old magazines or newspaper clippings when living at home, see if you can store them when he or she moves into the facility. They will be a great source of conversation for you both if you bring them with when you come to visit.

Continued Support

Frequent visits to your family member are the best way to be actively engaged in his or her life. If you have children, bring them along, so that they will have a connection to their family member. If you have a pet, inquire about the policy on bringing animals into the facility. They may restrict animals to an enclosed room so as not to harm or frighten other residents. Studies have shown, however, that pet therapy does result in social and health benefits to seniors in institutional settings, so bringing a pet may even be encouraged.

Studies also have shown that reminiscing with seniors is a good way to help prevent them from becoming depressed. If you are able, bring an album of your family member's old photos to look through. Allow the senior to talk about the stories behind the pictures, even if you have heard them many times before.

If you are unable to pay frequent visits to your loved one, consider making videotapes of you and the rest of your family to send to the senior. If you are unable to make videos, make an audio tape instead. Take photographs of your family while you are making the tape and send them along.

Another way to actively participate in your loved one's life is to attend social events at the facility specifically for family members. Many facilities hold special events, such as holiday parties, to which the residents' families are invited. Some might even have events that are open to the public to help form a positive relationship between the residents and the local community. One example might be a Halloween trick-or-treat event for children in the neighborhood of the facility. Residents dress up in costume and the facility provides candy for the residents to hand out to the local children. This encourages community support for the facility by providing a safe place for children to trick-or-treat.

You also can volunteer to help out at activities if you are able. If you work during the day, volunteer to run an occasional activity for residents in the evening. One suggestion would be to bring a movie from home to show to residents after dinner. You also could offer to bring popcorn or could request the kitchen staff provide a snack for residents. Afterward, lend a hand cleaning up and bringing residents back to their rooms. Not only will it benefit your own family member to have you present, your visit will bring enjoyment to many other residents as well, some of whom may not have many visitors. In addition, you will get to know the staff better, which is always a good idea. Moreover, they will appreciate your efforts, especially your assistance in lightening their workload.

Giving continued support also means being an advocate for your loved one. Insist on quality care by monitoring your loved one's living situation to be sure the plan of care is being followed. Be sure to attend care conferences and be an active member of the family council, if the facility has one. If they only have a resident council, encourage your loved one to join it. This too will give him or her a feeling of self-determination. If you have any questions or concerns about your family member's care, or physical or emotional condition, ask. Continue to ask questions until you receive a satisfactory answer.

You may find that your own feelings of guilt, sadness, depression, or even resentment persist, even after your loved one seems to have adapted to life in the facility. If this is the case, you might consider joining a support group for family members. Ask the administrator or the facility social worker for a recommendation. They undoubtedly have referred a number of families to such groups and can direct you to an organization that is suited to the your particular needs.

Chapter 8

Handling Problems with the Facility

Occasionally, a resident or the resident's family may find themselves at odds with a particular policy of the facility, with the way the policy is carried out by the staff, with the staff itself, or with another resident. It may be an occasional occurrence or a continuous problem. In any event, a grievance should be addressed and the situation corrected so that the resident's quality of life does not suffer.

Grievances are quite different from instances of nursing home abuse, which are circumstances requiring a much more urgent response. Abuse encompasses treatment ranging from neglect to emotional harm to physical mistreatment. Misappropriation of a resident's property also can amount to abuse.

Residents' Rights

The federal *Nursing Home Reform Act* specifically enumerates *a bill of rights* for residents of skilled care facilities. The bill of rights includes the following.

- ◆ The right to choose a personal attending physician.
- ◆ The right to be fully informed in advance about care and treatment.
- ◆ The right to be fully informed in advance of any changes in care or treatment that may affect the resident's well being.

- ◆ The right to participate in planning care and treatment or changes in care and treatment.
- ◆ The right to be free from physical or mental abuse, corporal punishment, involuntary seclusion, and any physical or chemical restraints imposed for purposes of discipline or convenience and not required to treat the resident's medical symptoms.
- ◆ The right to privacy with regard to accommodations, medical treatment, written and telephonic communications, visits, and meetings of family and of resident groups.
- ◆ The right to visits with and access to the resident's doctor, family, social service workers, ombudsmen, and state survey agency personnel.
- ◆ The right to confidentiality of personal and clinical records.
- ◆ The right to access current clinical records of the resident upon request by the resident or the resident's legal representative, within twenty-four (24) hours (excluding hours occurring during a weekend or holiday) after making such a request.
- ◆ The right to reside and receive services with reasonable accommodation of individual needs and preferences, except where the health or safety of the individual or other residents would be endangered.
- ◆ The right to receive notice before the room or roommate of the resident in the facility is changed.
- ◆ The right to voice grievances with respect to treatment or care that is (or is not) given, without discrimination or reprisal.
- ◆ The right to prompt efforts by the facility to resolve grievances the resident may have, including those with respect to the behavior of other residents.
- ◆ The right to organize and participate in resident groups in the facility (and the right of the resident's family to meet in the facility with the families of other residents).

◆ The right to participate in social, religious, and community activities, so long as they do not interfere with the rights of other residents in the facility.

◆ The right to examine, upon reasonable request, the results of the most recent state survey of the facility and any plan of correction in effect with respect to the facility.

◆ The right to refuse a transfer to another room within the facility, if a purpose of the transfer is to relocate the resident from a portion of the facility that is a skilled care facility to a nonskilled care portion of the facility.

◆ The right to remain in the facility unless transfer or discharge is appropriate due to medical concerns, safety concerns, nonpayment of charges, or closure of the facility.

◆ The right to thirty days notice of transfer or discharge.

◆ The right to manage one's own finances.

Appendix F contains selected sections of the U.S. Code of Federal Regulations that include expanded provisions on residents' rights. The resident also has the right to receive a written copy of these rights from the facility. If at any time the resident or family believes that any of these rights are being denied to the resident, the problem should be addressed with the staff or administration. The severity of the situation should determine the action that is taken.

Grievances

Grievances are complaints over incidents that do not amount to life- or health-threatening treatment. Examples of typical grievances would be a particular staff member repeatedly entering the resident's room without knocking or a roommate refusing to turn the sound down on his or her television set during the late evening hours. These complaints should be handled differently than situations of abuse or neglect, which are much more serious and need to be resolved immediately.

The best advice for a resident or family member with a complaint is to *document* the situation. As soon as you realize that there is a problem, start a file and write a brief summary of the facts. Be sure to note the date and the names of the people involved. Include a description of any consequences resulting from the situation, in particular, the effect the problem is having on the resident. Follow this procedure every time you believe an incident has occurred.

If the complaint involves a staff member, start by talking to him or her about the problem. Try not to be combative or accusatory, but explain your concerns and allow the staff member the chance to respond. If you believe you have a solution to the problem, make your ideas known. Remain firm in your concerns if the employee attempts to trivialize them or if his or her response is not satisfactory. You may wish to have another family member present when you speak to the employee. That other family member will serve as a witness to the conversation should the problem continue and it becomes necessary to take the grievance to another level.

If the response of the staff member is not adequate to resolve the problem, take the matter to his or her immediate superior, the department head. At this point, because you are taking your complaint to someone other than the particular employee, you should put your complaint in writing, with a copy to the administrator. The facility should have an official procedure for making complaints and now is the time to initiate that procedure. Keep copies of the correspondence in your file. Again, it will be more constructive if you speak with the department head in a calm but firm manner. If the department head does not provide the family with an acceptable solution, follow up with the administrator.

In the case where a grievance concerns a roommate, you should take your complaint directly to the administrator. Do not try to speak with the roommate's family, because they may become defensive over the situation and dig in their heels. This may result in the escalation of your grievance to a conflict. The administrator should serve as an objective third party in this situation by suggesting possible solutions, or if necessary by separating the residents.

The administrator should also be directly approached if the grievance concerns a policy of the facility, because the administrator is the one who most likely will have the authority to change the policy or allow an exception. As always, be sure to document events and conversations.

Councils

There are other options for assistance with a grievance within the facility organization. First is the resident or family council. Ultimately it will probably fall to the administrator to make any corrections, however, because these councils generally will not have the power to change policies or to address a particular resident's troubles. The main advantage to meeting with a resident or family council is to voice concerns in order to find out if anyone else has had a similar problem and to see how a previous situation was handled.

Corporate Ethics Committees

Corporations that run long-term care facilities often employ various support staff charged with the responsibility of mediating resident grievances. A concept that is growing in popularity among nursing homes is a corporate ethics committee to assist the administration in making decisions that affect the resident. One example of a decision an ethics committee might be called upon to make is when a health-care decision must be made on behalf of an incapacitated resident who has no advance directives in place and family members disagree on the proper course of action. The ethics committee may be necessary to determine who should have the authority to make the decision for the resident.

Ombudsman

If you feel you have exhausted all of your avenues within the facility's organization, you may be able to receive assistance from the local long-term care ombudsman's office. As discussed in Chapter 3, the ombudsman serves as an advocate for nursing home residents by providing consumer information and also by looking into resident's complaints against nursing homes and intervening on the resident's behalf, if necessary. Start with the *National Long-Term Care Ombudsman Resource Center* at **www.ltcombudsman.org** or 202-332-2275. They can provide contact information for your state ombudsman's office, which can direct you to the appropriate local office for your area.

Geriatric Care Manager

A geriatric care manager may be useful in a dispute situation with a facility, when the family feels that the facility is not sufficiently responding to concerns. Geriatric care managers are professionals who have experience with problem solving in all aspects of long-term care communities. A good resource for locating a geriatric care manager is the *National Association of Professional Geriatric Care Managers*, for which contact information is included in Appendix E.

Abuse

For most families placing elderly relatives in skilled care or assisted living, the possibility that their loved one will become a victim of abuse is the single greatest concern. Abuse can take a number of forms. Physical abuse includes conduct such as shoving or slapping, but it also can mean the use of unnecessary restraints. Emotional abuse includes yelling at or demeaning residents. Financial abuse arises in cases of property theft or embezzlement of residents' funds. Neglect, also a form of abuse, can occur when the nursing staff fails to respond to a resident's call light in a timely fashion, a resident does not receive adequate food or hydration, or when the staff does not frequently change a bedridden resident's position in the bed or properly attend to the resident's hygiene. Although abuse could come at the hands of any facility personnel, it is the nursing staff that has the most direct contact with the residents. Therefore, abuse complaints are most likely to be directed at those personnel.

Not all cases of abuse are intentional. Sometimes harm done to a resident is the result of negligence, or carelessness, on the part of the direct caregiver or even the supervisor. Keep in mind, too, that abusers are not always nursing home employees. Other residents and even family members can endanger the health and safety of residents.

Typically, there are one or more of a number of factors that lead health-care personnel to cause harm to those they are supposed to be caring for. Not surprisingly, experts point to the high level of work-related stress in an industry where employee turnover is high and staffing levels are low. The fact that wages are usually at the low end of the health-care pay scale contributes to the situation, as does the low morale often felt by these workers due to the lack of opportunities for advancement in their field and the lack of respect that others have for the job they do. As a result, less qualified and ultimately less satisfied workers are the ones who will end up as the primary caregivers. Other possible factors cited by experts are cultural differences between residents and staff and abusive or violent behavior on the part of a resident, such as striking or spitting at the employee, which triggers a retaliatory reaction. In fact, some nurses' aides have reported suffering aggressive treatment from residents' families and even from their own supervisors. It is not difficult to see how these factors can cause employee burnout, which could lead to a life-threatening situation for a helpless resident.

Resident maltreatment is a serious problem in the nursing home industry—how serious a problem, however, is subject to dispute. A recent Congressional report estimated that 30% of nursing homes in the United States have been cited in the previous two years for violations having the potential to cause a resident more than minimal harm. The *American Health Care Association*, the professional organization representing the long-term care industry, took exception to the report, claiming that fewer than 3% of United States facilities were cited for instances of actual harm. The discrepancy was attributed to the Congressional report's inclusion of complaints relating to procedural issues rather than actual instances of mistreatment. There are several other difficulties in fixing statistics. States have different standards for reporting and citing violations and in many cases, instances of abuse may go unreported. This happens either because the resident is afraid that no one will believe him or her or that the abuser will retaliate, or because there is no family or other concerned individual to monitor the resident's well-being.

Regardless of the extent of long-term care abuse, it is a problem that does exist in facilities. However, you can take steps to protect your loved one. Most important is that you do whatever you can to prevent a situation from even occurring and that you are able to identify signs of abuse in your family member in the event an incident does occur.

Prevention

Unfortunately, abuse in various forms can occur in assisted living and skilled care facilities. One of the best ways to prevent a situation is to ensure that your resident's facility has adequate staffing levels. Many experts agree that this is the single most important factor in determining the quality of care that long-term residents receive. Under the federal *Nursing Home Reform Act*, skilled care facilities are required to have twenty-four-hour licensed nursing service at a level adequate to meet nursing needs of all residents and must use the services of a registered professional nurse (RN) at least eight consecutive hours a day, seven days a week.

Beyond that, there is no minimum federal standard, although states may have their own rules regarding staffing levels. There should be enough *direct caregivers*, in other words nurses or nurses aides who provide nursing care and personal assistance directly to residents, to ensure that each resident's individual care needs are met on a daily basis. This usually translates to a recommended minimum staff level that is higher during the day, when demands on the staff are higher, than at night, when most residents would be expected to be asleep.

Some organizations that advocate for quality long-term nursing care have attempted to develop minimum recommended staff levels in the hope that eventually the federal government will pass laws requiring facilities in all states to provide adequate staff levels. The *National Citizen's Coalition for Nursing Home Reform* has proposed a standard of one direct caregiver for every five residents during the day shift, one for every ten residents during the evening shift, and one for every fifteen during the night shift. More staff would be necessary during mealtimes, because feeding residents who have trouble feeding themselves is more time-consuming. These standards would include all nursing personnel responsible for the hands-on caregiving for residents and would not count anyone whose sole duty was administrative or supervisory.

This minimum standard gives you a benchmark for evaluating whether the staffing at a facility that you are considering is sufficient to allow quality long-term care on a regular basis. However, because it is not a legal requirement, it may not be realistic to expect that any of these facilities will meet this standard. You can get some idea of nursing home staffing from Medicare's online *Nursing Home Compare* at **www.medicare.gov**. Nursing Home Compare includes a category for nursing staff hours per resident. Take the figures with a grain of salt, however, because they probably include staff hours for personnel who actually spend very little time providing care directly to the residents themselves. The most useful application for the nursing staff category is to compare the staffing figures with those of other facilities. The numbers in and of themselves may not accurately reflect the quality of care given at a particular facility.

Background Checks

Another step you can take to help ensure a safe environment for your loved one is to be sure that all employees of the facility have undergone thorough background checks prior to being hired and have participated in abuse prevention training. A background check should provide, at a minimum, a thorough criminal history, including any criminal assault charges, domestic batteries, DUI arrests, or drug offenses. You also can do some checking of your own. Federal law requires states to operate a nurses' aide registry that lists the names of all individuals who have completed a state-approved training program. The federal statute can be found in the United States Code, title 42, Section 1396r (42 USC Sec. 396r) and states:

> ...[T]he State shall establish and maintain a registry of all individuals who have satisfactorily completed a nurse aide training and competency evaluation program....The registry...shall provide for the inclusion of specific documented findings by a State ...of resident neglect or abuse or misappropriation of resident property involving an individual listed in the registry, as well as any brief statement of the individual disputing the findings. The State shall make available to the public information in the

registry. In the case of inquiries to the registry concerning an individual listed in the registry, any information disclosed concerning such a finding shall also include disclosure of any such statement in the registry relating to the finding or a clear and accurate summary of such a statement.

Aides who have completed state-mandated training are listed in the registry, along with information about any confirmed findings of abusive treatment of residents. The information in the registry is a matter of public record. (Appendix B lists Nurse Aide Registries for each state.) Contact the registry in the state of the facility for which you want information. You will need the names of the nurses' aides employed by the facility. The administration should make a list available to you for this purpose. Because of the high level of turnover among nurses' aides, you probably will want to periodically request an updated list so that you can continue to monitor the nursing staff on your own.

Granny Cams

Some experts believe that the wave of the future in long-term care security is the *granny cam,* a remote video monitoring system that allows the family of a nursing home or assisted living resident to monitor their loved one via the Internet on a twenty-four-hour basis. At present, the price of these systems start in the area of $600, with an additional monthly cost for an Internet service provider of around $20 and up. Although cost-prohibitive for many families, as the idea gains popularity it may become less expensive to purchase or rent video equipment for placement in residents' rooms. Some families with relatives in shared rooms might even consider splitting the cost of a system. For many families, the peace of mind in being able to check up on the family member would be well worth the cost.

Family Presence

Another one of the best ways to keep your loved one safe in a long-term care facility is for your family to maintain a presence at the facility, by being actively involved in your loved one's life, by visiting often and at different times during the week, and by questioning operating procedures at the facility any time they seem to be ineffective in protecting residents or potentially harmful to them. Although this may not be as effective in heading off negligent actions of staff members, it certainly may help keep a predatory situation from arising. Employees who see that a resident's family is fully involved in the resident's life and are on the lookout for signs of abuse may be more likely to take extra care with that resident, even when the family is not present.

Spotting the Signs of Neglect or Abuse

It is a good idea to familiarize yourself with signs of potential abuse or neglect, even if your family member is competent and able to express him- or herself. Sometimes an abusive staff member may try to use intimidation to keep the resident quiet about any mistreatment. In the case of a confused or incapacitated resident, it is especially important to recognize indicators that a family member is being abused.

The *National Center on Elder Abuse* has put together a list of potential abuse signs. Some of the things to look for include:

◆ bruises on wrists or ankles (improper use of restraints);

◆ bruises in genital area (possible sexual abuse);

◆ other signs of physical injury—broken bones, cuts, burns;

◆ bedsores or pressure ulcers (possible neglect);

◆ signs of neglect in appearance—unclean, unshaven, dirty or uncombed hair, urine or feces odor;

◆ severe weight loss or dehydration (possible dietary neglect or depression causing refusal to eat);

◆ loss of interest in normal activities;

◆ depression;

◆ emotional agitation;

◆ refusal to communicate;

◆ refusal to socialize;

◆ display of fear toward direct caregivers;

◆ aggressive conduct directed at family or other residents;

◆ disappearance of personal property; or,

◆ unexplained depletion of personal funds (possible financial abuse).

Gathering Evidence

If a family suspects that their loved one has suffered abuse or neglect at the hands of an employee or other resident, they need to decide what course of action to take. Some instances of neglect are unintentional and can be corrected by working with the facility administration and staff to ensure that proper care is given. In such a case, the family may decide to give the staff the opportunity to resolve the situation in-house, without making any formal report to state authorities. If, however, the resident is displaying some of the effects of abuse from the previous list, and there is no reasonable explanation for the appearance of these signs, the family needs to take quick action to stop the problem. *If the family believes that the resident is in immediate danger, they should contact local law enforcement right away.* They also should call the state agency for the reporting of elder abuse. (Appendix C lists each state's hotline telephone number for reporting elder abuse.)

If the family suspects abuse, but the resident is not in an immediately life-threatening situation, the first thing the family should do is speak to the resident about their suspicions. Even seniors who are confused and unable to remember or explain exactly what happened to them may be able to provide other clues, such as other injury sites that the family previously had not noticed. The family should ask questions and document the resident's responses. Sometimes a discussion will be more productive if a relative other than the resident's children speak with him or her, because he or she may be uncomfortable talking about certain situations such as sexual abuse with his or her children.

The person who speaks with the resident should take notes of dates, times, and names of anyone the resident was in contact with. The family also should take photographs of the resident's physical appearance, particularly where there are specific visible injuries. If the resident is unwilling or unable to communicate regarding the family's suspicions, the family will have to continue the investigation with the use of other evidence.

Reporting Abuse

Once the resident's family has documented as many facts as possible, they should contact the local agency for the reporting of elder abuse. This may be a local office of adult protective services or may be the local ombudsman. The ombudsman serves as an advocate for skilled care residents and helps to investigate and advise families who find circumstances of possible nursing home abuse. Ombudsmen have experience with these situations, and if necessary, can act as a go-between in the family's dealings with the facility administration.

After the matter is documented as thoroughly as possible and adult protective services has been contacted, the family should approach the administrator with their suspicions. Documenting the problem before approaching the administration will keep anyone from interfering with the evidence in order to cover up the situation. The family should remain calm when speaking with the administrator but should insist that protection is provided to the family member immediately or else should demand that the family member be transported to another local facility, on a temporary basis and at the facility's expense, for the resident's own safety. Once the family is satisfied that the resident is safe, they should follow up with a formal written complaint to the administrator. If the facility is corporate-run, a copy of the complaint should go to the corporate offices as well.

The next step, unless it is a case of suspected financial abuse, is to have a physician examine the resident. If possible, the family should contact a doctor who is not affiliated with the facility. If there are signs of physical abuse, the doctor may be able to give an opinion as to the cause. If the problem appears to be one of emotional abuse, it is possible that the resident will open up to a physician when otherwise hesitant to talk to family members. If the physician feels that abuse indeed may have occurred, he or she can suggest a course of treatment to correct the resident's condition, if necessary.

The family also should report incidents of abuse to the survey agency for the state in which the facility is located. (Appendix A gives contact information for each state's survey agency.) The agency can guide a family through that state's complaint and investigation process and can give a time frame for the investigation. Although each state is different in its approach to abuse situations, families should expect the process to take weeks rather than days and should contact the survey agency periodically to check on progress.

If a violation is found, the state survey agency will cite the facility for a deficiency and may impose a penalty, typically a monetary fine, according to state law. It is likely that results of an investigation will come more slowly than the family would like. In the meantime, it will become necessary for the family to decide what to do about their loved one's care on a long-term basis, especially if he or she has been removed from the facility. The local long-term care ombudsman may be able to provide advice to a family in this difficult situation.

Even if the resident is not in a situation of immediate danger, the family should still consider reporting the incident to local law enforcement, with the possibility that criminal charges will be brought against the abuser. Unfortunately, however, it is the exception rather than the rule that anyone will be prosecuted in a nursing home abuse case. On the other hand, it is usually advisable to make a police report, because a similar occurrence may happen in the future at the same facility. Whether the victim is the same resident or someone else, it is a good idea for the family to have a law enforcement agency document the complaint. Even if charges are brought, the case is prosecuted, and a conviction is won, this will not directly benefit the resident unless the judge in the criminal case orders that restitution is to be paid to the resident.

Pursuing Legal Action

In addition to reporting abuse to adult protective services, the state survey agency, and law enforcement personnel, families have another option in the form of a lawsuit filed in civil court. In a civil action, the injured person is the complainant (plaintiff), rather than the government as in a criminal matter. The abuser, and more often than not, the facility itself, are named as defendants. The facility usually is added to a lawsuit on the theory that the abuser, assuming he or she is an employee, is an agent of the facility and that it is the facility's fault that the employee was working in the facility where he or she could do harm to the resident/plaintiff. If someone other than an employee is the abuser, the facility still may be added on the theory that the facility did not provide adequate security to protect residents from predatory outsiders.

Any family that wishes to pursue a civil action against an abusive employee or a facility should hire a competent attorney who has experience dealing with personal injury cases in general and if possible with nursing home abuse cases in particular. It is difficult to present a lawsuit such as this without the assistance of a lawyer for two reasons. One reason is the complicated evidentiary issues involved, such as the use of expert medical testimony. The other is the licensing rules for attorneys in most states, which generally do not allow a nonlawyer to represent another person in court. In other words, the injured party is the resident so he or she is the only one other than a lawyer who could represent him- or herself in such a lawsuit.

A family who retains a personal injury lawyer should obtain references from the lawyer and should check them. There should be a written fee agreement for the services to be provided. The attorney may require a monetary *retainer*, which is similar to a deposit, before he or she will begin work on a case. Some attorneys charge hourly for their services and some take personal injury cases on a *contingent-fee basis*, which means they will handle the case and take a percentage of any money the plaintiff wins by either a court judgment or a settlement agreement with the defendants. One-third of the amount of a judgment or settlement in the case is typical, but some attorneys require as much as 40% as their fee. No matter what the contingent fee arrangement is, a plaintiff can expect to have to pay all of the court costs in the case, such as document filing fees, regardless of whether any money is ever won.

Monetary recovery in most personal injury cases, if the injured person prevails, should approximately cover medical expenses arising from the injury as well as some amount of restitution for the plaintiff's pain and suffering. Occasionally in nursing home cases, a jury will award a large amount in *punitive damages* as punishment against the wrongdoers, but generally these are cases of especially egregious conduct on the part of the facility personnel. Again, an experienced attorney can advise a family as whether they have a winning case and if so, what kind of recovery they might be able to obtain on behalf of their loved one.

Conclusion

Even though we all know that advanced age brings the possibility of illness, injury, or the inability to care for oneself, it still can be overwhelming to see any of these things happen to our parents or other loved ones. These are the people who cared for us when we were young and we may feel that we are letting them down by placing them in an institutional setting rather than keeping them in their own home or taking them into ours.

Try not to let feelings of guilt get to you if you are considering assisted living or skilled care for your family member. If he or she has been thoroughly evaluated by a physician, and if necessary, by a mental health professional, and a placement is found to be appropriate, recognize that you are, in fact, doing what is best for your family member. Keep in mind that, for a great many people living in skilled care or assisted living facilities, life is actually an improvement over remaining alone in one's home.

Today, extensive activity schedules are commonplace in both nursing and assisted living facilities. Residents have the freedom of choice to participate or not participate in the activities. Many facilities own their own vans, which they use to take residents on shopping trips, to sporting events or concerts, or other outings. For some people, the many opportunities to socialize and take part in activities are worth the trade-off for the advantages of remaining in their own homes.

Ask questions, research and observe the facilities, and follow up with assistance for your loved one as he or she makes the transition to the new surroundings. Remain a consistent participant in your family member's care and continue to monitor his or her progress even after he or she has adjusted to life as a resident of the facility.

You can be sure that, if you are an active advocate for your loved one, you are taking care of him or her to the best of your ability.

Glossary

A

AARP (formerly American Association of Retired People). An organization that advocates on behalf of persons age 50 and older.

activities of daily living (ADL). Benchmarks used to measure a person's ability to care for oneself, such as dressing, bathing, grooming, and cooking.

adult day care. Daily care provided by a facility to nonresident adults, usually for the purpose of allowing the primary caregivers to go to work.

advance medical directive. A type of document instructing health-care personnel as to the wishes of the maker of the document regarding health-care decisions, to be used in the event the maker of the document becomes terminally ill or incapacitated and is unable to communicate his or her wishes.

Alzheimer's disease. A degenerative disease of the brain, marked by loss of cognitive functions and dementia, usually associated with the elderly.

American Medical Association (AMA). The national professional organization for doctors.

ancillary services. Additional services provided by an assisted living or skilled care facility, beyond basic care, such as rehabilitative services like physical therapy or hospice services.

assisted living facility. An institutional lifestyle option for a senior citizen or disabled person needing some assistance with self care, but not needing skilled nursing care. Assisted living staff assists the resident with various tasks, such as grooming and housekeeping, as needed.

C

Centers for Medicare and Medicaid Services (CMS). The federal office that administers Medicare, and in conjunction with the individual states, Medicaid.

certified nurses aide (CNA). A health-care professional who has received state certification upon completion of required training, but who is not a licensed nursing professional.

continuing care retirement community (CCRC). A lifestyle option for seniors that provides a range of services and accommodations in a single facility or complex. Typically, a CCRC will contain some type of independent living accommodations, assisted living, skilled nursing facilities, and in some cases, specialized units, such as an Alzheimer's disease wing.

corporate ethics committee. In the case of company-owned long-term care facilities, a committee made up of corporate support staff to address topics that are germane to such facilities, including ethical health-care issues and certain resident grievances.

D

direct caregiver. A nursing staff member of a long-term care facility who provides one-on-one care directly to a resident.

do not resuscitate (DNR). An advance directive instructing that cardiopulmonary resuscitation not be administered to a patient suffering sudden cardiac or respiratory arrest.

E

elimination period. For purposes of long-term care insurance, a period of time during which the insured person must pay out-of-pocket for long-term care expenses before insurance coverage will begin.

F

Federal Long-Term Care Insurance Program (FLTCIP). A federal agency providing long-term care insurance to active and retired employees of the federal government, as well as certain members of their families.

G

geriatric care manager. A professional service provider who assists in long-term care planning by seeking suitable facilities for the elderly.

guardianship. A legal proceeding whereby a court appoints a representative to manage the affairs of an individual who has been deemed incompetent.

H

health care proxy. A type of advance medical directive executed by a person that makes another person his or her agent for the purpose of making health-care decisions on his or her behalf, in the event he or she becomes incapacitated and is unable to make such decisions on his or her own.

Home Equity Conversion Mortgage Program (HECM). A federally-insured reverse mortgage program by which a senior (aged 62 years and older) may receive a loan for long-term care expenses based on the equity in the senior's home.

home health care. A lifestyle option for a senior, wherein assistance with daily living activities, as well as any necessary medical care, is provided by a health-care aide in the senior's home, allowing the senior to maintain his or her own residence rather than relocating to an assisted living or nursing facility.

hospice. Care provided for the terminally ill, focusing on pain relief and emotional support for the patient, as well as bereavement assistance for the surviving family members.

I

independent living community. A community that typically is limited to those above a certain age (for example, the resident or spouse must be over the age of 55), with residents maintaining their own homes or apartments. The community provides no health care, but in some cases there is an activities staff to facilitate social interaction among the members of the community.

L

living will. A type of advance medical directive instructing that no extraordinary life-prolonging treatments are to be administered to the person making the directive, in the event the person becomes incapacitated and is unable to express his or her wishes.

long-term care facility. A lifestyle option for seniors who require skilled medical care or are otherwise unable to care for themselves. Nursing care and many basic activities of daily living are provided by the facility staff.

long-term care insurance. An insurance policy providing coverage of costs for various long-term care options for seniors or disabled persons. Policies and their coverage vary widely.

look back period. A three- to five-year period of time prior to applying for Medicaid, during which certain transfers of the applicant's property for less than fair market value will trigger a period of Medicaid ineligibility for the applicant.

M

Medicaid. A financial assistance program for certain low-income Americans and legal immigrants that is funded and administered by both the federal government and the state in which the recipient lives.

Medicare. Federally funded health insurance provided to persons aged 65 and older, certain younger disabled persons, and certain persons with permanent kidney failure.

Medigap. Supplemental health insurance to cover gaps in Medicare coverage.

N

nursing home. *See long-term care facility.*

O

ombudsman. An advocate on behalf of nursing home and assisted living facility residents who is responsible for addressing residents' disputes with facilities, and in some cases, for investigating complaints of elder abuse.

P

penalty period. A period of time during which a Medicaid applicant is ineligible for enrollment, because of certain transfers of the applicant's property for less than fair market value.

Q

qualifying hospital stay. Inpatient hospital stay, occurring just before admission to a nursing home, that is required before Medicare will pay for nursing home care. A qualifying hospital stay must be at least three consecutive days.

R

Resident Assessment Instrument (RAI). A form used to evaluate a long-term care facility resident's physical and emotional health and capabilities.

resident's representative. An agent of a nursing home resident designated to represent the resident in dealings with the facility and others; usually a family member of the resident.

resource allowance. A certain amount of marital assets, determined by federal law, that a noninstitutionalized spouse may own, regardless of the institutionalized spouse's resources for purposes of Medicaid eligibility.

respite care. Occasional care provided by a facility to a nonresident senior in order to give the primary caregivers temporary relief from their caregiving responsibility.

retirement community. *See independent living community.*

registered nurse (RN). A highly skilled nursing professional who is licensed pursuant to statutory requirements of the state in which the RN practices.

S

skilled care facility. *See long-term care facility.*

skilled nursing facility (SNF). *See long-term care facility.*

spending down. The transfer of an individual's assets in a certain manner that is allowable under federal Medicaid statutes and allows the individual to reach the threshold level for resources below which the individual is eligible for Medicaid.

T

toileting. The process of urinating and defecating.

V

Veterans Affairs, Department of (VA). An agency of the United States government that manages various programs and benefits for veterans of the Armed Services.

Veterans Health Administration (VHA). An agency under the VA that provides health services to military veterans.

Appendix A

State Senior Agencies & State Nursing Home Survey Agencies

ALABAMA
Department of Senior Services
www.adss.state.al.us
877-425-2243
334-242-5743

State Survey Agency
Department of Public Health
of Alabama—
Division of Health Care Facilities
800-356-9596 (In-State Calls Only)
334-206-5111

ALASKA
Senior and Disabilities Services
www.hss.state.ak.us/dsds
907-465-3165
866-465-3165

Alaska Commission on Aging
www.alaskaaging.org
907-465-4879

State Survey Agency
Department of Health and Social
Services of Alaska—
Department of Medical Assistance
Health Facilities:
Licensing and Certification
888-387-9387 *(In-State Calls Only)*
907-334-2483

ARIZONA
Aging and Adult Administration
www.de.state.az.us/aaa
602-542-4446

State Survey Agency
*Department of Health Services
 of Arizona—
Assurance and Licensure Division of
 Long-term Care*
602-364-2690

ARKANSAS
Division of Aging and Adult Services
www.arkansas.gov/dhs/aging
501-682-2441

State Survey Agency
*Department of Human Services
 of Arkansas—
Office of Long-term Care*
800-582-4887 *(Complaint Hotline)*
501-682-8487

CALIFORNIA
Department of Aging
www.aging.ca.gov
800-510-2020
916-322-3887

California Care Network
www.calcarenet.ca.gov

State Survey Agency
*Department of Health Services
 of California—
Licensing and Certification Program*
800-236-9747

COLORADO
Division of Aging and Adult Services
www.cdhs.state.co.us/ADRS/AAS/
 index1.html
303-866-2800

State Survey Agency
*Department of Public Health and
 Environment of Colorado—
Health Facilities Division*
800-886-7689 *(In-State Calls Only)*
303-692-2800

CONNECTICUT

Elderly Services Division
www.ctelderlyservices.state.ct.us
800-994-9422

State Survey Agency
Department of Public Health
* of Connecticut—*
Division of Health Systems Regulation
P.O. Box 340308
MS # 12 HSR
410 Capitol Avenue
Hartford, CT 06134-0308
860-509-7400
860-509-8000 *(Emergency after hours)*

DELAWARE

Division of Services for Aging and
* Adults with Physical Disabilities*
www.dsaapd.com
800-223-9074

State Survey Agency
Health and Social Services
* of Delaware—*
Division of Long-term Care and
* Resident Protection*
877-453-0012 *(In-State Calls Only)*
302-577-6661

DISTRICT OF COLUMBIA

Office on Aging
www.dcoa.dc.gov/dcoa/site/
    default.asp
202-724-5622

State Survey Agency
Department of Health of
* Washington, D.C.*
Health Regulation Administration
Health Care Facilities Division
202-442-5888

FLORIDA

Adult Services Program
www.dcf.state.fl.us/as
(separate telephone numbers
* by county)*

Department of Elder Affairs
http://elderaffairs.state.fl.us
850-414-2000

State Survey Agency
Agency for Health Care
Administration of Florida
888-419-3456

GEORGIA

Division of Aging Services
www2.state.ga.us/departments/dhr/
   aging.html
404-657-5258

State Survey Agency
*Department of Human Resources
   of Georgia—
Office of Regulatory Services*
800-878-6442 *(In-State Calls Only)*
404-657-5728

HAWAII

Adult Services
www.state.hi.us/dhs
808-832-5115

State Survey Agency
*Department of Health of Hawaii—
Office of Health Care Assurance*
808-692-7420

IDAHO

Commission on Aging
www.idahoaging.com/abouticoa/
   index.htm
877-471-2777
208-334-3833

State Survey Agency
*Department of Health and Welfare
   of Idaho*
208-334-6626

ILLINOIS

Department on Aging
www.state.il.us/aging
800-252-8966

State Survey Agency
*Department of Public Health
   of Illinois—
Central Complaint Registry*
800-252-4343 *(In-State Calls Only)*
217-782-4977

INDIANA

Bureau of Aging and In-Home Services
www.in.gov/fssa/elderly/aging/
   index.html
317-233-4454

State Survey Agency
*Department of Health of Indiana—
   Long-term Care Division*
800-246-8909 *(Complaint Hotline)*
317-233-7442

IOWA

Department of Elder Affairs
www.state.ia.us/elderaffairs
515-242-3333

State Survey Agency
*Department of Inspections and
   Appeals of Iowa—
Health Facilities Division*
877-686-0027 *(Complaint Hotline)*

KANSAS

Department on Aging
www.agingkansas.org/kdoa
800-432-3535
785-296-4986

State Survey Agency
*Department of Health and
Environment of Kansas—
Bureau of Health Facilities*
800-842-0078

KENTUCKY

Office of Aging Services
www.chs.state.ky.us/aging
502-564-6930

State Survey Agency
*Office of Inspector General
of Kentucky—
Division of Long-Term Care*
502-564-2800

LOUISIANA

Governor's Office of Elderly Affairs
www.gov.state.la.us/depts/
elderly.htm
800-259-4990
225-342-7100

State Survey Agency
*Department of Health and Hospitals
of Louisiana—
Health Standards Section*
888-810-1819

MAINE

Bureau of Elder and Adult Services
www.state.me.us/dhs/beas
800-262-2232

State Survey Agency
*Department of Human Services
of Maine—
Division of Licensing and Certification*
207-287-9300

MARYLAND

Office of Adult Services
www.dhr.state.md.us/csa/oas.htm
410-767-7384

Department of Aging
www.mdoa.state.md.us/services
800-243-3425

State Survey Agency
*Department of Health and Mental
Hygiene of Maryland*
877-402-8219

MASSACHUSETTS

Executive Office of Elder Affairs
www.800ageinfo.com
800-243-4636
617-727-7750

State Survey Agency
*Department of Public Health
of Massachusetts*
800-462-5540 *(In-State Calls Only)*
617-753-8000

MICHIGAN
Adult Services Program
www.michigan.gov
517-373-2035

Michigan Aging Services System
www.miseniors.net
517-373-8230

State Survey Agency
Department of Consumer and
  Industrial Services of Michigan—
Bureau of Health Division
  of Operations
800-882-6006

MINNESOTA
Board on Aging
www.mnaging.org
800-882-6262
651-296-2770

Aging Initiative
www.dhs.state.mn.us/Agingint
651-296-2544

State Survey Agency
Health Facility Complaints and
  Provider Compliance Division
  of Minnesota
800-369-7994

MISSISSIPPI
Division of Aging and Adult Services
www.mdhs.state.ms.us/aas.html
800-948-3090
601-359-4929

State Survey Agency
Department of Health of Mississippi—
  License and Certification
800-227-7308

MISSOURI
Division of Senior Services
www.dhss.state.mo.us/
  Senior_Services
800-235-5503

State Survey Agency
Elder Abuse and Neglect Hotline
  of Missouri
800-392-0210

MONTANA
Senior and Long-term Care Division
www.dphhs.state.mt.us/sltc
800-332-2272
406-444-4077

State Survey Agency
Department of Health and Human
  Services of Montana—
  Quality Assurance, Certification
  Bureau
406-444-2099

NEBRASKA

Division of Aging and
  Disability Services
www.hhs.state.ne.us/ags/
  agsindex.htm
800-942-7830
402-471-4623

State Survey Agency
Health and Human Services
  of Nebraska—
Regulation and Licensure
  Credentialing Division
402-471-0316

NEVADA

Division for Aging Services
www.aging.state.nv.us
702-486-3545 *(Las Vegas)*
775-687-4210 *(Carson City)*

State Survey Agency
State Health Division of Nevada
800-225-3414

NEW HAMPSHIRE

Division of Elderly and Adult Services
www.dhhs.state.nh.us/DHHS/DEAS/
  default.htm
800-351-1888
603-271-4680

State Survey Agency
Health Facility Administration of
  New Hampshire
800-852-3345 *(In-State Calls Only)*
603-271-4592

NEW JERSEY

Division of Senior Affairs
www.state.nj.us/health/senior
877-222-3737

State Survey Agency
Department of Health and Senior
  Services of New Jersey
800-792-9770 *(In-State Calls Only)*
609-633-8991

NEW MEXICO

Aging and Long-term Care
  Department
www.nmaging.state.nm.us
800-432-2080 (Santa Fe)
866-842-9230 (Albuquerque)
800-762-8690 (Las Cruces)

State Survey Agency
Department of Health of New Mexico
  Bureau of Health Facility—
Licensing and Certification
800-752-8649 *(In-State Calls Only)*
505-476-9025

NEW YORK

Office for the Aging
www.aging.state.ny.us
800-342-9871

State Survey Agency
New York State Department of Health
888-201-4563

NORTH CAROLINA
Adult and Family Services Section
www.dhhs.state.nc.us/dss/afs/
  afs_hm.htm

Division of Aging
www.dhhs.state.nc.us/aging
919-733-3983

State Survey Agency
*Division of Facility Services
  of North Carolina—
Licensure and Certification*
800-624-3004 *(In-State Calls Only)*
919-733-7461

NORTH DAKOTA
Aging Services Division
www.state.nd.us/humanservices/
  services/adultsaging
701-328-4601
800-451-8693

State Survey Agency
*Department of Health
  of North Dakota—
Division of Health Facilities:
Health Resources Section*
701-328-2352

OHIO
Department of Aging
www.aging.ohio.gov
614-466-5500

State Survey Agency
*Bureau of Long-term Care of Ohio—
  Quality Assurance*
800-342-0553 *(In-State Calls Only)*
614-752-9524

OKLAHOMA
Aging Services Division
www.okdhs.org/aging
800-211-2116
405-521-2327

State Survey Agency
*Department of Health of Oklahoma—
  Protective Health Services:
  Medical Facilities Division*
800-522-0203 *(In-State Calls Only)*
405-271-6868

OREGON
Seniors and People with Disabilities
www.dhs.state.or.us/seniors
800-282-8096 (In-State Calls Only)

State Survey Agency
Seniors and People with Disabilities
800-232-3020 (In-State Calls Only)

PENNSYLVANIA
Department of Aging
www.aging.state.pa.us
717-783-1550

State Survey Agency
Department of Health of Pennsylvania
800-254-5164

RHODE ISLAND
Department of Elderly Affairs
www.dea.state.ri.us
401-222-2000

State Survey Agency
Department of Health of Rhode Island
401-222-2566

SOUTH CAROLINA
Bureau of Senior Services
www.dhhs.state.sc.us/InsideDHHS/
  Bureaus/BureauofSeniorServices/
  default.htm
803-898-2850

State Survey Agency
Department of Health and
  Environmental Control
  of South Carolina—
Bureau of Certification
800-922-6735 *(In-State Calls Only)*
803-898-2590

SOUTH DAKOTA
Office of Adult Services and Aging
www.state.sd.us/social/ASA/
  index.htm
866-854-5465
605-773-3656

State Survey Agency
Department of Health
  of South Dakota—
Licensing and Certification
605-773-3656

TENNESSEE
Commission on Aging and Disability
www.state.tn.us/comaging
615-741-2056
866-836-6678

State Survey Agency
Department of Health of Tennessee—
  Division of Health Care Facilities
800-778-4504

TEXAS
Department on Aging
www.tdoa.state.tx.us
512-438-3200

State Survey Agency
Department of Human Services
  of Texas—
  Long-Term Care Regulatory
800-458-9858

UTAH
Division of Aging and Adult Services
www.hsdaas.utah.gov
801-538-3910

State Survey Agency
Department of Health of Utah—
   Bureau of Medicare/Medicaid Program:
   Certification and Resident Assessment
800-662-4157 *(In-State Calls Only)*
801-538-6158

VERMONT
Department of Aging and
   Adult Services
www.dad.state.vt.us
802-241-2400

State Survey Agency
Department of Aging and Disabilities
   of Vermont—
   Division of Licensing and Protection
802-241-2345

VIRGINIA
Department for the Aging
www.aging.state.va.us
800-552-3402
804-662-9333

State Survey Agency
Department of Health of Virginia—
   Center for Quality Health Care
   Services and Consumer Protection
800-955-1819 *(In-State Calls Only)*
804-367-2106

WASHINGTON
Aging and Disability Services
   Administration
www.aasa.dshs.wa.gov
800-422-3263

State Survey Agency
Department of Social and Health
   Services of Washington—
   Aging and Adult Services
   Administration:
   Residential Care
800-562-6078 *(Complaint Hotline)*
360-725-2300

WEST VIRGINIA
Bureau of Senior Services
www.state.wv.us/seniorservices
304-558-3317

State Survey Agency
Department of Health and Human
   Resources of West Virginia—
   Office of Health Facility Licensure and
   Certification
800-442-2888 *(In-State Calls Only)*
304-558-0050

WISCONSIN

Bureau of Aging and Long-term
  Care Resources
www.dhfs.state.wi.us/aging/
  baltcr_aging.htm
608-266-4448

State Survey Agency

Department of Health and Family
  Services of Wisconsin—
  Division of Supportive Living:
  Bureau of Quality Assurance
800-642-6552 *(In-State Calls Only)*
608-266-8481

WYOMING

Aging Division
wdhfs.state.wy.us/aging
800-442-2766
307-777-7986

State Survey Agency

Office of Health Quality of Wyoming
307-777-7123

Appendix B

State Nurse Aide Registries

(Source: Wisconsin Department of Health & Family Services)

ALABAMA
Department of Public Health—
Division of Licensure and Certification
201 Monroe Street
Montgomery, AL 36130-1701
334-206-5169

ALASKA
Department of
  Community and Economic
  Development—
Division of Occupational Licensing:
Nurse Aide Registry
3601 C Street, Suite 722
Anchorage, AK 99503-5986
907-269-8169

ARIZONA
Board of Nursing—
Nurse Aide Registration Program
1651 E. Morten Avenue, Suite 210
Phoenix, AZ 85020
602-331-8111 ext. 126

ARKANSAS
Department of Human Services
Nurse Aide Registry:
Office of Long Term Care
P.O. Box 8059, Slot 405
Little Rock, AR 72203-8059
501-682-8484

CALIFORNIA
Nurse Aide Registry
P.O. Box 942732
Sacramento, CA 94234
916-327-2445

COLORADO
Board of Nursing—
Nurse Aide Registry
1560 Broadway, Suite 880
Denver, CO 80202
303-894-2816

CONNECTICUT
Department of Public Health—
Division of Health Systems Regulation
410 Capitol Ave. MS #12 INV
P.O. Box 340308
Hartford, CT 06134-0308
860-509-7596

DELAWARE
Social and Health Services—
Division of Long Term Care
  Residents Protection
3 Mill Road, Suite 308
Wilmington, DE 19806
302-577-6661

DISTRICT OF COLUMBIA
Nurse Aide Registry
P.O. Box 13785
Philadelphia, PA 19101
800-566-8668

FLORIDA
Department of Health—
MQA/CNA Program
4052 Bald Cypress Way BIN #C13
Tallahassee, FL 32399-3263
850-245-4294

GEORGIA
Health Partnership
1455 Lincoln Parkway East, Suite 750
Atlanta, GA 30346-2200
800-414-4358

HAWAII
Department of Consumers Affairs—
Professional and Vocational
  Licensing Branch:
Nurse Aide Program
P.O. Box 3469
Honolulu, HI 96816
808-739-8122

IDAHO
Board of Nursing
P.O. Box 83720
Boise, ID 83720-5864
208-334-3110 ext. 21

ILLINOIS
Department of Public Health—
Education and Training Section
525 W. Jefferson Street
Springfield, IL 62761
217-785-5133

INDIANA
State Department of Health—
Division of Long Term Care
2 N Meridian Street, Section 4B
Indianapolis, IN 46204
317-233-7479

IOWA
Department of Inspections and
  Appeals—
Health Facilities Division:
Nurse Aide Registry
Lucas State Office Building
Des Moines, IA 50319-0083
515-281-4963

KANSAS
Department of Health and
  Environment—
Landon State Office Building,
  Suite 1051-S
900 SW Jackson Street
Topeka, KS 66612-1290
785-296-6877

KENTUCKY
Nurse Aide Registry
312 Whittington Parkway, Suite 300A
Louisville, KY 40222-5172
502-329-7047

LOUISIANA
Nurse Aide Registry
5615 Corporate Boulevard, Suite 8-D
Baton Rouge, LA 70808
225-925-4132

MAINE
Department of Human Services—
CNA Registry
State House Station 11
35 Anthony Avenue
Augusta, ME 04333
207-624-5205

MARYLAND
Board of Nursing
4140 Patterson Avenue
Baltimore, MD 21215-2254
410-585-1900

MASSACHUSETTS
Department of Public Health—
Nurse Aide Registry
10 West Street
Boston, MA 02111
617-753-8000

MICHIGAN
Nurse Aide Registry—
The Chauncey Group International
664 Rosedale Road
Princeton, NJ 08540
517-241-2881

MINNESOTA
Department of Health—
Nursing Aide Registry
85 East 7th Place, Suite 300
P.O. Box 64501
St. Paul, MN 55164-0501
651-215-8705

MISSISSIPPI
Nurse Aide Registry
P.O. Box 13785
Philadelphia, PA 19101
800-204-6215

MISSOURI
Department of Social Services—
Division of Aging:
Health Education Unit
P.O. Box 1337
Jefferson City, MO 65102
573-751-3082

MONTANA
Department of Public Health and
  Human Services—
Certification Bureau:
Nurse Aide Registry
2401 Colonial Drive
Helena, MT 59620-2953
406-444-4980

NEBRASKA
Health and Human Services—
Department of Regulation and
  Licensure
P.O. Box 94986
Lincoln, NE 68509-4986
402-471-0537

NEVADA
State Board of Nursing
4330 South Valley View, Suite 106
Las Vegas, NV 89103
702-486-5800

NEW HAMPSHIRE
Board of Nursing
P.O. Box 3898
Concord, NH 03302
603-271-6282

NEW JERSEY
Nurse Aide Registry
P.O. Box 13785
Philadelphia, PA 19101
800-274-8970

NEW MEXICO
Public Health Division—
Long Term Care Program
525 Camino De Los Marquez, Suite 2
Sante Fe, NM 87501
505-827-4200

NEW YORK
Nurse Aide Registry
P.O. Box 13785
Philadelphia, PA 19101
800-274-7181

NORTH CAROLINA
Division of Health and
  Human Services—
Nurse Aide Registry
P.O. Box 29530
Raleigh, NC 27626-0530
919-733-2786

NORTH DAKOTA
Board of Nursing—
Nurse Assistant Registry
919 South 7th Street, Suite 501
Bismarck, ND 58504-5881
701-328-9784

OHIO
Department of Health—
Nurse Aide Registry
P.O. Box 118
Columbus, OH 43266-0118
614-752-9500

OKLAHOMA
Department of Health—
Nurse Aide Registry
1000 NE 10th Street
Oklahoma City, OK 73117-1299
405-271-4085

OREGON
Board of Nursing
800 NE Oregon Street, Suite 465
Portland, OR 97232
503-731-3459

PENNSYLVANIA
Nurse Aide Registry
P.O. Box 13785
Philadelphia, PA 19101
800-852-0518

RHODE ISLAND
Department of Health Professionals
3 Capitol Hill, Room 105
Providence, RI 02908-5097
401-222-5888

SOUTH CAROLINA
Nurse Aide Registry
P.O. Box 13785
Philadelphia, PA 19101
800-475-8290

SOUTH DAKOTA
Board of Nursing
4300 S. Louise Avenue, Suite C-1
Sioux Falls, SD 57106
605-362-2760

TENNESSEE
Department of Health—
Division of Health Care Facilities
Cordell Hull Building, 1st floor
425 5 th Avenue North
Nashville, TN 37247-0560
888-310-4650

TEXAS
Department of Human Services—
Nurse Aide Registry
P.O. Box 149030, MC Y-977
Austin, TX 78714-9030
512-231-5829

UTAH
Health Technology Certification Center
550 E. 300 South
Kaysville, UT 84037
801-547-9947

VERMONT
Board of Nursing
109 State Street
Montpelier, VT 05609-1106
802-828-2819

VIRGINIA
Board of Nursing—
Nurse Aide Registry
6606 W. Broad Street, 4th Floor
Richmond, VA 23230-1717
804-662-7310

WASHINGTON
Nurse Aide Registry
P.O. Box 45600
Olympia, WA 98504-5600
360-725-2596

WEST VIRGINIA
Division of Health—
Office of Health Facilities Licensure
350 Capitol Street, Room 206
Charleston, WV 25305
304-558-0688

WISCONSIN
Nurse Aide Registry
P.O. Box 13785
Philadelphia, PA 19101
877-329-8760

WYOMING
Board of Nursing
2020 Carey Avenue, Suite 110
Cheyenne, WY 82002
307-777-7601

Appendix C:

Elder Abuse Reporting Numbers

ALABAMA
800-458-7214

ALASKA
800-730-6393
907-334-4483

ARIZONA
877-767-2385

ARKANSAS
800-582-4887

CALIFORNIA
800-231-4024

COLORADO
800-773-1366

CONNECTICUT
888-385-4225
860-424-5241

DELAWARE
800-223-9074

DISTRICT OF COLUMBIA
202-434-2140

FLORIDA
800-962-2873

GEORGIA
404-657-5726

HAWAII
808-241-3432

IDAHO
208-364-1899

ILLINOIS
800-252-4343

INDIANA
800-992-6978

IOWA
515-281-4115

KANSAS
800-842-0078

KENTUCKY
800-752-6200

LOUISIANA
800-259-4990

MAINE
800-624-8404

MARYLAND
800-917-7383

MASSACHUSETTS
800-462-5540

MICHIGAN
800-882-6006

MINNESOTA
800-333-2433

MISSISSIPPI
800-227-7308

MISSOURI
800-392-0210

MONTANA
800-332-2272

NEBRASKA
800-652-1999

NEVADA
800-992-5757

NEW HAMPSHIRE
800-442-5640
603-271-4396

NEW JERSEY
800-792-8820

NEW MEXICO
800-797-3260
505-841-6100

NEW YORK
800-342-9871

NORTH CAROLINA
800-662-7030

NORTH DAKOTA
800-451-8693

OHIO
800-282-1206

OKLAHOMA
800-522-3511

OREGON
800-232-3020

PENNSYLVANIA
800-254-5164

RHODE ISLAND
401-785-3340

SOUTH CAROLINA
800-898-2850

SOUTH DAKOTA
605-773-3656

TENNESSEE
888-277-8366

TEXAS
800-458-9858
512-438-2633

UTAH
801-264-7669 *(Salt Lake City County)*
800-371-7897 *(all other counties)*

VERMONT
800-564-1612

VIRGINIA
888-832-3858
804-371-0896

WASHINGTON
800-562-6078

WEST VIRGINIA
800-352-6513

WISCONSIN
800-815-0015
608-246-7013

WYOMING
307-777-7123

Appendix D

State Medicaid Offices

(Source: Centers for Medicare and Medicaid Services)

ALABAMA

Medicaid Agency of Alabama
501 Dexter Avenue
P.O. Box 5624
Montgomery, AL 36103-5624
334-242-5000
800-362-1504 (In-State only)

ALASKA

Department of Health and Social
  Services of Alaska
350 Main Street, Room 229
P.O. Box 110601
Juneau, AK 99811-0601
907-465-3030
800-211-7470

ARIZONA

Health Care Cost Containment
  of Arizona
801 E. Jefferson
Phoenix, AZ 85034
602-417-7000
800-962-6690
602-417-7700 (Spanish)

ARKANSAS

Department of Human Services
  of Arkansas
P.O. Box 1437, Slot 1100
Donaghey Plaza South
Little Rock, AR 72203-1437
501-682-8292
800-482-5431

CALIFORNIA

California Department
  of Health Services
P.O. Box 942732
Sacramento, CA 94234-7320
916-445-4171
800-952-5253 (Spanish)

COLORADO

Department of Health Care Policy and
  Financing of Colorado
1570 Sherman Street
Denver, CO 80203-1818
303-866-2993
800-221-3943
888-367-6557 (Spanish)

CONNECTICUT
Department of Social Services
  of Connecticut
25 Sigourney Street
Hartford, CT 06106-5033
860-424-4908
800-842-1508

DELAWARE
Health and Social Services of Delaware
1901 N. DuPont Highway
P.O. Box 906, Lewis Building
New Castle, DE 19720
302-255-9040

DISTRICT OF COLUMBIA
Department of Health
  of Washington, D.C.
825 North Capitol Street, NE
  5th Floor
Washington, DC 20002
202-442-5999

FLORIDA
Agency for Health Care
  Administration of Florida
P.O. Box 13000
Tallahassee, FL 32317-3000
888-419-3456

GEORGIA
Department of Community Health
  of Georgia
2 Peachtree Street, NW
Atlanta, GA 30303
770-570-3300
866-322-4260

HAWAII
Department of Human Services
  of Hawaii
P.O. Box 339
Honolulu, HI 96809
808-524-3370
800-316-8005

IDAHO
Department of Health and Welfare
  of Idaho
450 West State Street
Boise, ID 83720-0036
208-334-5500

ILLINOIS
Department of Public Aid of Illinois
201 South Grand Avenue, East
Chicago, IL 60607
217-782-2570
800-226-0768 (In-State only)

INDIANA
Family and Social Services
 Administration of Indiana
402 W. Washington Street
P.O. Box 7083
Indianapolis, IN 46207-7083
317-232-4966
800-457-4584
317-234-0225 (Spanish)

IOWA
Department of Human Services
 of Iowa
Hoover State Office Building, 5th Floor
1305 E. Court
Des Moines, IA 50319-0114
515-327-5121
800-338-8366

KANSAS
Department of Social and
 Rehabilitation Services of Kansas
915 SW Harrison Street
Topeka, KS 66612
785-274-4200
800-792-4884

KENTUCKY
Cabinet for Health Services
 of Kentucky
P.O. Box 2110
Frankfort, KY 40602-2110
502-564-2687
800-635-2570

LOUISIANA
Department of Health and
 Hospital of Louisiana
1201 Capitol Access Road
P.O. Box 629
Baton Rouge, LA 70821-0629
225-342-9500

MAINE
Department of Human Services
 of Maine
442 Civic Center Drive
11 State House Station
Augusta, ME 04333-0011
207-287-3094
800-321-5557 (In-State only)

MARYLAND
Department of Human Resources
 of Maryland
P.O. Box 17259
Baltimore, MD 21203-7259
410-767-5800
800-492-5231

MASSACHUSETTS
Office of Health and Human
 Services of Massachusetts
600 Washington Street
Boston, MA 02111
617-628-4141
800-325-5231

MICHIGAN

Department of Community Health
  of Michigan
Medical Services Administration
Lewis Class Building, Sixth Floor
320 South Walnut Street
Lansing, MI 48913
517-335-5500 (for verification only)
800-292-2550
888-367-6557 (Outside of Michigan)
888-367-6557 (Spanish)

MINNESOTA

Department of Human Services
  of Minnesota
444 Lafayette Road North
St. Paul, MN 55155
651-297-3933
800-366-8930

MISSISSIPPI

Office of the Governor of Mississippi
Robert E. Lee Building, Suite 801
239 North Lamar Street
Jackson, MS 39201-1399
601-359-6050
800-421-2408 (In-State only)

MISSOURI

Department of Social Services
  of Missouri
221 West High Street
P.O. Box 1527
Jefferson City, MO 65102-1527
573-751-4815
800-392-2161 (In-State only)

MONTANA

Department of Public Health and
  Human Services of Montana
1400 Broadway, Cogswell Building
P.O. Box 8005
Helena, MT 59604-8005
406-444-5900
800-362-8312

NEBRASKA

Department of Health and Human
  Services System of Nebraska
P.O. Box 95044
Lincoln, NE 68509-5044
402-471-3121

NEVADA

Department of Human Resources
  of Nevada
Aging Division
1100 East William Street, Suite 101
Carson City, NV 89701
702-486-5000

NEW HAMPSHIRE

Department of Health and Human
  Services of New Hampshire
129 Pleasant Street
Concord, NH 03301-3857
603-271-4238

NEW JERSEY
Department of Human Services
  of New Jersey
Quakerbridge Plaza, Building 6
P.O. Box 716
Trenton, NJ 08625-0716
609-588-2600
800-356-1561 (In-State only)

NEW MEXICO
Department of Human Services
  of New Mexico
P.O. Box 2348
Sante Fe, NM 87504-2348
505-827-3100
888-997-2583
800-432-6217 (Spanish)

NEW YORK
New York State Department of Health
  Office of Medicaid Management
Governor Nelson A. Rockefeller
  Empire State Plaza
Corning Tower Building
Albany, NY 12237
518-747-8887
800-541-2831

NORTH CAROLINA
Department of Health and Human
  Services of North Carolina
1918 Umstead Drive
Kirby Building
Raleigh, NC 27699-2501
919-857-4011
800-662-7030

NORTH DAKOTA
Department of Human Services
  of North Dakota
600 E. Boulevard Avenue
Bismarck, ND 58505-0250
701-328-2332
800-755-2604 (In-State only)

OHIO
Department of Job and Family Services
  of Ohio
Ohio Health Plans
30 East Broad Street, 31st Floor
Columbus, OH 43215-3414
614-728-3288
800-324-8680

OKLAHOMA
Health Care Authority of Oklahoma
4545 N. Lincoln Boulevard, Suite 124
Oklahoma City, OK 73105
405-522-7300
800-522-0114

OREGON
Department of Human Services
  of Oregon
500 Summer Street, NE, 3rd Floor
Salem, OR 94310-1014
503-945-5772
800-527-5772

PENNSYLVANIA
*Department of Public Welfare
  of Pennsylvania*
Health and Welfare Building
Room 515
P.O. Box 2675
Harrisburg, PA 17105
717-787-1870
800-692-7462

PUERTO RICO
*Medicaid Office of Puerto Rico and
  Virgin Islands*
GPO Box 70184
San Juan, PR 00936
787-765-1230

RHODE ISLAND
*Department of Human Services
  of Rhode Island*
Louis Pasteur Building
600 New London Avenue
Cranston, RI 02921
401-462-5300
401-462-1500 (Spanish)

SOUTH CAROLINA
*Department of Health and Human
Services of South Carolina*
P.O. Box 8206
Columbia, SC 29202-8206
803-898-2500

SOUTH DAKOTA
*Department of Social Services
  of South Dakota*
700 Governors Drive
Richard F. Kneip Building
Pierre, SD 57501
605-773-3495
800-452-7691

TENNESSEE
*Department of Finance and
  Administration of Tennessee*
729 Church Street
Nashville, TN 37247
615-741-4800
800-669-1851
800-254-7568 (Spanish)

TEXAS
*Health and Human Services
  Commission of Texas*
4900 N. Lamar Boulevard, 4th Floor
Austin, TX 78701
512-424-6500
888-834-7406

UTAH
Department of Health of Utah
288 North 1460 West
P.O. Box 143101
Salt Lake City, UT 84114-3101
801-538-6155
800-662-9651
800-662-9651 (Spanish)

VERMONT

Agency of Human Services of Vermont
103 South Main Street
Waterbury, VT 05676-1201
802-241-2800
800-250-8427 (In-State only)

VIRGINIA

*Department of Social Services
  of Virginia*
600 East Broad Street, Suite 1300
Richmond, VA 23219
804-726-4231

WASHINGTON

*Department of Social and Health
  Services of Washington*
P.O. Box 45505
Olympia, WA 98504-5505
800-562-6188
800-562-3022 (In-State only)

WEST VIRGINIA

*Department of Health and Human
  Resources of West Virginia*
350 Capitol Street, Room 251
Charleston, WV 25301-3709
304-558-1700

WISCONSIN

*Department of Health and Family
  Services of Wisconsin*
1 West Wilson Street
P.O. Box 309
Madison, WI 53701-0309
608-221-5720
800-362-3002

WYOMING

Department of Health of Wyoming
147 Hathaway Building
Cheyenne, WY 82002
307-777-6964
888-996-8678 (In-State only)

Appendix E

Additional Resources

(Publishers Note: the following contacts are provided for informa-tional purposes only. No endorsement by the author or publisher of any of the following sites is to be implied.)

LONG-TERM CARE
American Association of Homes and Services for the Aging
2519 Connecticut Avenue, NW
Washington, DC 20008
202-783-2242
www2.aahsa.org
Association for the advancement of quality, affordable care for seniors

American Health Care Association
1201 L Street, N.W.
Washington, DC 20005
202-842-4444
www.ahca.org
Association representing long-term care providers

Long-term Care Living
www.longtermcareliving.com
Consumer information about long-term care

MemberoftheFamily.net
www.memberofthefamily.net
Information about Medicare- and Medicaid-certified nursing homes;
National Nursing Home Watch List

National Association of Professional Geriatric Care Managers
1604 N. Country Club Road
Tucson, AZ 85716-3102
520-881-8008
www.caremanager.org
Association of professionals specializing in assisting families with long-term care planning

National Center for Assisted Living
1201 L Street, N.W.
Washington, DC 20005
202-842-4444
www.ncal.org
Provides consumer information regarding assisted living facilities

National Citizens' Coalition for Nursing Home Reform
www.nccnhr.org
Grassroots advocacy for quality long-term care

GOVERNMENT AGENCIES
Eldercare Locator
www.eldercare.gov
Finds local services for seniors

Medicare
www.medicare.gov
Official government website for Medicare recipients;
Medicare eligibility tool;
Nursing Home Compare

U.S. Administration on Aging
Washington, DC 20201
202-619-0724
www.aoa.gov
Government agency promoting independence of elderly persons

Veteran's Health Administration
810 Vermont Avenue, NW
Washington, DC 20420
877-222-8387
www.va.gov
Information on veteran's health benefits

ELDER ABUSE
Clearinghouse on Abuse and Neglect of the Elderly (CANE)
National Center on Elder Abuse
1201 15th Street, NW, Suite 350
Washington, DC 20005-2842
202-898-2586
www.elderabusecenter.org
Information and assistance on issues pertaining to abuse of seniors
Online resources pertaining to elder abuse

HOSPICE CARE
American Hospice Foundation
2120 L Street, NW, Suite 200
Washington, DC 20037
202-223-0204
www.americanhospice.org
Advocacy and educational organization

National Hospice and Palliative Care Organization
1700 Diagonal Road, Suite 625
Alexandria, VA 22314
703-837-1500
www.nho.org
Organization promoting quality end-of-life care

ALZHEIMER'S DISEASE

Alzheimer's Association
225 North Michigan Avenue, Suite 1700
Chicago, IL 60601-7633
800-272-3900
www.alz.org
Alzheimer's disease research and support site

Alzheimer's Disease Education and Referral Center
P.O. Box 8250
Silver Spring, MD 20907-8250
800-438-4380
www.alzheimers.org
Provides information on Alzheimer's disease to professionals and families

ORGANIZATIONS

AARP (formerly American Association of Retired People)
601 E. Street NW
Washington, DC 20049
888-OUR-AARP (888-687-2277)
www.aarp.org
Advocacy organization for people age 50 and older

Families 4 Care
www.families4care.org
Family Alliance for Compassionate Eldercare

National Academy of Elder Law Attorneys
1604 North Country Club Rd.
Tucson, Arizona 85716
520-881-4005
www.naela.org
Locates attorneys concentrating in legal issues relating to the elderly

National Council on the Aging
300 D Street, SW, Suite 801
Washington, D.C. 20024
202-479-1200
www.ncoa.org
Organization promoting self-determination and health of the elderly

**National Long-Term Care Ombudsman
Resource Center**
1424 16th Street, NW, Suite 202
Washington, DC 20036
202-332-2275
www.ltcombudsman.org
Listing of state ombudsman's offices

Appendix F

Selected Federal Regulations Relating to Skilled Care Facilities

(From 42 C.F.R. 483)

Subpart B—Requirements for Long Term Care Facilities

• • •

Sec. 483.10 Resident rights.

The resident has a right to a dignified existence, self-determination, and communication with and access to persons and services inside and outside the facility. A facility must protect and promote the rights of each resident, including each of the following rights:

Exercise of rights. (1) The resident has the right to exercise his or her rights as a resident of the facility and as a citizen or resident of the United States.

(2) The resident has the right to be free of interference, coercion, discrimination, and reprisal from the facility in exercising his or her rights.

(3) In the case of a resident adjudged incompetent under the laws of a State by a court of competent jurisdiction, the rights of the resident are exercised by the person appointed under State law to act on the resident's behalf.

(4) In the case of a resident who has not been adjudged incompetent by the State court, any legal-surrogate designated in accordance with State law may exercise the resident's rights to the extent provided by State law.

(b) Notice of rights and services. (1) The facility must inform the resident both orally and in writing in a language that the resident understands of his or her rights and all rules and regulations governing resident conduct and responsibilities during the stay in the facility.

• • •

(2) The resident or his or her legal representative has the right—

(i) Upon an oral or written request, to access all records pertaining to himself or herself including current clinical records within 24 hours (excluding weekends and holidays); and

(ii) After receipt of his or her records for inspection, to purchase at a cost not to exceed the community standard photocopies of the records or any portions of them upon request and 2 working days advance notice to the facility.

(3) The resident has the right to be fully informed in language that he or she can understand of his or her total health status, including but not limited to, his or her medical condition;

(4) The resident has the right to refuse treatment, to refuse to participate in experimental research, and to formulate an advance directive as specified in paragraph (8) of this section; and

(5) The facility must—

Inform each resident who is entitled to Medicaid benefits, in writing, at the time of admission to the nursing facility or, when the resident becomes eligible for Medicaid of—

(A) The items and services that are included in nursing facility services under the State plan and for which the resident may not be charged;

(B) Those other items and services that the facility offers and for which the resident may be charged, and the amount of charges for those services; and

(ii) Inform each resident when changes are made to the items and services specified in paragraphs (5)(i) (A) and (B) of this section.

(6) The facility must inform each resident before, or at the time of admission, and peri-

odically during the resident's stay, of services available in the facility and of charges for those services, including any charges for services not covered under Medicare or by the facility's per diem rate.

(7) The facility must furnish a written description of legal rights which includes—

(i) A description of the manner of protecting personal funds, under paragraph (c) of this section;

(ii) A description of the requirements and procedures for establishing eligibility for Medicaid, including the right to request an assessment under section 1924(c) which determines the extent of a couple's nonexempt resources at the time of institutionalization and attributes to the community spouse an equitable share of resources which cannot be considered available for payment toward the cost of the institutionalized spouse's medical care in his or her process of spending down to Medicaid eligibility levels;

(iii) A posting of names, addresses, and telephone numbers of all pertinent State client advocacy groups such as the State survey and certification agency, the State licensure office, the State ombudsman program, the protection and advocacy network, and the Medicaid fraud control unit; and

(iv) A statement that the resident may file a complaint with the State survey and certification agency concerning resident abuse, neglect, misappropriation of resident property in the facility, and non-compliance with the advance directives requirements.

(8) The facility must comply with the requirements specified in subpart I of part 489 of this chapter relating to maintaining written policies and procedures regarding advance directives. These requirements include provisions to inform and provide written information to all adult residents concerning the right to accept or refuse medical or surgical treatment and, at the individual's option, formulate an advance directive. This includes a written description of the facility's policies to implement advance directives and applicable State law. Facilities are permitted to contract with other entities

to furnish this information but are still legally responsible for ensuring that the requirements of this section are met. If an adult individual is incapacitated at the time of admission and is unable to receive information (due to the incapacitating condition or a mental disorder) or articulate whether or not he or she has executed an advance directive, the facility may give advance directive information to the individual's family or surrogate in the same manner that it issues other materials about policies and procedures to the family of the incapacitated individual or to a surrogate or other concerned persons in accordance with State law. The facility is not relieved of its obligation to provide this information to the individual once he or she is no longer incapacitated or unable to receive such information. Follow-up procedures must be in place to provide the information to the individual directly at the appropriate time.

(9) The facility must inform each resident of the name, specialty, and way of contacting the physician responsible for his or her care.

(10) The facility must prominently display in the facility written information, and provide to residents and applicants for admission oral and written information about how to apply for and use Medicare and Medicaid benefits, and how to receive refunds for previous payments covered by such benefits.

(11) Notification of changes. (i) A facility must immediately inform the resident; consult with the resident's physician; and if known, notify the resident's legal representative or an interested family member when there is—

(A) An accident involving the resident which results in injury and has the potential for requiring physician intervention;

(B) A significant change in the resident's physical, mental, or psychosocial status (i.e., a deterioration in health, mental, or psychosocial status in either life-threatening conditions or clinical complications);

(C) A need to alter treatment significantly (i.e., a need to discontinue an existing form of treatment due to adverse consequences, or to commence a new form of treatment); or

(D) A decision to transfer or discharge the resident from the facility as specified in Sec. 483.12(a).

(ii) The facility must also promptly notify the resident and, if known, the resident's legal representative or interested family member when there is—

(A) A change in room or roommate assignment as specified in Sec. 483.15(e)(2); or

(B) A change in resident rights under Federal or State law or regulations as specified in paragraph (b)(1) of this section.

(iii) The facility must record and periodically update the address and phone number of the resident's legal representative or interested family member.

• • •

(c) Protection of resident funds. (1) The resident has the right to manage his or her financial affairs, and the facility may not require residents to deposit their personal funds with the facility.

(2) Management of personal funds. Upon written authorization of a resident, the facility must hold, safeguard, manage, and account for the personal funds of the resident deposited with the facility, as specified in paragraphs (c)(3)-(8) of this section.

(3) Deposit of funds. (i) Funds in excess of $50. The facility must deposit any residents' personal funds in excess of $50 in an interest bearing account (or accounts) that is separate from any of the facility's operating accounts, and that credits all interest earned on resident's funds to that account. (In pooled accounts, there must be a separate accounting for each resident's share.)

(ii) Funds less than $50. The facility must maintain a resident's personal funds that do not exceed $50 in a non-interest bearing account, interest-bearing account, or petty cash fund.

(4) Accounting and records. The facility must establish and maintain a system that assures a full and complete and separate accounting, according to generally accepted accounting principles, of each resident's personal funds entrusted to the facility on the

resident's behalf.

(i) The system must preclude any commingling of resident funds with facility funds or with the funds of any person other than another resident.

(ii) The individual financial record must be available through quarterly statements and on request to the resident or his or her legal representative.

(5) Notice of certain balances. The facility must notify each resident that receives Medicaid benefits—

(i) When the amount in the resident's account reaches $200 less than the SSI resource limit for one person, specified in section 1611(a)(3)(B) of the Act; and

(ii) That, if the amount in the account, in addition to the value of the resident's other nonexempt resources, reaches the SSI resource limit for one person, the resident may lose eligibility for Medicaid or SSI.

(6) Conveyance upon death. Upon the death of a resident with a personal fund deposited with the facility, the facility must convey within 30 days the resident's funds, and a final accounting of those funds, to the individual or probate jurisdiction administering the resident's estate.

(7) Assurance of financial security. The facility must purchase a surety bond, or otherwise provide assurance satisfactory to the Secretary, to assure the security of all personal funds of residents deposited with the facility.

(8) Limitation on charges to personal funds. The facility may not impose a charge against the personal funds of a resident for any item or service for which payment is made under Medicaid or Medicare (except for applicable deductible and coinsurance amounts). The facility may charge the resident for requested services that are more expensive than or in excess of covered services in accordance with Sec. 489.32 of this chapter.

• • •

(i) Services included in Medicare or Medicaid payment. During the course of a covered Medicare or Medicaid stay, facilities may not charge a resident for the following categories of items and services:

(A) Nursing services as required at Sec.

483.30 of this subpart.

(B) Dietary services as required at Sec. 483.35 of this subpart.

(C) An activities program as required at Sec. 483.15(f) of this subpart.

(D) Room/bed maintenance services.

(E) Routine personal hygiene items and services as required to meet the needs of residents, including, but not limited to, hair hygiene supplies, comb, brush, bath soap, disinfecting soaps or specialized cleansing agents when indicated to treat special skin problems or to fight infection, razor, shaving cream, toothbrush, toothpaste, denture adhesive, denture cleaner, dental floss, moisturizing lotion, tissues, cotton balls, cotton swabs, deodorant, incontinence care and supplies, sanitary napkins and related supplies, towels, washcloths, hospital gowns, over the counter drugs, hair and nail hygiene services, bathing, and basic personal laundry.

(F) Medically-related social services as required at Sec. 483.15(g) of this subpart.

(ii) Items and services that may be charged to residents' funds. Listed below are general categories and examples of items and services that the facility may charge to residents' funds if they are requested by a resident, if the facility informs the resident that there will be a charge, and if payment is not made by Medicare or Medicaid:

(A) Telephone.

(B) Television/radio for personal use.

(C) Personal comfort items, including smoking materials, notions and novelties, and confections.

(D) Cosmetic and grooming items and services in excess of those for which payment is made under Medicaid or Medicare.

(E) Personal clothing.

(F) Personal reading matter.

(G) Gifts purchased on behalf of a resident.

(H) Flowers and plants.

(I) Social events and entertainment offered outside the scope of the activities program, provided under Sec. 483.15(f) of this subpart.

(J) Noncovered special care services such as privately hired nurses or aides.

(K) Private room, except when therapeutically required (for example, isolation for infection control).

(L) Specially prepared or alternative food requested instead of the food generally prepared by the facility, as required by Sec. 483.35 of this subpart.

(iii) Requests for items and services. (A) The facility must not charge a resident (or his or her representative) for any item or service not requested by the resident.

(B) The facility must not require a resident (or his or her representative) to request any item or service as a condition of admission or continued stay.

(C) The facility must inform the resident (or his or her representative) requesting an item or service for which a charge will be made that there will be a charge for the item or service and what the charge will be.

(d) Free choice. The resident has the right to—

(1) Choose a personal attending physician;

(2) Be fully informed in advance about care and treatment and of any changes in that care or treatment that may affect the resident's well-being; and

(3) Unless adjudged incompetent or otherwise found to be incapacitated under the laws of the State, participate in planning care and treatment or changes in care and treatment.

(e) Privacy and confidentiality. The resident has the right to personal privacy and confidentiality of his or her personal and clinical records.

(1) Personal privacy includes accommodations, medical treatment, written and telephone communications, personal care, visits, and meetings of family and resident groups, but this does not require the facility to provide a private room for each resident;

(2) Except as provided in paragraph (e)(3) of this section, the resident may approve or refuse the release of personal and clinical records to any individual outside the facility;

(3) The resident's right to refuse release of personal and clinical records does not apply when—

(i) The resident is transferred to another health care institution; or

(ii) Record release is required by law.

(f) Grievances. A resident has the right to—

(1) Voice grievances without discrimination or reprisal. Such grievances include those with respect to treatment which has been furnished as well as that which has not been furnished; and

(2) Prompt efforts by the facility to resolve grievances the resident may have, including those with respect to the behavior of other residents.

(g) Examination of survey results. A resident has the right to—

(1) Examine the results of the most recent survey of the facility conducted by Federal or State surveyors and any plan of correction in effect with respect to the facility. The facility must make the results available for examination in a place readily accessible to residents, and must post a notice of their availability; and

(2) Receive information from agencies acting as client advocates, and be afforded the opportunity to contact these agencies.

(h) Work. The resident has the right to—

(1) Refuse to perform services for the facility;

(2) Perform services for the facility, if he or she chooses, when—

(i) The facility has documented the need or desire for work in the plan of care;

(ii) The plan specifies the nature of the services performed and whether the services are voluntary or paid;

(iii) Compensation for paid services is at or above prevailing rates; and

(iv) The resident agrees to the work arrangement described in the plan of care.

(i) Mail. The resident has the right to privacy in written communications, including the right to—

(1) Send and promptly receive mail that is unopened; and

(2) Have access to stationery, postage, and writing implements at the resident's own expense.

(j) Access and visitation rights. (1) The resident has the right and the facility must provide immediate access to any resident by the following:

(i) Any representative of the Secretary;

(ii) Any representative of the State:

(iii) The resident's individual physician;

(iv) The State long term care ombudsman (established under section 307(a)(12) of the Older Americans Act of 1965);

(v) The agency responsible for the protection and advocacy system for developmentally disabled individuals (established under part C of the Developmental Disabilities Assistance and Bill of Rights Act);

(vi) The agency responsible for the protection and advocacy system for mentally ill individuals (established under the Protection and Advocacy for Mentally Ill Individuals Act);

(vii) Subject to the resident's right to deny or withdraw consent at any time, immediate family or other relatives of the resident; and

(viii) Subject to reasonable restrictions and the resident's right to deny or withdraw consent at any time, others who are visiting with the consent of the resident.

(2) The facility must provide reasonable access to any resident by any entity or individual that provides health, social, legal, or other services to the resident, subject to the resident's right to deny or withdraw consent at any time.

(3) The facility must allow representatives of the State Ombudsman, described in paragraph (j)(1)(iv) of this section, to examine a resident's clinical records with the permission of the resident or the resident's legal representative, and consistent with State law.

(k) Telephone. The resident has the right to have reasonable access to the use of a telephone where calls can be made without being overheard.

(l) Personal property. The resident has the right to retain and use personal possessions, including some furnishings, and appropriate clothing, as space permits, unless to do so would infringe upon the rights or health and safety of other residents.

(m) Married couples. The resident has the right to share a room with his or her spouse when married residents live in the same facility and both spouses consent to the arrangement.

(n) Self-Administration of Drugs. An individual resident may self-administer drugs if the interdisciplinary team, as defined by Sec. 483.20(d)(2)(ii), has determined that this practice is safe.

(o) Refusal of certain transfers. (1) An individual has the right to refuse a transfer to another room within the institution, if the purpose of the transfer is to relocate—

(i) A resident of a SNF from the distinct part of the institution that is a SNF to a part of the institution that is not a SNF, or

(ii) A resident of a NF from the distinct part of the institution that is a NF to a distinct part of the institution that is a SNF.

(2) A resident's exercise of the right to refuse transfer under paragraph (o)(1) of this section does not affect the individual's eligibility or entitlement to Medicare or Medicaid benefits.

• • •

Sec. 483.12 Admission, transfer and discharge rights.

(a) Transfer and discharge—

(1) Definition: Transfer and discharge includes movement of a resident to a bed outside of the certified facility whether that bed is in the same physical plant or not. Transfer and discharge does not refer to movement of a resident to a bed within the same certified facility.

(2) Transfer and discharge requirements. The facility must permit each resident to remain in the facility, and not transfer or discharge the resident from the facility unless—

(i) The transfer or discharge is necessary for the resident's welfare and the resident's needs cannot be met in the facility;

(ii) The transfer or discharge is appropriate because the resident's health has improved sufficiently so the resident no longer needs the services provided by the facility;

(iii) The safety of individuals in the facility is endangered;

(iv) The health of individuals in the facility would otherwise be endangered;

(v) The resident has failed, after reasonable and appropriate notice, to pay for (or to have paid under Medicare or Medicaid) a stay at the facility. For a resident who becomes eligible for Medicaid after admission to a facility, the facility may charge a

resident only allowable charges under Medicaid; or

(vi) The facility ceases to operate.

(3) Documentation. When the facility transfers or discharges a resident under any of the circumstances specified in paragraphs (a)(2)(i) through (v) of this section, the resident's clinical record must be documented. The documentation must be made by—

(i) The resident's physician when transfer or discharge is necessary under paragraph (a)(2)(i) or paragraph (a)(2)(ii) of this section; and

(ii) A physician when transfer or discharge is necessary under paragraph (a)(2)(iv) of this section.

(4) Notice before transfer. Before a facility transfers or discharges a resident, the facility must—

(i) Notify the resident and, if known, a family member or legal representative of the resident of the transfer or discharge and the reasons for the move in writing and in a language and manner they understand.

(ii) Record the reasons in the resident's clinical record; and

(iii) Include in the notice the items described in paragraph (a)(6) of this section.

(5) Timing of the notice. (i) Except when specified in paragraph (a)(5)(ii) of this section, the notice of transfer or discharge required under paragraph (a)(4) of this section must be made by the facility at least 30 days before the resident is transferred or discharged.

(ii) Notice may be made as soon as practicable before transfer or discharge when—

(A) the safety of individuals in the facility would be endangered under paragraph (a)(2)(iii) of this section;

(B) The health of individuals in the facility would be endangered, under paragraph (a)(2)(iv) of this section;

(C) The resident's health improves sufficiently to allow a more immediate transfer or discharge, under paragraph (a)(2)(ii) of this section;

(D) An immediate transfer or discharge is required by the resident's urgent medical needs, under paragraph (a)(2)(i) of this section; or

(E) A resident has not resided in the facility for 30 days.

(6) Contents of the notice. The written notice specified in paragraph (a)(4) of this section must include the following:

(i) The reason for transfer or discharge;

(ii) The effective date of transfer or discharge;

(iii) The location to which the resident is transferred or discharged;

(iv) A statement that the resident has the right to appeal the action to the State;

(v) The name, address and telephone number of the State long term care ombudsman;

• • •

(7) Orientation for transfer or discharge. A facility must provide sufficient preparation and orientation to residents to ensure safe and orderly transfer or discharge from the facility.

(8) Room changes in a composite distinct part. Room changes in a facility that is a composite distinct part (as defined in Sec. 483.5(c)) must be limited to moves within the particular building in which the resident resides, unless the resident voluntarily agrees to move to another of the composite distinct part's locations.

(b) Notice of bed-hold policy and readmission—(1) Notice before transfer. Before a nursing facility transfers a resident to a hospital or allows a resident to go on therapeutic leave, the nursing facility must provide written information to the resident and a family member or legal representative that specifies—

(i) The duration of the bed-hold policy under the State plan, if any, during which the resident is permitted to return and resume residence in the nursing facility; and

(ii) The nursing facility's policies regarding bed-hold periods, which must be consistent with paragraph (b)(3) of this section, permitting a resident to return.

(2) Bedhold notice upon transfer. At the time of transfer of a resident for hospitalization or therapeutic leave, a nursing facility must provide to the resident and a family member or legal representative written notice which specifies the duration of the bed-hold policy described in paragraph (b)(1) of this section.

(3) Permitting resident to return to facility. A nursing facility must establish and follow a written policy under which a resident, whose hospitalization or therapeutic leave exceeds the bed-hold period under the State plan, is readmitted to the facility immediately upon the first availability of a bed in a semi-private room if the resident—

(i) Requires the services provided by the facility; and

(ii) Is eligible for Medicaid nursing facility services.

(4) Readmission to a composite distinct part. When the nursing facility to which a resident is readmitted is a composite distinct part (as defined in Sec. 483.5(c) of this subpart), the resident must be permitted to return to an available bed in the particular location of the composite distinct part in which he or she resided previously. If a bed is not available in that location at the time of readmission, the resident must be given the option to return to that location upon the first availability of a bed there.

(c) Equal access to quality care.

(1) A facility must establish and maintain identical policies and practices regarding transfer, discharge, and the provision of services under the State plan for all individuals regardless of source of payment;

• • •

(d) Admissions policy.

The facility must—

(i) Not require residents or potential residents to waive their rights to Medicare or Medicaid; and

(ii) Not require oral or written assurance that residents or potential residents are not eligible for, or will not apply for, Medicare or Medicaid benefits.

(2) The facility must not require a third party guarantee of payment to the facility as a condition of admission or expedited admission, or continued stay in the facility. However, the facility may require an individual who has legal access to a resident's income or resources available to pay for facility care to sign a contract, without incurring personal financial liability, to provide facility payment from the resident's income or resources.

(3) In the case of a person eligible for

Medicaid, a nursing facility must not charge, solicit, accept, or receive, in addition to any amount otherwise required to be paid under the State plan, any gift, money, donation, or other consideration as a precondition of admission, expedited admission or continued stay in the facility. However—

(i) A nursing facility may charge a resident who is eligible for Medicaid for items and services the resident has requested and received, and that are not specified in the State plan as included in the term "nursing facility services" so long as the facility gives proper notice of the availability and cost of these services to residents and does not condition the resident's admission or continued stay on the request for and receipt of such additional services; and

(ii) A nursing facility may solicit, accept, or receive a charitable, religious, or philanthropic contribution from an organization or from a person unrelated to a Medicaid eligible resident or potential resident, but only to the extent that the contribution is not a condition of admission, expedited admission, or continued stay in the facility for a Medicaid eligible resident.

(4) States or political subdivisions may apply stricter admissions standards under State or local laws than are specified in this section, to prohibit discrimination against individuals entitled to Medicaid.

Sec. 483.13 Resident behavior and facility practices.

(a) Restraints. The resident has the right to be free from any physical or chemical restraints imposed for purposes of discipline or convenience, and not required to treat the resident's medical symptoms.

(b) Abuse. The resident has the right to be free from verbal, sexual, physical, and mental abuse, corporal punishment, and involuntary seclusion.

(c) Staff treatment of residents. The facility must develop and implement written policies and procedures that prohibit mistreatment, neglect, and abuse of residents and misappropriation of resident property.

(1) The facility must—

(i) Not use verbal, mental, sexual, or physical abuse, corporal punishment, or involuntary seclusion;

(ii) Not employ individuals who have been—

(A) Found guilty of abusing, neglecting, or mistreating residents by a court of law; or

(B) Have had a finding entered into the State nurse aide registry concerning abuse, neglect, mistreatment of residents or misappropriation of their property; and

(iii) Report any knowledge it has of actions by a court of law against an employee, which would indicate unfitness for service as a nurse aide or other facility staff to the State nurse aide registry or licensing authorities.

(2) The facility must ensure that all alleged violations involving mistreatment, neglect, or abuse, including injuries of unknown source, and misappropriation of resident property are reported immediately to the administrator of the facility and to other officials in accordance with State law through established procedures (including to the State survey and certification agency).

(3) The facility must have evidence that all alleged violations are thoroughly investigated, and must prevent further potential abuse while the investigation is in progress.

(4) The results of all investigations must be reported to the administrator or his designated representative and to other officials in accordance with State law (including to the State survey and certification agency) within 5 working days of the incident, and if the alleged violation is verified appropriate corrective action must be taken.

• • •

Sec. 483.15 Quality of life.

A facility must care for its residents in a manner and in an environment that promotes maintenance or enhancement of each resident's quality of life.

(a) Dignity. The facility must promote care for residents in a manner and in an environment that maintains or enhances each resident's dignity and respect in full recognition of his or her individuality.

Self-determination and participation. The resident has the right to—

(1) Choose activities, schedules, and health

care consistent with his or her interests, assessments, and plans of care;

(2) Interact with members of the community both inside and outside the facility; and

(3) Make choices about aspects of his or her life in the facility that are significant to the resident.

(c) Participation in resident and family groups. (1) A resident has the right to organize and participate in resident groups in the facility;

(2) A resident's family has the right to meet in the facility with the families of other residents in the facility;

(3) The facility must provide a resident or family group, if one exists, with private space;

(4) Staff or visitors may attend meetings at the group's invitation;

(5) The facility must provide a designated staff person responsible for providing assistance and responding to written requests that result from group meetings;

(6) When a resident or family group exists, the facility must listen to the views and act upon the grievances and recommendations of residents and families concerning proposed policy and operational decisions affecting resident care and life in the facility.

(d) Participation in other activities. A resident has the right to participate in social, religious, and community activities that do not interfere with the rights of other residents in the facility.

(e) Accommodation of needs. A resident has the right to—

(1) Reside and receive services in the facility with reasonable accommodation of individual needs and preferences, except when the health or safety of the individual or other residents would be endangered; and

(2) Receive notice before the resident's room or roommate in the facility is changed.

(f) Activities. (1) The facility must provide for an ongoing program of activities designed to meet, in accordance with the comprehensive assessment, the interests and the physical, mental, and psychosocial well-being of each resident.

(1) The activities program must be directed

by a qualified professional who—

(I) Is a qualified therapeutic recreation specialist or an activities professional who—

(A) Is licensed or registered, if applicable, by the State in which practicing; and

(B) Is eligible for certification as a therapeutic recreation specialist or as an activities professional by a recognized accrediting body on or after October 1, 1990; or

(ii) Has 2 years of experience in a social or recreational program within the last 5 years, 1 of which was full-time in a patient activities program in a health care setting; or

(iii) Is a qualified occupational therapist or occupational therapy assistant; or

(iv) Has completed a training course approved by the State.

(g) Social Services. (1) The facility must provide medically-related social services to attain or maintain the highest practicable physical, mental, and psychosocial well-being of each resident.

(2) A facility with more than 120 beds must employ a qualified social worker on a full-time basis.

(3) Qualifications of social worker. A qualified social worker is an individual with—

(i) A bachelor's degree in social work or a bachelor's degree in a human services field including but not limited to sociology, special education, rehabilitation counseling, and psychology; and

(ii) One year of supervised social work experience in a health care setting working directly with individuals.

(h) Environment. The facility must provide—

(1) A safe, clean, comfortable, and homelike environment, allowing the resident to use his or her personal belongings to the extent possible;

(2) Housekeeping and maintenance services necessary to maintain a sanitary, orderly, and comfortable interior;

(3) Clean bed and bath linens that are in good condition;

(4) Private closet space in each resident room, as specified in Sec. 483.70(d)(2)(iv) of this part;

(5) Adequate and comfortable lighting levels in all areas;

(6) Comfortable and safe temperature levels. Facilities initially certified after October 1, 1990 must maintain a temperature range of 71-81 degrees F.
(7) For the maintenance of comfortable sound levels.

Sec. 483.20 Resident assessment.

The facility must conduct initially and periodically a comprehensive, accurate, standardized, reproducible assessment of each resident's functional capacity.
(a) Admission orders. At the time each resident is admitted, the facility must have physician orders for the resident's immediate care.
(b) Comprehensive assessments.
(1) Resident assessment instrument. A facility must make a comprehensive assessment of a resident's needs, using the resident assessment instrument (RAI) specified by the State. The assessment must include at least the following:
(i) Identification and demographic information.
(ii) Customary routine.
(iii) Cognitive patterns.
(iv) Communication.
(v) Vision.
(vi) Mood and behavior patterns.
(vii)Psychosocial well-being.
(viii)Physical functioning and structural problems.
(ix) Continence.
(x) Disease diagnoses and health conditions.
(xi) Dental and nutritional status.
(xii) Skin condition.
(xiii)Activity pursuit.
(xiv) Medications.
(xv) Special treatments and procedures.
(xvi) Discharge potential.
(xvii)Documentation of summary information regarding the additional assessment performed through the resident assessment protocols.
(xviii)Documentation of participation in assessment.
The assessment process must include direct observation and communication with the resident, as well as communication with

licensed and nonlicensed direct care staff members on all shifts.
(2) When required.
• • •
(i) Within 14 calendar days after admission, excluding re-admissions in which there is no significant change in the resident's physical or mental condition. (For purposes of this section, "readmission" means a return to the facility following a temporary absence for hospitalization or for therapeutic leave.)
(ii) Within 14 calendar days after the facility determines, or should have determined, that there has been a significant change in the resident's physical or mental condition. (For purposes of this section, a "significant change" means a major decline or improvement in the resident's status that will not normally resolve itself without further intervention by staff or by implementing standard disease-related clinical interventions, that has an impact on more than one area of the resident's health status, and requires interdisciplinary review or revision of the care plan, or both.)
(iii) Not less often than once every 12 months.
(c) Quarterly review assessment. A facility must assess a resident using the quarterly review instrument specified by the State and approved by CMS not less frequently than once every 3 months.
(d) Use. A facility must maintain all resident assessments completed within the previous 15 months in the resident's active record and use the results of the assessments to develop, review, and revise the resident's comprehensive plan of care.
• • •
(g) Accuracy of assessments. The assessment must accurately reflect the resident's status.
(h) Coordination. A registered nurse must conduct or coordinate each assessment with the appropriate participation of health professionals.
(i) Certification. (1) A registered nurse must sign and certify that the assessment is completed.
(2) Each individual who completes a portion of the assessment must sign and certify the accuracy of that portion of the assessment.

• • •

(k) Comprehensive care plans. (1) The facility must develop a comprehensive care plan for each resident that includes measurable objectives and timetables to meet a resident's medical, nursing, and mental and psychosocial needs that are identified in the comprehensive assessment. The care plan must describe the following—

(i) The services that are to be furnished to attain or maintain the resident's highest practicable physical, mental, and psychosocial well-being[. . .]

• • •

A comprehensive care plan must be—

(i) Developed within 7 days after completion of the comprehensive assessment;

(ii) Prepared by an interdisciplinary team, that includes the attending physician, a registered nurse with responsibility for the resident, and other appropriate staff in disciplines as determined by the resident's needs, and, to the extent practicable, the participation of the resident, the resident's family or the resident's legal representative; and

(iii) Periodically reviewed and revised by a team of qualified persons after each assessment.

• • •

Sec. 483.25 Quality of care.

Each resident must receive and the facility must provide the necessary care and services to attain or maintain the highest practicable physical, mental, and psychosocial well-being, in accordance with the comprehensive assessment and plan of care.

(a) Activities of daily living. Based on the comprehensive assessment of a resident, the facility must ensure that—

(1) A resident's abilities in activities of daily living do not diminish unless circumstances of the individual's clinical condition demonstrate that diminution was unavoidable. This includes the resident's ability to—

(i) Bathe, dress, and groom;

(ii) Transfer and ambulate;

(iii) Toilet;

(iv) Eat; and

(v) Use speech, language, or other functional communication systems.

(2) A resident is given the appropriate treatment and services to maintain or improve his or her abilities specified in paragraph (a)(1) of this section; and

(3) A resident who is unable to carry out activities of daily living receives the necessary services to maintain good nutrition, grooming, and personal and oral hygiene.

(c) Vision and hearing. To ensure that residents receive proper treatment and assistive devices to maintain vision and hearing abilities, the facility must, if necessary, assist the resident—

(1) In making appointments, and

(2) By arranging for transportation to and from the office of a practitioner specializing in the treatment of vision or hearing impairment or the office of a professional specializing in the provision of vision or hearing assistive devices.

(c) Pressure sores. Based on the comprehensive assessment of a resident, the facility must ensure that—

(1) A resident who enters the facility without pressure sores does not develop pressure sores unless the individual's clinical condition demonstrates that they were unavoidable; and

(2) A resident having pressure sores receives necessary treatment and services to promote healing, prevent infection and prevent new sores from developing.

(c) Urinary Incontinence. Based on the resident's comprehensive assessment, the facility must ensure that—

(1) A resident who enters the facility without an indwelling catheter is not catheterized unless the resident's clinical condition demonstrates that catheterization was necessary; and

(2) A resident who is incontinent of bladder receives appropriate treatment and services to prevent urinary tract infections and to restore as much normal bladder function as possible.

(e) Range of motion. Based on the comprehensive assessment of a resident, the facility must ensure that—

(1) A resident who enters the facility without a limited range of motion does not experience reduction in range of motion unless the resident's clinical condition demonstrates that a reduction in range of motion is unavoidable; and

(2) A resident with a limited range of motion receives appropriate treatment and services to increase range of motion and/or to prevent further decrease in range of motion.

(f) Mental and Psychosocial functioning. Based on the comprehensive assessment of a resident, the facility must ensure that—

(1) A resident who displays mental or psychosocial adjustment difficulty, receives appropriate treatment and services to correct the assessed problem, and

(2) A resident whose assessment did not reveal a mental or psychosocial adjustment difficulty does not display a pattern of decreased social interaction and/or increased withdrawn, angry, or depressive behaviors, unless the resident's clinical condition demonstrates that such a pattern was unavoidable.

(g) Naso-gastric tubes. Based on the comprehensive assessment of a resident, the facility must ensure that—

(1) A resident who has been able to eat enough alone or with assistance is not fed by naso-gastric tube unless the resident's clinical condition demonstrates that use of a naso-gastric tube was unavoidable; and

(2) A resident who is fed by a naso-gastric or gastrostomy tube receives the appropriate treatment and services to prevent aspiration pneumonia, diarrhea, vomiting, dehydration, metabolic abnormalities, and nasalpharyngeal ulcers and to restore, if possible, normal eating skills.

(h) Accidents. The facility must ensure that—

(1) The resident environment remains as free of accident hazards as is possible; and

(2) Each resident receives adequate supervision and assistance devices to prevent accidents.

(i) Nutrition. Based on a resident's comprehensive assessment, the facility must ensure that a resident—

(1) Maintains acceptable parameters of nutritional status, such as body weight and protein levels, unless the resident's clinical condition demonstrates that this is not possible; and

(2) Receives a therapeutic diet when there is a nutritional problem.

(j) Hydration. The facility must provide each resident with sufficient fluid intake to maintain proper hydration and health.

(k) Special needs. The facility must ensure that residents receive proper treatment and care for the following special services:

(1) Injections;

(2) Parenteral and enteral fluids;

(3) Colostomy, ureterostomy, or ileostomy care;

(4) Tracheostomy care;

(5) Tracheal suctioning;

(6) Respiratory care;

(7) Foot care; and

(8) Prostheses.

(l) Unnecessary drugs—(1) General. Each resident's drug regimen must be free from unnecessary drugs. An unnecessary drug is any drug when used:

(i) In excessive dose (including duplicate drug therapy); or

(ii) For excessive duration; or

(iii) Without adequate monitoring; or

(iv) Without adequate indications for its use; or

(v) In the presence of adverse consequences which indicate the dose should be reduced or discontinued; or

(vi) Any combinations of the reasons above.

(2) Antipsychotic Drugs. Based on a comprehensive assessment of a resident, the facility must ensure that—

(i) Residents who have not used antipsychotic drugs are not given these drugs unless antipsychotic drug therapy is necessary to treat a specific condition as diagnosed and documented in the clinical record; and

(ii) Residents who use antipsychotic drugs receive gradual dose reductions, and behavioral interventions, unless clinically contraindicated, in an effort to discontinue these drugs.

(m) Medication Errors. The facility must

ensure that—
(1) It is free of medication error rates of five percent or greater; and
(2) Residents are free of any significant medication errors.

Sec. 483.30 Nursing services.

The facility must have sufficient nursing staff to provide nursing and related services to attain or maintain the highest practicable physical, mental, and psychosocial well-being of each resident, as determined by resident assessments and individual plans of care.

(a) Sufficient staff. (1) The facility must provide services by sufficient numbers of each of the following types of personnel on a 24-hour basis to provide nursing care to all residents in accordance with resident care plans:
(i) Except when waived under paragraph (c) of this section, licensed nurses; and
(ii) Other nursing personnel.
(2) Except when waived under paragraph (c) of this section, the facility must designate a licensed nurse to serve as a charge nurse on each tour of duty.
(b) Registered nurse. (1) Except when waived under paragraph (c) or (d) of this section, the facility must use the services of a registered nurse for at least 8 consecutive hours a day, 7 days a week.
(2) Except when waived under paragraph (c) or (d) of this section, the facility must designate a registered nurse to serve as the director of nursing on a full time basis.
(3) The director of nursing may serve as a charge nurse only when the facility has an average daily occupancy of 60 or fewer residents.
(c)Nursing facilities: Waiver of requirement to provide licensed nurses on a 24-hour basis. To the extent that a facility is unable to meet the requirements of paragraphs (a)(2) and (b)(1) of this section, a State may waive such requirements with respect to the facility if—
(1) The facility demonstrates to the satisfaction of the State that the facility has been unable, despite diligent efforts (including

offering wages at the community prevailing rate for nursing facilities), to recruit appropriate personnel;
(2) The State determines that a waiver of the requirement will not endanger the health or safety of individuals staying in the facility;
(3) The State finds that, for any periods in which licensed nursing services are not available, a registered nurse or a physician is obligated to respond immediately to telephone calls from the facility;
(4) A waiver granted under the conditions listed in paragraph (c) of this section is subject to annual State review;
(5) In granting or renewing a waiver, a facility may be required by the State to use other qualified, licensed personnel;
(6) The State agency granting a waiver of such requirements provides notice of the waiver to the State long term care ombudsman (established under section 307(a)(12) of the Older Americans Act of 1965) and the protection and advocacy system in the State for the mentally ill and mentally retarded; and
(7) The nursing facility that is granted such a waiver by a State notifies residents of the facility (or, where appropriate, the guardians or legal representatives of such residents) and members of their immediate families of the waiver.
(d) SNFs: Waiver of the requirement to provide services of a registered nurse for more than 40 hours a week.
(1) The Secretary may waive the requirement that a SNF provide the services of a registered nurse for more than 40 hours a week, including a director of nursing specified in paragraph (b) of this section, if the Secretary finds that—
(i) The facility is located in a rural area and the supply of skilled nursing facility services in the area is not sufficient to meet the needs of individuals residing in the area;
(ii) The facility has one full-time registered nurse who is regularly on duty at the facility 40 hours a week; and
(iii) The facility either—
(A) Has only patients whose physicians have indicated (through physicians' orders or

admission notes) that they do not require the services of a registered nurse or a physician for a 48-hours period, or

(B) Has made arrangements for a registered nurse or a physician to spend time at the facility, as determined necessary by the physician, to provide necessary skilled nursing services on days when the regular full-time registered nurse is not on duty;

(iv) The Secretary provides notice of the waiver to the State long-term care ombudsman (established under section 307(a)(12) of the Older Americans Act of 1965) and the protection and advocacy system in the State for the mentally ill and mentally retarded; and

(v) The facility that is granted such a waiver notifies residents of the facility (or, where appropriate, the guardians or legal representatives of such residents) and members of their immediate families of the waiver.

(2) A waiver of the registered nurse requirement under paragraph (d)(1) of this section is subject to annual renewal by the Secretary.

Sec. 483.35 Dietary services.

The facility must provide each resident with a nourishing, palatable, well-balanced diet that meets the daily nutritional and special dietary needs of each resident.

(a) Staffing. The facility must employ a qualified dietitian either full-time, part-time, or on a consultant basis.

• • •

(b) Sufficient staff. The facility must employ sufficient support personnel competent to carry out the functions of the dietary service.

(c) Menus and nutritional adequacy. Menus must—

(1) Meet the nutritional needs of residents in accordance with the recommended dietary allowances of the Food and Nutrition Board of the National Research Council, National Academy of Sciences;

(2) Be prepared in advance; and

(3) Be followed.

(d) Food. Each resident receives and the facility provides—

(1) Food prepared by methods that conserve nutritive value, flavor, and appearance;

(2) Food that is palatable, attractive, and at the proper temperature;

(3) Food prepared in a form designed to meet individual needs; and

(4) Substitutes offered of similar nutritive value to residents who refuse food served.

(e) Therapeutic diets. Therapeutic diets must be prescribed by the attending physician.

(f) Frequency of meals. (1) Each resident receives and the facility provides at least three meals daily, at regular times comparable to normal mealtimes in the community.

(2) There must be no more than 14 hours between a substantial evening meal and breakfast the following day, except as provided in (4) below.

(3) The facility must offer snacks at bedtime daily.

(4) When a nourishing snack is provided at bedtime, up to 16 hours may elapse between a substantial evening meal and breakfast the following day if a resident group agrees to this meal span, and a nourishing snack is served.

(g) Assistive devices. The facility must provide special eating equipment and utensils for residents who need them.

(h) Paid feeding assistants—(1) State-approved training course. A facility may use a paid feeding assistant, as defined in Sec. 488.301 of this chapter, if—

(i) The feeding assistant has successfully completed a State-approved training course that meets the requirements of Sec. 483.160 before feeding residents; and

(ii) The use of feeding assistants is consistent with State law.

(2) Supervision. (i) A feeding assistant must work under the supervision of a registered nurse (RN) or licensed practical nurse (LPN).

(ii) In an emergency, a feeding assistant must call a supervisory nurse for help on the resident call system.

(3) Resident selection criteria.

(i) A facility must ensure that a feeding assistant feeds only residents who have no complicated feeding problems.

(ii) Complicated feeding problems include, but are not limited to, difficulty swallowing, recurrent lung aspirations, and tube or par-enteral/IV feedings.

(iii) The facility must base resident selection on the charge nurse's assessment and the resident's latest assessment and plan of care.

(i) Sanitary conditions. The facility must—

(1) Procure food from sources approved or considered satisfactory by Federal, State, or local authorities;

(2) Store, prepare, distribute, and serve food under sanitary conditions; and

(3) Dispose of garbage and refuse properly.

Sec. 483.40 Physician services.

A physician must personally approve in writing a recommendation that an individual be admitted to a facility. Each resident must remain under the care of a physician.

(a) Physician supervision. The facility must ensure that—

(1) The medical care of each resident is supervised by a physician; and

(2) Another physician supervises the medical care of residents when their attending physician is unavailable.

• • •

(c) Frequency of physician visits.

(1) The resident must be seen by a physician at least once every 30 days for the first 90 days after admission, and at least once every 60 days thereafter.

(2) A physician visit is considered timely if it occurs not later than 10 days after the date the visit was required.

(3) Except as provided in paragraphs (c)(4) and (f) of this section, all required physician visits must be made by the physician personally.

(4) At the option of the physician, required visits in SNFs after the initial visit may alternate between personal visits by the physician and visits by a physician assistant, nurse practitioner, or clinical nurse specialist in accordance with paragraph (e) of this section.

(d) Availability of physicians for emergency care. The facility must provide or arrange for the provision of physician services 24 hours a day, in case of an emergency.

(e) Physician delegation of tasks in SNFs.

• • •

(2) A physician may not delegate a task when the regulations specify that the physician must perform it personally, or when the delegation is prohibited under State law or by the facility's own policies.

• • •

Sec. 483.45 Specialized rehabilitative services.

(a) Provision of services. If specialized rehabilitative services such as but not limited to physical therapy, speech-language pathology, occupational therapy, and mental health rehabilitative services for mental illness and mental retardation, are required in the resident's comprehensive plan of care, the facility must—

(1) Provide the required services; or

(2) Obtain the required services from an outside resource (in accordance with Sec. 483.75(h) of this part) from a provider of specialized rehabilitative services.

(b) Qualifications. Specialized rehabilitative services must be provided under the written order of a physician by qualified personnel.

Sec. 483.55 Dental services.

The facility must assist residents in obtaining routine and 24-hour emergency dental care.

(a) Skilled nursing facilities. A facility (1) Must provide or obtain from an outside resource, in accordance with Sec. 483.75(h) of this part, routine and emergency dental services to meet the needs of each resident;

(2) May charge a Medicare resident an additional amount for routine and emergency dental services;

(3) Must if necessary, assist the resident—

(i) In making appointments; and

(ii) By arranging for transportation to and from the dentist's office; and

(4) Promptly refer residents with lost or damaged dentures to a dentist.

(b) Nursing facilities. The facility (1) Must provide or obtain from an outside resource, in accordance with Sec. 483.75(h) of this part, the following dental services to meet the needs of each resident:

(i) Routine dental services (to the extent covered under the State plan); and

(ii) Emergency dental services;

Must, if necessary, assist the resident—

(i) In making appointments; and

(ii) By arranging for transportation to and from the dentist's office; and

(3) Must promptly refer residents with lost or damaged dentures to a dentist.

Sec. 483.60 Pharmacy services.

The facility must provide routine and emergency drugs and biologicals to its residents, or obtain them under an agreement described in Sec. 483.75(h) of this part. The facility may permit unlicensed personnel to administer drugs if State law permits, but only under the general supervision of a licensed nurse.

(a) Procedures. A facility must provide pharmaceutical services (including procedures that assure the accurate acquiring, receiving, dispensing, and administering of all drugs and biologicals) to meet the needs of each resident.

• • •

(c) Drug regimen review. (1) The drug regimen of each resident must be reviewed at least once a month by a licensed pharmacist.

(2) The pharmacist must report any irregularities to the attending physician and the director of nursing, and these reports must be acted upon.

(d) Labeling of drugs and biologicals. Drugs and biologicals used in the facility must be labeled in accordance with currently accepted professional principles, and include the appropriate accessory and cautionary instructions, and the expiration date when applicable.

(e) Storage of drugs and biologicals.

(1) In accordance with State and Federal laws, the facility must store all drugs and biologicals in locked compartments under proper temperature controls, and permit only authorized personnel to have access to the keys.

• • •

Sec. 483.65 Infection control.

The facility must establish and maintain an infection control program designed to provide a safe, sanitary, and comfortable environment and to help prevent the development and transmission of disease and infection.

(a) Infection control program. The facility must establish an infection control program under which it—

(1) Investigates, controls, and prevents infections in the facility;

(2) Decides what procedures, such as isolation, should be applied to an individual resident; and

(3) Maintains a record of incidents and corrective actions related to infections.

(b) Preventing spread of infection. (1) When the infection control program determines that a resident needs isolation to prevent the spread of infection, the facility must isolate the resident.

(2) The facility must prohibit employees with a communicable disease or infected skin lesions from direct contact with residents or their food, if direct contact will transmit the disease.

(3) The facility must require staff to wash their hands after each direct resident contact for which hand washing is indicated by accepted professional practice.

(c) Linens. Personnel must handle, store, process, and transport linens so as to prevent the spread of infection.

Sec. 483.70 Physical environment.

The facility must be designed, constructed, equipped, and maintained to protect the health and safety of residents, personnel and the public.

(a) Life safety from fire. Except as otherwise provided in this section, the facility must meet the applicable provisions of the 2000 edition of the Life Safety Code of the National Fire Protection Association.

• • •

(b) Emergency power. (1) An emergency electrical power system must supply power adequate at least for lighting all entrances and exits; equipment to maintain the fire detection, alarm, and extinguishing systems; and life support systems in the event the normal electrical supply is interrupted.

(2) When life support systems are used, the facility must provide emergency electrical

power with an emergency generator (as defined in NFPA 99, Health Care Facilities) that is located on the premises.

(c) Space and equipment. The facility must—

(1) Provide sufficient space and equipment in dining, health services, recreation, and program areas to enable staff to provide residents with needed services as required by these standards and as identified in each resident's plan of care; and

(2) Maintain all essential mechanical, electrical, and patient care equipment in safe operating condition.

(d) Resident rooms. Resident rooms must be designed and equipped for adequate nursing care, comfort, and privacy of residents. Bedrooms must—

(i) Accommodate no more than four residents;

(ii) Measure at least 80 square feet per resident in multiple resident bedrooms, and at least 100 square feet in single resident rooms;

(iii) Have direct access to an exit corridor;

(iv) Be designed or equipped to assure full visual privacy for each resident;

(v) In facilities initially certified after March 31, 1992, except in private rooms, each bed must have ceiling suspended curtains, which extend around the bed to provide total visual privacy in combination with adjacent walls and curtains;

(vi) Have at least one window to the outside; and

(vii) Have a floor at or above grade level.

(2) The facility must provide each resident with—

(i) A separate bed of proper size and height for the convenience of the resident;

(ii) A clean, comfortable mattress;

(iii) Bedding appropriate to the weather and climate; and

(iv) Functional furniture appropriate to the resident's needs, and individual closet space in the resident's bedroom with clothes racks and shelves accessible to the resident.

(3) CMS, or in the case of a nursing facility the survey agency, may permit variations in requirements specified in paragraphs (d)(1) (i) and (ii) of this section relating to rooms in individual cases when the facility demonstrates in writing that the variations—

(i) Are in accordance with the special needs of the residents; and

(ii) Will not adversely affect residents' health and safety.

(e) Toilet facilities. Each resident room must be equipped with or located near toilet and bathing facilities.

(f) Resident call system. The nurse's station must be equipped to receive resident calls through a communication system from—

(1) Resident rooms; and

(2) Toilet and bathing facilities.

(g) Dining and resident activities. The facility must provide one or more rooms designated for resident dining and activities. These rooms must—

(1) Be well lighted;

(2) Be well ventilated, with nonsmoking areas identified;

(3) Be adequately furnished; and

(4) Have sufficient space to accommodate all activities.

(h) Other environmental conditions. The facility must provide a safe, functional, sanitary, and comfortable environment for the residents, staff and the public. The facility must—

(1) Establish procedures to ensure that water is available to essential areas when there is a loss of normal water supply;

(2) Have adequate outside ventilation by means of windows, or mechanical ventilation, or a combination of the two;

(3) Equip corridors with firmly secured handrails on each side; and

(4) Maintain an effective pest control program so that the facility is free of pests and rodents.

Sec. 483.75 Administration.

A facility must be administered in a manner that enables it to use its resources effectively and efficiently to attain or maintain the highest practicable physical, mental, and psychosocial well-being of each resident.

(a) Licensure. A facility must be licensed under applicable State and local law.

(b) Compliance with Federal, State, and local laws and professional standards. The facility must operate and provide services in compliance with all applicable Federal, State, and local laws, regulations, and codes, and with accepted professional standards and principles that apply to professionals providing services in such a facility.

(c) Relationship to other HHS regulations. In addition to compliance with the regulations set forth in this subpart, facilities are obliged to meet the applicable provisions of other HHS regulations, including but not limited to those pertaining to nondiscrimination on the basis of race, color, or national origin (45 CFR part 80); nondiscrimination on the basis of handicap (45 CFR part 84); nondiscrimination on the basis of age (45 CFR part 91); protection of human subjects of research (45 CFR part 46); and fraud and abuse (42 CFR part 455). Although these regulations are not in themselves considered requirements under this part, their violation may result in the termination or suspension of, or the refusal to grant or continue payment with Federal funds.

(d) Governing body. (1) The facility must have a governing body, or designated persons functioning as a governing body, that is legally responsible for establishing and implementing policies regarding the management and operation of the facility; and

(2) The governing body appoints the administrator who is—

(i) Licensed by the State where licensing is required; and

(ii) Responsible for management of the facility.

(e) Required training of nursing aides—(1) Definitions.

Licensed health professional means a physician; physician assistant; nurse practitioner; physical, speech, or occupational therapist; physical or occupational therapy assistant; registered professional nurse; licensed practical nurse; or licensed or certified social worker. Nurse aide means any individual providing nursing or nursing-related services to residents in a facility who is not a licensed health professional, a registered dietitian, or someone who volunteers to provide such services without pay. Nurse aides do not include those individuals who furnish services to residents only as paid feeding assistants as defined in Sec. 488.301 of this chapter.

(2) General rule. A facility must not use any individual working in the facility as a nurse aide for more than 4 months, on a full-time basis, unless:

(i) That individual is competent to provide nursing and nursing related services; and

(ii)(A) That individual has completed a training and competency evaluation program, or a competency evaluation program approved by the State as meeting the requirements of Secs. 483.151-483.154 of this part; or

(B) That individual has been deemed or determined competent as provided in Sec. 483.150 (a) and (b).

(3) Non-permanent employees. A facility must not use on a temporary, per diem, leased, or any basis other than a permanent employee any individual who does not meet the requirements in paragraphs (e)(2)(i) and (ii) of this section.

(4) Competency. A facility must not use any individual who has worked less than 4 months as a nurse aide in that facility unless the individual—

(i) Is a full-time employee in a State-approved training and competency evaluation program;

(ii) Has demonstrated competence through satisfactory participation in a State-approved nurse aide training and competency evaluation program or competency evaluation program; or

(iii) Has been deemed or determined competent as provided in Sec. 483.150 (a) and (b).

(5) Registry verification. Before allowing an individual to serve as a nurse aide, a facility must receive registry verification that the individual has met competency evaluation requirements unless—

(i) The individual is a full-time employee in a training and competency evaluation program approved by the State; or

(ii) The individual can prove that he or she has recently successfully completed a training and competency evaluation program or competency evaluation program approved by the State and has not yet been included in the registry. Facilities must follow up to ensure that such an individual actually becomes registered.

(6) Multi-State registry verification. Before allowing an individual to serve as a nurse aide, a facility must seek information from every State registry established under sections 1819(e)(2)(A) or 1919(e)(2)(A) of the Act the facility believes will include information on the individual.

(7) Required retraining. If, since an individual's most recent completion of a training and competency evaluation program, there has been a continuous period of 24 consecutive months during none of which the individual provided nursing or nursing-related services for monetary compensation, the individual must complete a new training and competency evaluation program or a new competency evaluation program.

(8) Regular in-service education. The facility must complete a performance review of every nurse aide at least once every 12 months, and must provide regular in-service education based on the outcome of these reviews. The in-service training must—
(i) Be sufficient to ensure the continuing competence of nurse aides, but must be no less than 12 hours per year;
(ii) Address areas of weakness as determined in nurse aides' performance reviews and may address the special needs of residents as determined by the facility staff; and
(iii) For nurse aides providing services to individuals with cognitive impairments, also address the care of the cognitively impaired.

(f) Proficiency of Nurse aides. The facility must ensure that nurse aides are able to demonstrate competency in skills and techniques necessary to care for residents' needs, as identified through resident assessments, and described in the plan of care.

• • •

(i) Medical director. (1) The facility must designate a physician to serve as medical director.
(2) The medical director is responsible for—
(i) Implementation of resident care policies; and

(ii) The coordination of medical care in the facility.

(j) Level B requirement: Laboratory services.
(1) The facility must provide or obtain laboratory services to meet the needs of its residents. The facility is responsible for the quality and timeliness of the services.

• • •

(k) Radiology and other diagnostic services.
(1) The facility must provide or obtain radiology and other diagnostic services to meet the needs of its residents. The facility is responsible for the quality and timeliness of the services.

• • •

(l) Clinical records. (1) The facility must maintain clinical records on each resident in accordance with accepted professional standards and practices that are—
(i) Complete;
(ii) Accurately documented;
(iii) Readily accessible; and
(iv) Systematically organized.
(2) Clinical records must be retained for—
(i) The period of time required by State law; or
(ii) Five years from the date of discharge when there is no requirement in State law; or
(iii) For a minor, three years after a resident reaches legal age under State law.
(3) The facility must safeguard clinical record information against loss, destruction, or unauthorized use;
(4) The facility must keep confidential all information contained in the resident's records, regardless of the form or storage method of the records, except when release is required by—
(i) Transfer to another health care institution;
(ii) Law;
(iii) Third party payment contract; or
(iv) The resident.
(5) The clinical record must contain—
(i) Sufficient information to identify the resident;
(ii) A record of the resident's assessments;
(iii) The plan of care and services provided;
(iv) The results of any preadmission screening conducted by the State; and

(v) Progress notes.

(m) Disaster and emergency preparedness. (1) The facility must have detailed written plans and procedures to meet all potential emergencies and disasters, such as fire, severe weather, and missing residents.

(2) The facility must train all employees in emergency procedures when they begin to work in the facility, periodically review the procedures with existing staff, and carry out unannounced staff drills using those procedures.

(n) Transfer agreement. (1) In accordance with section 1861(l) of the Act, the facility (other than a nursing facility which is located in a State on an Indian reservation) must have in effect a written transfer agreement with one or more hospitals approved for participation under the Medicare and Medicaid programs that reasonably assures that—

(i) Residents will be transferred from the facility to the hospital, and ensured of timely admission to the hospital when transfer is medically appropriate as determined by the attending physician; and

(ii) Medical and other information needed for care and treatment of residents, and, when the transferring facility deems it appropriate, for determining whether such residents can be adequately cared for in a less expensive setting than either the facility or the hospital, will be exchanged between the institutions.

(2) The facility is considered to have a transfer agreement in effect if the facility has attempted in good faith to enter into an agreement with a hospital sufficiently close to the facility to make transfer feasible.

(o) Quality assessment and assurance. (1) A facility must maintain a quality assessment and assurance committee consisting of—

(i) The director of nursing services;

(ii) A physician designated by the facility; and

(iii) At least 3 other members of the facility's staff.

(2) The quality assessment and assurance committee—

(i) Meets at least quarterly to identify issues with respect to which quality assessment and assurance activities are necessary; and

(ii) Develops and implements appropriate plans of action to correct identified quality deficiencies.

(3) A State or the Secretary may not require disclosure of the records of such committee except in so far as such disclosure is related to the compliance of such committee with the requirements of this section.

(4) Good faith attempts by the committee to identify and correct quality deficiencies will not be used as a basis for sanctions.

(p) Disclosure of ownership. (1) The facility must comply with the disclosure requirements of Secs. 420.206 and 455.104 of this chapter.

(2) The facility must provide written notice to the State agency responsible for licensing the facility at the time of change, if a change occurs in—

(i) Persons with an ownership or control interest, as defined in Secs. 420.201 and 455.101 of this chapter;

(ii) The officers, directors, agents, or managing employees;

(iii) The corporation, association, or other company responsible for the management of the facility; or

(iv) The facility's administrator or director of nursing.

(3) The notice specified in paragraph (p)(2) of this section must include the identity of each new individual or company.

• • •

(q) Required training of feeding assistants. A facility must not use any individual working in the facility as a paid feeding assistant unless that individual has successfully completed a State-approved training program for feeding assistants, as specified in Sec. 483.160 of this part.

• • •

Subpart D—Requirements That Must Be Met by States and State Agencies:
Nurse Aide Training and Competency Evaluation; and Paid Feeding Assistants

• • •

Sec. 483.152 Requirements for approval of a nurse aide training and competency evaluation program.

(a) For a nurse aide training and competency evaluation program to be approved by the State, it must, at a minimum—

(1) Consist of no less than 75 clock hours of training;

(2) Include at least the subjects specified in paragraph (b) of this section;

(3) Include at least 16 hours of supervised practical training. Supervised practical training means training in a laboratory or other setting in which the trainee demonstrates knowledge while performing tasks on an individual under the direct supervision of a registered nurse or a licensed practical nurse;

(4) Ensure that—

(i) Students do not perform any services for which they have not trained and been found proficient by the instructor; and

(ii) Students who are providing services to residents are under the general supervision of a licensed nurse or a registered nurse;

(5) Meet the following requirements for instructors who train nurse aides;

(i) The training of nurse aides must be performed by or under the general supervision of a registered nurse who possesses a minimum of 2 years of nursing experience, at least 1 year of which must be in the provision of long term care facility services;

(ii) Instructors must have completed a course in teaching adults or have experience in teaching adults or supervising nurse aides;

(iii) In a facility-based program, the training of nurse aides may be performed under the general supervision of the director of nursing for the facility who is prohibited from performing the actual training; and

(iv) Other personnel from the health professions may supplement the instructor, including, but not limited to, registered nurses, licensed practical/vocational nurses, pharmacists, dietitians, social workers, sanitarians, fire safety experts, nursing home administrators, gerontologists, psychologists, physical and occupational therapists, activities specialists, speech/language/hearing therapists, and resident rights experts. Supplemental personnel must have at least 1 year of experience in their fields;

(6) Contain competency evaluation procedures specified in Sec. 483.154.

• • •

Subpart E—Appeals of Discharges, Transfers, and Preadmission Screening and Annual Resident Review (PASARR) Determinations

• • •

Sec. 483.202 Definitions.

For purposes of this subpart and subparts B and C—

Discharge means movement from an entity that participates in Medicare as a skilled nursing facility, a Medicare certified distinct part, an entity that participates in Medicaid as a nursing facility, or a Medicaid certified distinct part to a noninstitutional setting when the discharging facility ceases to be legally responsible for the care of the resident.

Individual means an individual or any legal representative of the individual.

Resident means a resident of a SNF or NF or any legal representative of the resident.

Transfer means movement from an entity that participates in Medicare as a skilled nursing facility, a Medicare certified distinct part, an entity that participates in Medicaid as a nursing facility or a Medicaid certified distinct part to another institutional setting when the legal responsibility for the care of the resident changes from the transferring facility to the receiving facility.

Sec. 483.204 Provision of a hearing and appeal system.

(a) Each State must provide a system for:

(1) A resident of a SNF or a NF to appeal a notice from the SNF or NF of intent to discharge or transfer the resident; and

(2) An individual who has been adversely affected by any PASARR determination made by the State in the context of either a preadmission screening or an annual resident review under subpart C of part 483 to appeal that determination.

(b) The State must provide an appeals system that meets the requirements of this subpart, Sec. 483.12 of this part, and part 431 subpart E of this chapter.

Sec. 483.206 Transfers, discharges and relocations subject to appeal.

(a) "Facility" means a certified entity, either a Medicare SNF or a Medicaid NF (see Secs. 483.5 and 483.12(a)(1)).

(b) A resident has appeal rights when he or she is transferred from-

(1) A certified bed into a noncertified bed; and

(2) A bed in a certified entity to a bed in an entity which is certified as a different provider.

(c) A resident has no appeal rights when he or she is moved from one bed in the certified entity to another bed in the same certified entity.

• • •

Subpart F—Requirements That Must be Met by States and State Agencies, Resident Assessment

• • •

Sec. 483.315 Specification of resident assessment instrument.

• • •

(e) Minimum data set (MDS). The MDS includes assessment in the following areas:

(1) Identification and demographic information, which includes information to identify the resident and facility, the resident's residential history, education, the reason for the assessment, guardianship status and information regarding advance directives, and information regarding mental health history.

(2) Customary routine, which includes the resident's lifestyle prior to admission to the facility.

(3) Cognitive patterns, which include memory, decision making, consciousness, behavioral measures of delirium, and stability of condition.

(4) Communication, which includes scales for measuring hearing and communication skills, information on how the resident expresses himself or herself, and stability of communicative ability.

(5) Vision pattern, which includes a scale for measuring vision and vision problems.

(6) Mood and behavior patterns, which include scales for measuring behavioral indicators and symptoms, and stability of condition.

(7) Psychosocial well-being, which includes the resident's interpersonal relationships and adjustment factors.

(8) Physical functioning and structural problems, which contains scales for measuring activities of daily living, mobility, potential for improvement, and stability of functioning.

(9) Continence, which includes assessment scales for bowel and bladder incontinence, continence patterns, interventions, and stability of continence status.

(10) Disease diagnoses and health conditions, which includes active medical diagnoses, physical problems, pain assessment, and stability of condition.

(11) Dental and nutritional status, which includes information on height and weight, nutritional problems and accommodations, oral care and problems, and measure of nutritional intake.

(12) Skin condition, which includes current and historical assessment of skin problems, treatments, and information regarding foot care.

(13) Activity pursuit, which gathers information on the resident's activity preferences and the amount of time spent participating in activities.

(14) Medications, which contains information on the types and numbers of medications the resident receives.

(15) Special treatments and procedures, which includes measurements of therapies, assessment of rehabilitation/restorative care, special programs and interventions, and information on hospital visits and physician involvement.

(16) Discharge potential, which assesses the possibility of discharging the resident and discharge status.

(17) Documentation of summary information regarding the additional assessment performed through the resident assessment protocols.

(18) Documentation of participation in assessment.

(f) Resident assessment protocols (RAPs). At a minimum, the RAPs address the following domains:

(1) Delirium.

(2) Cognitive loss.

(3) Visual function.

(4) Communication.

(5) ADL functional/rehabilitation potential.

(6) Urinary incontinence and indwelling catheter.

(7) Psychosocial well-being.

(8) Mood state.

(9) Behavioral symptoms.

(10) Activities.

(11) Falls.

(12) Nutritional status.

(13) Feeding tubes.

(14) Dehydration/fluid maintenance.

(15) Dental care.

(16) Pressure ulcers.

(17) Psychotropic drug use.

(18) Physical restraints.

• • •

(j) Resident-identifiable data. (1) The State may not release information that is resident-identifiable to the public.

(2) The State may not release RAI data that is resident-identifiable except in accordance with a written agreement under which the recipient agrees to be bound by the restrictions described in paragraph (i) of this section.

Sample State Laws Relating to Assisted Living Facilities & CCRCs

(Illinois Compiled Statutes)

Assisted Living and Shared Housing Act

• • •

210 ILCS 9/10

Sec.10. Definitions. For purposes of this Act:

"Activities of daily living" means eating, dressing, bathing, toileting, transferring, or personal hygiene.

"Advisory Board" means the Assisted Living and Shared Housing Advisory Board.

"Assisted living establishment" or "establishment" means a home, building, residence, or any other place where sleeping accommodations are provided for at least 3 unrelated adults, at least 80% of whom are 55 years of age or older and where the following are provided consistent with the purposes of this Act:

(1) services consistent with a social model that is based on the premise that the resident's unit in assisted living and shared housing is his or her own home;

(2) community-based residential care for persons who need assistance with activities of daily living, including personal, supportive, and intermittent health-related services available 24 hours per day, if needed, to meet the scheduled and unscheduled needs of a resident;

(3) mandatory services, whether provided directly by the establishment or by another entity arranged for by the establishment, with the consent of the resident or resident's representative; and

(4) a physical environment that is a home-like setting that includes the following and such other elements as established by the Department in conjunction with the Assisted Living and Shared Housing Advisory Board: individual living units each of which shall accommodate small kitchen appliances and contain private bathing, washing, and toilet facilities, or private washing and toilet facilities with a common bathing room readily accessible to each resident. Units shall be maintained for single occupancy except in cases in which 2 residents choose to share a unit. Sufficient common space shall exist to permit individual and group activities.

"Assisted living establishment" or "establishment" does not mean any of the following:

(1) A home, institution, or similar place operated by the federal government or the State of Illinois.

(2) A long term care facility licensed under the Nursing Home Care Act. However, a long term care facility may convert distinct parts of the facility to assisted living. If the long term care facility elects to do so, the facility shall retain the Certificate of Need for its nursing and sheltered care beds that were converted.

(3) A hospital, sanitarium, or other institution, the principal activity or business of which is the diagnosis, care, and treatment of human illness and that is required to be licensed under the Hospital Licensing Act.

(4) A facility for child care as defined in the Child Care Act of 1969.

(5) A community living facility as defined in

the Community Living Facilities Licensing Act.

(6) A nursing home or sanitarium operated solely by and for persons who rely exclusively upon treatment by spiritual means through prayer in accordance with the creed or tenants of a well-recognized church or religious denomination.

(7) A facility licensed by the Department of Human Services as a community-integrated living arrangement as defined in the Community-Integrated Living Arrangements Licensure and Certification Act.

(8) A supportive residence licensed under the Supportive Residences Licensing Act.

(9) A life care facility as defined in the Life Care Facilities Act; a life care facility may apply under this Act to convert sections of the community to assisted living.

(10) A free-standing hospice facility licensed under the Hospice Program Licensing Act.

(11) A shared housing establishment.

(12) A supportive living facility as described in Section 5-5.0la of the Illinois Public Aid Code.

"Department" means the Department of Public Health.

"Director" means the Director of Public Health.

"Emergency situation" means imminent danger of death or serious physical harm to a resident of an establishment.

"License" means any of the following types of licenses issued to an applicant or licensee by the Department:

(1) "Probationary license" means a license issued to an applicant or licensee that has not held a license under this Act prior to its application or pursuant to a license transfer in accordance with Section 50 of this Act.

(2) "Regular license" means a license issued by the Department to an applicant or licensee that is in substantial compliance with this Act and any rules promulgated under this Act.

"Licensee" means a person, agency, association, corporation, partnership, or organization that has been issued a license to operate an assisted living or shared housing establishment.

"Licensed health care professional" means a registered professional nurse, an advanced practice nurse, a physician assistant, and a licensed practical nurse.

"Mandatory services" include the following:

(1) 3 meals per day available to the residents prepared by the establishment or an outside contractor;

(2) housekeeping services including, but not limited to, vacuuming, dusting, and cleaning the resident's unit;

(3) personal laundry and linen services available to the residents provided or arranged for by the establishment;

(4) security provided 24 hours each day including, but not limited to, locked entrances or building or contract security personnel;

(5) an emergency communication response system, which is a procedure in place 24 hours each day by which a resident can notify building management, an emergency response vendor, or others able to respond to his or her need for assistance; and

(6) assistance with activities of daily living as required by each resident.

"Negotiated risk" is the process by which a resident, or his or her representative, may formally negotiate with providers what risks each are willing and unwilling to assume in service provision and the resident's living environment. The provider assures that the resident and the resident's representative, if any, are informed of the risks of these decisions and of the potential consequences of assuming these risks.

"Owner" means the individual, partnership, corporation, association, or other person who owns an assisted living or shared housing establishment. In the event an assisted living or shared housing establishment is operated by a person who leases or manages the physical plant, which is owned by another person, "owner" means the person who operates the assisted living or shared housing establishment, except that if the person who owns the physical plant is an affiliate of the person who operates the assisted living or shared housing establishment and has significant control over the day to day operations of the assisted living or shared housing establishment, the person who owns the physical plant shall incur jointly and severally with the owner all liabilities imposed on an owner under this Act.

"Physician" means a person licensed under the Medical Practice Act of 1987 to practice medicine in all of its branches.

"Resident" means a person residing in an assisted living or shared housing establishment.

"Resident's representative" means a person, other than the owner, agent, or employee of an establishment or of the health care provider unless related to the resident, designated in writing by a resident to be his or her representative. This designation may be accomplished through the Illinois Power of Attorney Act, pursuant to the guardianship process under the Probate Act of 1975, or pursuant to an executed designation of representative form specified by the Department.

"Self" means the individual or the individual's designated representative.

"Shared housing establishment" or "establishment" means a publicly or privately operated free-standing residence for 12 or fewer persons, at least 80% of whom are 55 years of age or older and who are unrelated to the owners and one manager of the residence, where the following are provided:

(1) services consistent with a social model that is based on the premise that the resident's unit is his or her own home;

(2) community-based residential care for persons who need assistance with activities of daily living, including housing and personal, supportive, and intermittent health-related services available 24 hours per day, if needed, to meet the scheduled and unscheduled needs of a resident; and

(3) mandatory services, whether provided directly by the establishment or by another entity arranged for by the establishment, with the consent of the resident or the resident's representative.

"Shared housing establishment" or "establishment" does not mean any of the following:

(1) A home, institution, or similar place operated by the federal government or the State of Illinois.

(2) A long term care facility licensed under the Nursing Home Care Act. A long term care facility may, however, convert sections of the facility to assisted living. If the long term care facility elects to do so, the facility shall retain the Certificate of Need for its nursing beds that were converted.

(3) A hospital, sanitarium, or other institution, the principal activity or business of which is the diagnosis, care, and treatment of human illness and that is required to be licensed under the Hospital Licensing Act.

(4) A facility for child care as defined in the Child Care Act of 1969.

(5) A community living facility as defined in the Community Living Facilities Licensing Act.

(6) A nursing home or sanitarium operated solely by and for persons who rely exclusively upon treatment by spiritual means through prayer in accordance with the creed or tenants of a well-recognized church or religious denomination.

(7) A facility licensed by the Department of Human Services as a community-integrated living arrangement as defined in the Community-Integrated Living Arrangements Licensure and Certification Act.

(8) A supportive residence licensed under the Supportive Residences Licensing Act.

(9) A life care facility as defined in the Life Care Facilities Act; a life care facility may apply under this Act to convert sections of the community to assisted living.

(10) A free-standing hospice facility licensed under the Hospice Program Licensing Act.

(11) An assisted living establishment.

(12) A supportive living facility as described in Section 5-5.01a of the Illinois Public Aid Code.

"Total assistance" means that staff or another individual performs the entire activity of daily living without participation by the resident.

210 ILCS 9/15

Sec. 15. Assessment and service plan requirements. Prior to admission to any establishment covered by this Act, a comprehensive assessment that includes an evaluation of the prospective resident's physical, cognitive, and psychosocial condition shall be completed. At least annually, a comprehensive assessment shall be completed, and upon identification of a significant change in the resident's condition, the resident shall be reassessed. The Department may by rule specify circumstances under which more frequent assessments of skin integrity and nutritional status shall be required. The comprehensive assessment shall be completed by a physician. Based on the assessment, a written service plan shall be developed and mutually agreed upon by the provider and the resident. The service plan, which shall be reviewed annually, or more often as the resident's condition, preferences, or service needs change, shall serve as a basis for the service delivery contract between the provider and the resident. Based on the assessment, the service plan may provide for the disconnection or removal of any appliance.

210 ILCS 9/20

Sec. 20. Construction and operating standards. The Department, in consultation with the Advisory Board, shall prescribe minimum standards for establishments. These standards shall include:

(1) the location and construction of the establishment, including plumbing, heating, lighting, ventilation, and other physical conditions which shall ensure the health, safety, and comfort of residents and their protection from fire hazards; these standards shall include, at a minimum, compliance with the residential board and care occupancies chapter of the National Fire Protection Association's Life Safety Code, local and State building codes for the building type, and accessibility standards of the Americans with Disabilities Act;

(2) the number and qualifications of all personnel having responsibility for any part of the services provided for residents;

(3) all sanitary conditions within the establishment and its surroundings, including water supply, sewage disposal, food handling, infection control, and general hygiene, which shall ensure the health and comfort of residents;

(4) a program for adequate maintenance of physical plant and equipment;

(5) adequate accommodations, staff, and services for the number and types of residents for whom the establishment is licensed;

(6) the development of evacuation and other appropriate safety plans for use during weather, health, fire, physical plant, environmental, and national defense emergencies; and

7) the maintenance of minimum financial and other resources necessary to meet the standards established under this Section and to operate the establishment in accordance with this Act.

210 ILCS 9/25

Sec. 25. License requirement. No person may establish, operate, maintain, or offer an establishment as an assisted living establishment or shared housing establishment as defined by the Act within this State unless and until he or she obtains a valid license, which remains unsuspended, unrevoked, and unexpired. No public official, agent, or employee may place any person in, or recommend that any person be placed in, or directly or indirectly cause any person to be placed in any establishment that meets the definition under this Act that is being operated without a valid license. No public official, agent, or employee may place the name of an unlicensed establishment that is required to be licensed under this Act on a list of programs. An entity that operates as an assisted living or shared housing establishment as defined by this Act without a license shall be subject to the provisions, including penalties, of the Nursing Home Care Act. No entity shall use in its name or advertise "assisted living" unless licensed as an assisted living establishment under this Act or as a shelter care facility under the Nursing Home Care Act that also meets the definition of an assisted living establishment under this Act, except a shared housing establishment licensed under this Act may advertise assisted living services.

210 ILCS 9/30

Sec. 30. Licensing.
(a) The Department, in consultation with

the Advisory Board, shall establish by rule forms, procedures, and fees for the annual licensing of assisted living and shared housing establishments; shall establish and enforce sanctions and penalties for operating in violation of this Act, as provided in Section 135 of this Act and rules adopted under Section 110 of this Act. The Department shall conduct an annual on-site review for each establishment covered by this Act, which shall include, but not be limited to, compliance with this Act and rules adopted hereunder, focus on solving resident issues and concerns, and the quality improvement process implemented by the establishment to address resident issues. The quality improvement process implemented by the establishment must benchmark performance, be customer centered, be data driven, and focus on resident satisfaction.

(b) An establishment shall provide the following information to the Department to be considered for licensure:

(1) the business name, street address, mailing address, and telephone number of the establishment;

(2) the name and mailing address of the owner or owners of the establishment and if the owner or owners are not natural persons, identification of the type of business entity of the owners, and the names and addresses of the officers and members of the governing body, or comparable persons for partnerships, limited liability companies, or other types of business organizations;

(3) financial information, content and form to be determined by rules which may provide different standards for assisted living establishments and shared housing establishments, establishing that the project is financially feasible;

(4) the name and mailing address of the managing agent of the establishment, whether hired under a management agreement or lease agreement, if different from the owner or owners, and the name of the full-time director;

(5) verification that the establishment has entered or will enter into a service delivery contract as provided in Section 90, as required under this Act, with each resident or resident's representative;

(6) the name and address of at least one natural person who shall be responsible for dealing with the Department on all matters provided for in this Act, on whom personal service of all notices and orders shall be made, and who shall be authorized to accept service on behalf of the owner or owners and the managing agent. Notwithstanding a contrary provision of the Code of Civil Procedure, personal service on the person identified pursuant to this subsection shall be considered service on the owner or owners and the managing agent, and it shall not be a defense to any action that personal service was not made on each individual or entity;

(7) the signature of the authorized representative of the owner or owners;

(8) proof of an ongoing quality improvement program in accordance with rules adopted by the Department in collaboration with the Advisory Board;

(9) information about the number and types of units, the maximum census, and the services to be provided at the establishment, proof of compliance with applicable State and local residential standards, and a copy of the standard contract offered to residents;

(10) documentation of adequate liability insurance; and

(11) other information necessary to determine the identity and qualifications of an applicant or licensee to operate an establishment in accordance with this Act as required by the Department by rule.

(c) The information in the statement of ownership shall be public information and shall be available from the Department.

• • •

210 ILCS 9/75

Sec. 75. Residency Requirements.

(a) No individual shall be accepted for residency or remain in residence if the establishment cannot provide or secure appropriate services, if the individual requires a level of service or type of service for which the establishment is not licensed or which the establishment does not provide, or if the establishment does not have the staff appropriate in numbers and with appropriate skill to provide such services.

(b) Only adults may be accepted for residency.

(c) A person shall not be accepted for residency if:

(1) the person poses a serious threat to himself or herself or to others;

(2) the person is not able to communicate his or her needs and no resident representative residing in the establishment, and with a prior relationship to the person, has been appointed to direct the provision of services;

(3) the person requires total assistance with 2 or more activities of daily living;

(4) the person requires the assistance of more than one paid caregiver at any given time with an activity of daily living;

(5) the person requires more than minimal assistance in moving to a safe area in an emergency;

(6) the person has a severe mental illness, which for the purposes of this Section means a condition that is characterized by the presence of a major mental disorder as classified in the Diagnostic and Statistical Manual of Mental Disorders, Fourth Edition (DSM-IV) (American Psychiatric Association, 1994), where the individual is substantially disabled due to mental illness in the areas of self maintenance, social functioning, activities of community living and work skills, and the disability specified is expected to be present for a period of not less than one year, but does not mean Alzheimer's disease and other forms of dementia based on organic or physical disorders;

(7) the person requires intravenous therapy or intravenous feedings unless self-administered or administered by a qualified, licensed health care professional;

(8) the person requires gastrostomy feedings unless Self-administered or administered by a licensed health care professional;

(9) the person requires insertion, sterile irrigation, and replacement of catheter, except for routine maintenance of urinary catheters, unless the catheter care is self-administered or administered by a licensed health care professional;

(10) the person requires sterile wound care unless care is self-administered or administered by a licensed health care professional;

(11) the person requires sliding scale insulin administration unless self-performed or administered by a licensed health care professional;

(12) the person is a diabetic requiring routine insulin injections unless the injections are self-administered or administered by a licensed health care professional;

(13) the person requires treatment of stage 3 or stage 4 decubitus ulcers or exfoliative dermatitis;

(14) the person requires 5 or more skilled nursing visits per week for conditions other than those listed in items (13) and (15) of this subsection for a period of 3 consecutive weeks or more except when the course of treatment is expected to extend beyond a 3 week period for rehabilitative purposes and is certified as temporary by a physician; or

(15) other reasons prescribed by the Department by rule.

(d) A resident with a condition listed in items (1) through (15) of subsection (c) shall have his or her residency terminated.

(e) Residency shall be terminated when services available to the resident in the establishment are no longer adequate to meet the needs of the resident. This provision shall not be interpreted as limiting the authority of the Department to require the residency termination of individuals.

(f) Subsection (d) of this Section shall not apply to terminally ill residents who receive or would qualify for hospice care and such care is coordinated by a hospice licensed under the Hospice Program Licensing Act or other licensed health care professional employed by a licensed home health agency and the establishment and all parties agree to the continued residency.

(g) Items (3), (4), (5), and (9) of subsection (c) shall not apply to a quadriplegic, paraplegic, or individual with neuro-muscular diseases, such as muscular dystrophy and multiple sclerosis, or other chronic diseases and conditions as defined by rule if the individual is able to communicate his or her needs and does not require assistance with complex medical problems, and the establishment is able to accommodate the individual's needs. The Department shall prescribe rules pursuant to this Section that address special safety and service needs of these individuals.

(h) For the purposes of items (7) through (11) of subsection (c), a licensed health care professional may not be employed by the owner or operator of the establishment, its parent entity, or any other entity with ownership common to either the owner or operator of the establishment or parent entity, including but not limited to an affiliate of the owner or operator of the establishment. Nothing in this Section is meant to limit a resident's right to choose his or her health care provider.

210 ILCS 9/80

Sec. 80. Involuntary termination of residency.

(a) Residency shall be involuntarily terminated only for the following reasons:

(1) as provided in Section 75 of this Act;

(2) nonpayment of contracted charges after the resident and the resident's representative have received a minimum of 30-days written notice of the delinquency and the resident or the resident's representative has had at least 15 days to cure the delinquency; or

(3) failure to execute a service delivery contract or to substantially comply with its terms and conditions, failure to comply with the assessment requirements contained in Section 15, or failure to substantially comply with the terms and conditions of the lease agreement.

(b) A 30 day written notice of residency termination shall be provided to the resident, the resident's representative, or both, and the long term care ombudsman, which shall include the reason for the pending action, the date of the proposed move, and a notice, the content and form to be set forth by rule, of the resident's right to appeal, the steps that the resident or the resident's representative must take to initiate an appeal, and a statement of the resident's right to continue to reside in the establishment until a decision is rendered. The notice shall include a toll free telephone number to initiate an

appeal and a written hearing request form, together with a postage paid, pre-addressed envelope to the Department. If the resident or the resident's representative, if any, cannot read English, the notice must be provided in a language the individual receiving the notice can read or the establishment must provide a translator who has been trained to assist the resident or the resident's representative in the appeal process. In emergency situations as defined in Section 10 of this Act, the 30-day provision of the written notice may be waived.

(c) The establishment shall attempt to resolve with the resident or the resident's representative, if any, circumstances that if not remedied have the potential of resulting in an involuntary termination of residency and shall document those efforts in the resident's file. This action may occur prior to or during the 30-day notice period, but must occur prior to the termination of the residency. In emergency situations as defined in Section 10 of this Act, the requirements of this subsection may be waived.

(d) A request for a hearing shall stay an involuntary termination of residency until a decision has been rendered by the Department, according to a process adopted by rule. During this time period, the establishment may not terminate or reduce any service for the purpose of making it more difficult or impossible for the resident to remain in the establishment.

(e) The establishment shall offer the resident and the resident's representative, if any, residency termination and relocation assistance including information on available alternative placement. Residents shall be involved in planning the move and shall choose among the available alternative placements except when an emergency situation makes prior resident involvement impossible. Emergency placements are deemed temporary until the resident's input can be sought in the final placement decision. No resident shall be forced to remain in a temporary or permanent placement.

(f) The Department may offer assistance to the establishment and the resident in the preparation of residency termination and relocation plans to assure safe and orderly transition and to protect the resident's health, safety, welfare, and rights. In non-emergencies, and where possible in emergencies, the transition plan shall be designed and implemented in advance of transfer or residency termination.

210 ILCS 9/85

Sec. 85. Contract requirements. No entity may establish, operate, conduct, or maintain an establishment in this State unless a written service delivery contract is executed between the establishment and each resident or resident's representative in accordance with Section 90 and unless the establishment operates in accordance with the terms of the contract. The resident or the resident's representative shall be given a complete copy of the contract and all supporting documents and attachments and any changes whenever changes are made. If the resident does not understand English and if translated documents are not available, the establishment must explain its policies to a responsible relative or friend or another individual who has agreed to communicate the information to the resident.

210 ILCS 9/90

Sec. 90. Contents of service delivery contract. A contract between an establishment and a resident must be entitled "assisted living establishment contract" or "shared housing establishment contract" as applicable, shall be printed in no less than 12 point type, and shall include at least the following elements in the body or through supporting documents or attachments:

(1) the name, street address, and mailing address of the establishment;

(2) the name and mailing address of the owner or owners of the establishment and, if the owner or owners are not natural persons, the type of business entity of the owner or owners;

(3) the name and mailing address of the managing agent of the establishment, whether hired under a management agreement or lease agreement, if the managing agent is different from the owner or owners;

(4) the name and address of at least one natural person who is authorized to accept service on behalf of the owners and managing agent;

(5) a statement describing the license status of the establishment and the license status of all providers of health-related or supportive services to a resident under arrangement with the establishment;

(6) the duration of the contract;

(7) the base rate to be paid by the resident and a description of the services to be provided as part of this rate;

(8) a description of any additional services to be provided for an additional fee by the establishment directly or by a third party provider under arrangement with the establishment;

(9) the fee schedules outlining the cost of any additional services;

(10) a description of the process through which the contract may be modified, amended, or terminated;

(11) a description of the establishment's complaint resolution process available to residents and notice of the availability of the Department on Aging's Senior Helpline for complaints;

(12) the name of the resident's designated representative, if any;

(13) the resident's obligations in order to maintain residency and receive services including compliance with all assessments required under Section 15;

(14) the billing and payment procedures and requirements;

(15) a statement affirming the resident's freedom to receive services from service providers with whom the establishment does not have a contractual arrangement, which may also disclaim liability on the part of the establishment for those services;

(16) a statement that medical assistance under Article V or Article VI of the Illinois Public Aid Code is not available for payment for services provided in an establishment;

(17) a statement detailing the admission, risk management, and residency termination criteria and procedures;

(18) a statement listing the rights specified

in Section 95 and acknowledging that, by contracting with the assisted living or shared housing establishment, the resident does not forfeit those rights; and

(19) a statement detailing the Department's annual on-site review process including what documents contained in a resident's personal file shall be reviewed by the on-site reviewer as defined by rule.

210 ILCS 9/95

Sec. 95. Resident rights. No resident shall be deprived of any rights, benefits, or privileges guaranteed by law, the Constitution of the State of Illinois, or the Constitution of the United States solely on account of his or her status as a resident of an establishment, nor shall a resident forfeit any of the following rights:

(1) the right to retain and use personal property and a place to store personal items that is locked and secure;

(2) the right to refuse services and to be advised of the consequences of that refusal;

(3) the right to respect for bodily privacy and dignity at all times, especially during care and treatment;

(4) the right to the free exercise of religion;

(5) the right to privacy with regard to mail, phone calls, and visitors;

(6) the right to uncensored access to the State Ombudsman or his or her designee;

(7) the right to be free of retaliation for criticizing the establishment or making complaints to appropriate agencies;

(8) the right to be free of chemical and physical restraints;

(9) the right to be free of abuse or neglect or to refuse to perform labor;

(10) the right to confidentiality of the resident's medical records;

(11) the right of access and the right to copy the resident's personal files maintained by the establishment;

(12) the right to 24 hours access to the establishment;

(13) the right to a minimum of 90-days notice of a planned establishment closure;

(14) the right to a minimum of 30-days notice of an involuntary residency termination, except where the resident poses a threat to himself or others, or in other emergency situations, and the right to appeal such termination; and

(15) the right to a 30-day notice of delinquency and at least 15 days right to cure delinquency.

• • •

210 ILCS 9/110

Sec. 110. Powers and duties of the Department.

(a) The Department shall conduct an annual unannounced on-site visit at each assisted living and shared housing establishment to determine compliance with applicable licensure requirements and standards. Additional visits may be conducted without prior notice to the assisted living or shared housing establishment.

(b) Upon receipt of information that may indicate the failure of the assisted living or shared housing establishment or a service provider to comply with a provision of this Act, the Department shall investigate the matter or make appropriate referrals to other government agencies and entities having jurisdiction over the subject matter of the possible violation. The Department may also make referrals to any public or private agency that the Department considers available for appropriate assistance to those involved. The Department may oversee and coordinate the enforcement of State consumer protection policies affecting residents residing in an establishment licensed under this Act.

(c) The Department shall establish by rule complaint receipt, investigation, resolution, and involuntary residency termination procedures. Resolution procedures shall provide for on-site review and evaluation of an assisted living or shared housing establishment found to be in violation of this Act within a specified period of time based on the gravity and severity of the violation and any pervasive pattern of occurrences of the same or similar violations.

(d) The Governor shall establish an Assisted Living and Shared Housing Advisory Board.

(e) The Department shall by rule establish penalties and sanctions, which shall include, but need not be limited to, the creation of a schedule of graduated penalties and sanctions to include closure.

(f) The Department shall by rule establish procedures for disclosure of information to the public, which shall include, but not be limited to, ownership, licensure status, frequency of complaints, disposition of substantiated complaints, and disciplinary actions.

(g) The Department shall cooperate with, seek the advice of, and collaborate with the Assisted Living and Shared Housing Quality of Life Advisory Committee in the Department on Aging on matters related to the responsibilities of the Committee. Consistent with subsection (d) of Section 125, the Department shall provide to the Department on Aging for distribution to the committee copies of all administrative rules and changes to administrative rules for review and comment prior to notice being given to the public. If the Committee, having been asked for its review, fails to respond within 90 days, the rules shall be considered acted upon.

(h) Beginning January 1, 2000, the Department shall begin drafting rules necessary for the administration of this Act.

LIFE CARE FACILITIES ACT
• • •

210 ILCS 40/2

Sec. 2. As used in this Act, unless the context otherwise requires:

(a) "Department" means the Department of Public Health.

(b) "Director" means the Director of the Department.

(c) "Life care contract" means a contract to provide to a person for the duration of such person's life or for a term in excess of one year, nursing services, medical services or personal care services, in addition to maintenance services for such person in a facility, conditioned upon the transfer of an entrance fee to the provider of such services in addition to or in lieu of the payment of regular periodic charges for the care and services involved.

(d) "Provider" means a person who provides services pursuant to a life care contract.

(e) "Resident" means a person who enters into a life care contract with a provider, or who is designated in a life care contract to be a person provided with maintenance and nursing, medical or personal care services.

(f) "Facility" means a place or places in which a provider undertakes to provide a resident with nursing services, medical services or personal care services, in addition to maintenance services for a term in excess of one year or for life pursuant to a life care contract. The term also means a place or places in which a provider undertakes to provide such services to a non-resident.

(g) "Living unit" means an apartment, room or other area within a facility set aside for the exclusive use of one or more identified residents.

(h) "Entrance fee" means an initial or deferred transfer to a provider of a sum of money or property, made or promised to be made by a person entering into a life care contract, which assures a resident of services pursuant to a life care contract.

(i) "Permit" means a written authorization to enter into life care contracts issued by the Department to a provider.

(j) "Medical services" means those services

pertaining to medical or dental care that are performed in behalf of patients at the direction of a physician licensed under the Medical Practice Act of 1987 or a dentist licensed under the Illinois Dental Practice Act by such physicians or dentists, or by a registered or licensed practical nurse as defined in the Nursing and Advanced Practice Nursing Act or by other professional and technical personnel.

(k) "Nursing services" means those services pertaining to the curative, restorative and preventive aspects of nursing care that are performed at the direction of a physician licensed under the Medical Practice Act of 1987 by or under the supervision of a registered or licensed practical nurse as defined in the Nursing and Advanced Practice Nursing Act.

(l) "Personal care services" means assistance with meals, dressing, movement, bathing or other personal needs or maintenance, or general supervision and oversight of the physical and mental well being of an individual, who is incapable of maintaining a private, independent residence or who is incapable of managing his person whether or not a guardian has been appointed for such individual.

(m) "Maintenance services" means food, shelter and laundry services.

(n) "Certificates of Need" means those permits issued pursuant to the Illinois Health Facilities Planning Act as now or hereafter amended.

(o) "Non-resident" means a person admitted to a facility who has not entered into a life care contract.

• • •

210 ILCS 40/5

Sec. 5. (a) At the time of or prior to the execution of a life care contract and the transfer of any money or other property to a provider or escrow agent, the provider shall deliver to the resident a copy of a financial disclosure statement reflecting the provider's financial condition. This statement shall include, but not be limited to, disclosure of short term assets and liabilities.

(b) The life care contract shall provide that any person entering into the contract shall have a period of 14 days beginning with the first full calendar day following the execution of the contract, or the payment of an initial sum of money as a deposit or application fee, or receipt of the financial disclosure statement, whichever occurs last, within which to rescind the life care contract without penalty or further obligation. In the event of such rescission, all money or property paid or transferred by such person shall be fully refunded. No person shall be required to move into a facility until after the expiration of the 14 day rescission period. No permit shall be issued under this Act if the form of life care contract attached as an exhibit in support of the application for permit as provided in Section 4 does not contain the provisions required by this paragraph (b).

Appendix H

The Nursing Home Reform Act

(TITLE 42 UNITED STATES CODE)

Sec. 1395i-3 - Requirements for, and assuring quality of care in, skilled nursing facilities

• • •

(b) Requirements relating to provision of services
　(1) Quality of life
　　(A) In general, a skilled nursing facility must care for its residents in such a manner and in such an environment as will promote maintenance or enhancement of the quality of life of each resident.
　　(B) Quality assessment and assurance
　　A skilled nursing facility must maintain a quality assessment and assurance committee, consisting of the director of nursing services, a physician designated by the facility, and at least 3 other members of the facility's staff, which
　　　(i) meets at least quarterly to identify issues with respect to which quality assessment and assurance activities are necessary and
　　　(ii) develops and implements appropriate plans of action to correct identified quality deficiencies. A State or the Secretary may not require disclosure of the records of such committee except insofar as such disclosure is related to the compliance of such committee with the requirements of this subparagraph.
　(2) Scope of services and activities under plan of care
　A skilled nursing facility must provide services to attain or maintain the highest practicable physical, mental, and psychosocial well being of each resident, in accordance with a written plan of care which
　　(A) describes the medical, nursing, and psychosocial needs of the resident and how such needs will be met; and
　　(B) is initially prepared, with the participation to the extent practicable of the resident or the resident's family or legal representative, by a team which includes the resident's attending physician and a registered professional nurse with responsibility for the resident; and
　　(C) is periodically reviewed and revised by such team after each assessment under paragraph (3)
　(3) Residents' assessment
　　(A) Requirement. A skilled nursing facility must conduct a comprehensive, accurate, standardized, reproducible assessment of each resident's functional capacity, which assessment

(i) describes the resident's capability to perform daily life functions and significant impairments in functional capacity; and

(ii) is based on a uniform minimum data set specified by the Secretary under subsection (f)(6)(A) of this section; and

(iii) uses an instrument which is specified by the State under subsection (e)(5) of this section; and

(iv) includes the identification of medical problems.

(B) Certification

(i) In general

Each such assessment must be conducted or coordinated (with the appropriate participation of health professionals) by a registered professional nurse who signs and certifies the completion of the assessment. Each individual who completes a portion of such an assessment shall sign and certify as to the accuracy of that portion of the assessment.

• • •

(iii) Use of independent assessors

If a State determines, under a survey under subsection (g) of this section or otherwise, that there has been a knowing and willful certification of false assessments under this paragraph, the State may require (for a period specified by the State) that resident assessments under this paragraph be conducted and certified by individuals who are independent of the facility and who are approved by the State.

(C) Frequency

(i) In general

Subject to the timeframes prescribed by the Secretary under section 1395yy (e)(6) of this title, such an assessment must be conducted -

(I) promptly upon (but no later than 14 days after the date of) admission for each individual admitted on or after October 1, 1990, and by not later than January 1, 1991, for each resident of the facility on that date;

(II) promptly after a significant change in the resident's physical or mental condition; and

(III) in no case less often than once every 12 months.

(ii) Resident review

The skilled nursing facility must examine each resident no less frequently than once every 3 months and, as appropriate, revise the resident's assessment to assure the continuing accuracy of the assessment.

(D) Use the results of such an assessment shall be used in developing, reviewing, and revising the resident's plan of care under paragraph (2).

(E) Coordination. Such assessments shall be coordinated with any State-required preadmission screening program to the maximum extent practicable in order to avoid duplicative testing and effort.

(4) Provision of services and activities

(A) In general

To the extent needed to fulfill all plans of care described in paragraph (2), a skilled nursing facility must provide, directly or under arrangements (or, with respect to dental services, under agreements) with others for the provision of -

(i) nursing services and specialized rehabilitative services to attain or maintain the highest practicable physical, mental, and psychosocial well being of each resident;

(ii) medically related social services to attain or maintain the highest practicable physical, mental, and psychosocial well being of each resident;

(iii) pharmaceutical services (including procedures that assure the accurate acquiring, receiving, dispensing, and administering of all drugs and biologicals) to meet the needs of each resident;

(iv) dietary services that assure that the meals meet the daily nutritional and special dietary needs of each resident; and

(v) an on-going program, directed by a qualified professional, of activities designed to meet the interests and the physical, mental, and psychosocial well-being of each resident;

(vi) routine and emergency dental services to meet the needs of each resident; and

(vii) treatment and services required by mentally ill and mentally retarded residents not otherwise provided or arranged for (or required to be provided or arranged for) by the State.

The services provided or arranged by the facility must meet professional standards of quality. Nothing in clause (vi) shall be construed as requiring a facility to provide or arrange for dental services described in that clause without additional charge.

(B) Qualified persons providing services

Services described in clause (i), (ii), (iii), (iv), and (vi) of subparagraph (A) must be provided by qualified persons in accordance with each resident's written plan of care.

(C) Required nursing care

(i) In general

Except as provided in clause (ii), a skilled nursing facility must provide 24-hour licensed nursing service which is sufficient to meet nursing needs of its residents and must use the services of a registered professional nurse at least 8 consecutive hours a day, 7 days a week.

(ii) Exception

To the extent that clause (i) may be deemed to require that a skilled nursing facility engage the services of a registered professional nurse for more than 40 hours a week, the Secretary is authorized to waive such requirement if the Secretary finds that—

(I) the facility is located in a rural area and the supply of skilled nursing facility services in such area is not sufficient to meet the needs of individuals residing therein,

(II) the facility has one full-time registered professional nurse, who is regularly on duty at such facility 40 hours a week,

(III) the facility either has only patients whose physicians have indicated (through physicians' orders or admission notes) that each such patient does not require the services of a registered nurse or a physician for a 48-hour period, or has made arrangements for a registered professional nurse or a physician to spend such time at such facility as may be indicated as necessary by the physician to provide necessary skilled nursing services on days when the regular full-time registered professional nurse is not on duty,

(IV) the Secretary provides notice of the waiver to the State long-term care ombudsman (established under section 307(a)(12) [2] of the Older Americans Act of 1965) and the protection and advocacy system in the State for the mentally ill and the mentally retarded, and

(V) the facility that is granted such a waiver notifies residents of the facility (or, where appropriate, the guardians or legal representatives of such residents) and members of their immediate families of the waiver. A waiver under this subparagraph shall be subject to annual renewal.

(5) Required training of nurse aides
    (A) In general
        (i) Except as provided in clause (ii), a skilled nursing facility must not use on a full-time basis any individual as a nurse aide in the facility on or after October 1, 1990 for more than 4 months unless the individual -
            (I) has completed a training and competency evaluation program, or a competency evaluation program, approved by the State under subsection (e)(1)(A) of this section, and
            (II) is competent to provide nursing or nursing-related services.
                          • • •
    (C) Competency
    The skilled nursing facility must not permit an individual, other than in a training and competency evaluation program approved by the State, to serve as a nurse aide or provide services of a type for which the individual has not demonstrated competency and must not use such an individual as a nurse aide unless the facility has inquired of any State registry established under subsection (e)(2)(A) of this section that the facility believes will include information concerning the individual.
    (D) Re-training required
    For purposes of subparagraph (A), if, since an individual's most recent completion of a training and competency evaluation program, there has been a continuous period of 24 consecutive months during none of which the individual performed nursing or nursing-related services for monetary compensation, such individual shall complete a new training and competency evaluation program or a new competency evaluation program.
    (E) Regular in-service education
    The skilled nursing facility must provide such regular performance review and regular in-service education as assures that individuals used as nurse aides are competent to perform services as nurse aides, including training for individuals providing nursing and nursing-related services to residents with cognitive impairments.
                          • • •
(6) Physician supervision and clinical records
A skilled nursing facility must—
    (A) require that the medical care of every resident be provided under the supervision of a physician; and
    (B) provide for having a physician available to furnish necessary medical care in case of emergency; and
    (C) maintain clinical records on all residents, which records include the plans of care (described in paragraph (2)) and the residents' assessments (described in paragraph (3)).
(7) Required social services
In the case of a skilled nursing facility with more than 120 beds, the facility must have at least one social worker (with at least a bachelor's degree in social work or similar professional qualifications) employed full-time to provide or assure the provision of social services.
(c) Requirements relating to residents' rights
    (1) General rights
        (A) Specified rights
        A skilled nursing facility must protect and promote the rights of each resident, including each of the following rights:
            (i) Free choice. The right to choose a personal attending physician, to be fully informed in advance about care and treatment, to be fully informed in advance of any changes in care or treatment that may affect the resident's well-being, and (except with respect to a resident adjudged incompetent) to participate in planning

care and treatment or changes in care and treatment.

(ii) Free from restraints. The right to be free from physical or mental abuse, corporal punishment, involuntary seclusion, and any physical or chemical restraints imposed for purposes of discipline or convenience and not required to treat the resident's medical symptoms. Restraints may only be imposed -

(I) to ensure the physical safety of the resident or other residents, and

(II) only upon the written order of a physician that specifies the duration and circumstances under which the restraints are to be used (except in emergency circumstances specified by the Secretary until such an order could reasonably be obtained).

(iii) Privacy. The right to privacy with regard to accommodations, medical treatment, written and telephonic communications, visits, and meetings of family and of resident groups.

(iv) Confidentiality. The right to confidentiality of personal and clinical records and to access to current clinical records of the resident upon request by the resident or the resident's legal representative, within 24 hours (excluding hours occurring during a weekend or holiday) after making such a request.

(v) Accommodation of needs the right -

(I) to reside and receive services with reasonable accommodation of individual needs and preferences, except where the health or safety of the individual or other residents would be endangered, and

(II) to receive notice before the room or roommate of the resident in the facility is changed.

(vi) Grievances The right to voice grievances with respect to treatment or care that is (or fails to be) furnished, without discrimination or reprisal for voicing the grievances and the right to prompt efforts by the facility to resolve grievances the resident may have, including those with respect to the behavior of other residents.

(vii) Participation in resident and family groups The right of the resident to organize and participate in resident groups in the facility and the right of the resident's family to meet in the facility with the families of other residents in the facility.

(viii) Participation in other activities. The right of the resident to participate in social, religious, and community activities that does not interfere with the rights of other residents in the facility.

(ix) Examination of survey results. The right to examine, upon reasonable request, the results of the most recent survey of the facility conducted by the Secretary or a State with respect to the facility and any plan of correction in effect with respect to the facility.

(x) Refusal of certain transfers. The right to refuse a transfer to another room within the facility, if a purpose of the transfer is to relocate the resident from a portion of the facility that is a skilled nursing facility (for purposes of this subchapter) to a portion of the facility that is not such a skilled nursing facility.

(xi) Other rights

Any other right established by the Secretary.

Clause (iii) shall not be construed as requiring the provision of a private room. A resident's exercise of a right to refuse transfer under clause (x) shall not affect the resident's eligibility or entitlement to benefits under this subchapter or to medical assistance under subchapter XIX of this chapter.

(B) Notice of rights and services

A skilled nursing facility must -

(i) inform each resident, orally and in writing at the time of admission to the facility, of the resident's legal rights during the stay at the facility; and

(ii) make available to each resident, upon reasonable request, a written statement of such rights (which statement is updated upon changes in such rights) including the notice (if any) of the State developed under section 1396r(e)(6) of this title; and

(iii) inform each other resident, in writing before or at the time of admission and periodically during the resident's stay, of services available in the facility and of related charges for such services, including any charges for services not covered under this subchapter or by the facility's basic per diem charge.

The written description of legal rights under this subparagraph shall include a description of the protection of personal funds under paragraph (6) and a statement that a resident may file a complaint with a State survey and certification agency respecting resident neglect and abuse and misappropriation of resident property in the facility.

(C) Rights of incompetent residents

In the case of a resident adjudged incompetent under the laws of a State, the rights of the resident under this subchapter shall devolve upon, and, to the extent judged necessary by a court of competent jurisdiction, be exercised by, the person appointed under State law to act on the resident's behalf.

(D) Use of psychopharmacologic drugs

Psychopharmacologic drugs may be administered only on the orders of a physician and only as part of a plan (included in the written plan of care described in paragraph (2)) designed to eliminate or modify the symptoms for which the drugs are prescribed and only if, at least annually, an independent, external consultant reviews the appropriateness of the drug plan of each resident receiving such drugs. In determining whether such a consultant is qualified to conduct reviews under the preceding sentence, the Secretary shall take into account the needs of nursing facilities under this subchapter to have access to the services of such a consultant on a timely basis.

(E) Information respecting advance directives

A skilled nursing facility must comply with the requirement of section 1395cc(f) of this title (relating to maintaining written policies and procedures respecting advance directives).

(2) Transfer and discharge rights

(A) In general

A skilled nursing facility must permit each resident to remain in the facility and must not transfer or discharge the resident from the facility unless -

(i) the transfer or discharge is necessary to meet the resident's welfare and the resident's welfare cannot be met in the facility; and

(ii) the transfer or discharge is appropriate because the resident's health has improved sufficiently so the resident no longer needs the services provided by the facility; and

(iii) the safety of individuals in the facility is endangered; and

(iv) the health of individuals in the facility would otherwise be endangered; and

(v) the resident has failed, after reasonable and appropriate notice, to pay (or to have paid under this subchapter or subchapter XIX of this chapter on the resident's behalf) for a stay at the facility; or

(vi) the facility ceases to operate.

In each of the cases described in clause (i) through (v), the basis for the transfer or discharge must be documented in the resident's clinical record. In the cases described in clause (i) and (ii), the documentation must be made by the resident's physician, and in the cases described in clause (iii) and (iv) the documentation must be made by a physician.

(B) Pre-transfer and pre-discharge notice

(i) In general

Before effecting a transfer or discharge of a resident, a skilled nursing facility must -

(I) notify the resident (and, if known, a family member of the resident or legal representative) of the transfer or discharge and the reasons therefor,

(II) record the reasons in the resident's clinical record (including any documentation required under subparagraph (A)), and

(III) include in the notice the items described in clause (iii).

(ii) Timing of notice

The notice under clause (i)(I) must be made at least 30 days in advance of the resident's transfer or discharge except -

(I) in a case described in clause (iii) or (iv) of subparagraph (A);

(II) in a case described in clause (ii) of subparagraph (A), where the resident's health improves sufficiently to allow a more immediate transfer or discharge;

(III) in a case described in clause (i) of subparagraph (A), where a more immediate transfer or discharge is necessitated by the resident's urgent medical needs; or

(IV) in a case where a resident has not resided in the facility for 30 days. In the case of such exceptions, notice must be given as many days before the date of the transfer or discharge as is practicable.

(iii) Items included in notice

Each notice under clause (i) must include -

(I) for transfers or discharges effected on or after October 1, 1990, notice of the resident's right to appeal the transfer or discharge under the State process established under subsection (e)(3) of this section; and

(II) the name, mailing address, and telephone number of the State long-term care ombudsman (established under title III or VII of the Older Americans Act of 1965 (42 U.S.C. 3021et seq., 3058 et seq.) in accordance with section 712 of the Act 42 U.S.C. 3058g.

(C) Orientation

A skilled nursing facility must provide sufficient preparation and orientation to residents to ensure safe and orderly transfer or discharge from the facility.

(3) Access and visitation rights

A skilled nursing facility must -

(A) permit immediate access to any resident by any representative of the Secretary, by any representative of the State, by an ombudsman described in paragraph (2)(B)(iii)(II), or by the resident's individual physician;

(B) permit immediate access to a resident, subject to the resident's right to deny or withdraw consent at any time, by immediate family or other relatives of the resident;

(C) permit immediate access to a resident, subject to reasonable restrictions and the resident's right to deny or withdraw consent at any time, by others who are visiting with the consent of the resident;

(D) permit reasonable access to a resident by any entity or individual that provides health, social, legal, or other services to the resident, subject to the resident's right to deny or withdraw consent at any time; and

(E) permit representatives of the State ombudsman (described in paragraph

(2)(B)(iii)(II)), with the permission of the resident (or the resident's legal representative) and consistent with State law, to examine a resident's clinical records.

(4) Equal access to quality care

A skilled nursing facility must establish and maintain identical policies and practices regarding transfer, discharge, and covered services under this subchapter for all individuals regardless of source of payment.

(5) Admissions policy

(A) Admissions

With respect to admissions practices, a skilled nursing facility must –

(i)(I) not require individuals applying to reside or residing in the facility to waive their rights to benefits under this subchapter or under a State plan under subchapter XIX of this chapter,

(II) not require oral or written assurance that such individuals are not eligible for, or will not apply for, benefits under this subchapter or such a State plan, and

(III) prominently display in the facility and provide to such individuals written information about how to apply for and use such benefits and how to receive refunds for previous payments covered by such benefits; and

(ii) not require a third party guarantee of payment to the facility as a condition of admission (or expedited admission) to, or continued stay in, the facility.

(B) Construction

(i) No preemption of stricter standards

Subparagraph (A) shall not be construed as preventing States or political subdivisions therein from prohibiting, under State or local law, the discrimination against individuals who are entitled to medical assistance under this subchapter with respect to admissions practices of skilled nursing facilities.

(ii) Contracts with legal representatives

Subparagraph (A)(ii) shall not be construed as preventing a facility from requiring an individual, who has legal access to a resident's income or resources available to pay for care in the facility, to sign a contract (without incurring personal financial liability) to provide payment from the resident's income or resources for such care.

(6) Protection of resident funds

(A) In general

The skilled nursing facility -

(i) may not require residents to deposit their personal funds with the facility, and

(ii) upon the written authorization of the resident, must hold, safeguard, and account for such personal funds under a system established and maintained by the facility in accordance with this paragraph.

(B) Management of personal funds

Upon written authorization of a resident under subparagraph (A)(ii), the facility must manage and account for the personal funds of the resident deposited with the facility as follows:

(i) Deposit

The facility must deposit any amount of personal funds in excess of $100 with respect to a resident in an interest bearing account (or accounts) that is separate from any of the facility's operating accounts and credits all interest earned on such separate account to such account. With respect to any other personal funds, the facility must maintain such funds in a non-interest bearing account or petty cash fund.

(ii) Accounting and records

The facility must assure a full and complete separate accounting of each such res-

ident's personal funds, maintain a written record of all financial transactions involving the personal funds of a resident deposited with the facility, and afford the resident (or a legal representative of the resident) reasonable access to such record.
(iii) Conveyance upon death
Upon the death of a resident with such an account, the facility must convey promptly the resident's personal funds (and a final accounting of such funds) to the individual administering the resident's estate.
(C) Assurance of financial security
The facility must purchase a surety bond, or otherwise provide assurance satisfactory to the Secretary, to assure the security of all personal funds of residents deposited with the facility.
(D) Limitation on charges to personal funds
The facility may not impose a charge against the personal funds of a resident for any item or service for which payment is made under this subchapter or subchapter XIX of this chapter.
(d) Requirements relating to administration and other matters
  (1) Administration
    (A) In general
    A skilled nursing facility must be administered in a manner that enables it to use its resources effectively and efficiently to attain or maintain the highest practicable physical mental, and psychosocial well-being of each resident (consistent with requirements established under subsection (f)(5) of this section).
                              • • •
    (C) Skilled nursing facility administrator
    The administrator of a skilled nursing facility must meet standards established by the Secretary under subsection (f)(4) of this section.
  (2) Licensing and Life Safety Code
    (A) Licensing
    A skilled nursing facility must be licensed under applicable State and local law.
    (B) Life Safety Code
    A skilled nursing facility must meet such provisions of such edition (as specified by the Secretary in regulation) of the Life Safety Code of the National Fire Protection Association as are applicable to nursing homes; except that -
      (i) the Secretary may waive, for such periods as he deems appropriate, specific provisions of such Code which if rigidly applied would result in unreasonable hardship upon a facility, but only if such waiver would not adversely affect the health and safety of residents or personnel, and
      (ii) the provisions of such Code shall not apply in any State if the Secretary finds that in such State there is in effect a fire and safety code, imposed by State law, which adequately protects residents of and personnel in skilled nursing facilities.
  (3) Sanitary and infection control and physical environment
  A skilled nursing facility must -
    (A) establish and maintain an infection control program designed to provide a safe, sanitary, and comfortable environment in which residents reside and to help prevent the development and transmission of disease and infection, and
    (B) be designed, constructed, equipped, and maintained in a manner to protect the health and safety of residents, personnel, and the general public.
  (4) Miscellaneous
    (A) Compliance with Federal, State, and local laws and professional standards
    A skilled nursing facility must operate and provide services in compliance with all

applicable Federal, State, and local laws and regulations (including the requirements of section 1320a-3 of this title) and with accepted professional standards and principles which apply to professionals providing services in such a facility.

(B) Other

A skilled nursing facility must meet such other requirements relating to the health, safety, and well being of residents or relating to the physical facilities thereof as the Secretary may find necessary.

• • •

(g) (2) Surveys

(A) Standard survey

(i) In general

Each skilled nursing facility shall be subject to a standard survey, to be conducted without any prior notice to the facility. Any individual who notifies (or causes to be notified) a skilled nursing facility of the time or date on which such a survey is scheduled to be conducted is subject to a civil money penalty of not to exceed $2,000. The provisions of section 1320a-7aof this title (other than subsections (a) and (b)) shall apply to a civil money penalty under the previous sentence in the same manner as such provisions apply to a penalty or proceeding under section 1320a-7a (a) of this title. The Secretary shall review each State's procedures for the scheduling and conduct of standard surveys to assure that the State has taken all reasonable steps to avoid giving notice of such a survey through the scheduling procedures and the conduct of the surveys themselves.

(ii) Contents

Each standard survey shall include, for a case-mix-stratified sample of residents -

(I) a survey of the quality of care furnished, as measured by indicators of medical, nursing, and rehabilitative care, dietary and nutrition services, activities and social participation, and sanitation, infection control, and the physical environment,

(II) written plans of care provided under subsection (b)(2) of this section and an audit of the residents' assessments under subsection (b)(3) of this section to determine the accuracy of such assessments and the adequacy of such plans of care, and

(III) a review of compliance with residents' rights under subsection (c) of this section.

(iii) Frequency

(I) In general

Each skilled nursing facility shall be subject to a standard survey not later than 15 months after the date of the previous standard survey conducted under this subparagraph. The Statewide average interval between standard surveys of skilled nursing facilities under this subsection shall not exceed 12 months.

(II) Special surveys

If not otherwise conducted under subclause (I), a standard survey (or an abbreviated standard survey) may be conducted within 2 months of any change of ownership, administration, management of a skilled nursing facility, or the director of nursing in order to determine whether the change has resulted in any decline in the quality of care furnished in the facility.

(B) Extended surveys

(i) In general

Each skilled nursing facility which is found, under a standard survey, to have provided substandard quality of care shall be subject to an extended survey. Any other facility may, at the Secretary's or State's discretion, be subject to such an extended survey (or a partial extended survey).

(ii) Timing

The extended survey shall be conducted immediately after the standard survey (or, if not practicable, not later than 2 weeks after the date of completion of the standard survey).

(iii) Contents

In such an extended survey, the survey team shall review and identify the policies and procedures which produced such substandard quality of care and shall determine whether the facility has complied with all the requirements described in subsections (b), (c), and (d) of this section. Such review shall include an expansion of the size of the sample of residents' assessments reviewed and a review of the staffing, of in-service training, and, if appropriate, of contracts with consultants.

(iv) Construction

Nothing in this paragraph shall be construed as requiring an extended or partial extended survey as a prerequisite to imposing a sanction against a facility under subsection (h) of this section, on the basis of findings in a standard survey.

• • •

(E) (ii) Prohibition of conflicts of interest

A State may not use as a member of a survey team under this subsection an individual who is serving (or has served within the previous 2 years) as a member of the staff of, or as a consultant to, the facility surveyed respecting compliance with the requirements of subsections (b), (c), and (d) of this section, or who has a personal or familial financial interest in the facility being surveyed.

• • •

(5) Disclosure of results of inspections and activities

(A) Public information

Each State, and the Secretary, shall make available to the public—

(i) information respecting all surveys and certifications made respecting skilled nursing facilities, including statements of deficiencies, within 14 calendar days after such information is made available to those facilities, and approved plans of correction,

(ii) copies of cost reports of such facilities filed under this subchapter or subchapter XIX of this chapter,

(iii) copies of statements of ownership under section 1320a-3 of this title, and

(iv) information disclosed under section 1320a-5of this title.

(B) Notice to ombudsman

Each State shall notify the State long-term care ombudsman (established under title III or VII of the Older Americans Act of 1965 (42 U.S.C. 3021 et seq., 3058 et seq.) in accordance with section 712 of the Act (42 U.S.C. 3058g)) of the State's findings of noncompliance with any of the requirements of subsections (b), (c), and (d) of this section, or of any adverse action taken against a skilled nursing facility under paragraph (1), (2), or (4) of subsection (h) of this section, with respect to a skilled nursing facility in the State.

(C) Notice to physicians and skilled nursing facility administrator licensing board

If a State finds that a skilled nursing facility has provided substandard quality of care, the State shall notify -

(i) the attending physician of each resident with respect to which such finding is made, and

(ii) the State board responsible for the licensing of the skilled nursing facility administrator at the facility.

(D) Access to fraud control units

Each State shall provide its State Medicaid fraud and abuse control unit (established under section 1396b (q) of this title) with access to all information of the State agency responsible for surveys and certifications under this subsection.

(h) Enforcement process

(1) In general

If a State finds, on the basis of a standard, extended, or partial extended survey under subsection (g)(2) of this section or otherwise, that a skilled nursing facility no longer meets a requirement of subsection (b), (c), or (d) of this section, and further finds that the facility's deficiencies -

(A) immediately jeopardize the health or safety of its residents, the State shall recommend to the Secretary that the Secretary take such action as described in paragraph (2)(A)(i); or

(B) do not immediately jeopardize the health or safety of its residents, the State may recommend to the Secretary that the Secretary take such action as described in paragraph (2)(A)(ii).

If a State finds that a skilled nursing facility meets the requirements of subsections (b), (c), and (d) of this section, but, as of a previous period, did not meet such requirements, the State may recommend a civil money penalty under paragraph (2)(B)(ii) for the days in which it finds that the facility was not in compliance with such requirements.

(2) Secretarial authority

(A) In general

With respect to any skilled nursing facility in a State, if the Secretary finds, or pursuant to a recommendation of the State under paragraph (1) finds, that a skilled nursing facility no longer meets a requirement of subsection (b), (c), (d), or (e) of this section, and further finds that the facility's deficiencies -

(i) immediately jeopardize the health or safety of its residents, the Secretary shall take immediate action to remove the jeopardy and correct the deficiencies through the remedy specified in subparagraph (B)(iii), or terminate the facility's participation under this subchapter and may provide, in addition, for one or more of the other remedies described in subparagraph (B); or

(ii) do not immediately jeopardize the health or safety of its residents, the Secretary may impose any of the remedies described in subparagraph (B).

Nothing in this subparagraph shall be construed as restricting the remedies available to the Secretary to remedy a skilled nursing facility's deficiencies. If the Secretary finds, or pursuant to the recommendation of the State under paragraph (1) finds, that a skilled nursing facility meets such requirements but, as of a previous period, did not meet such requirements, the Secretary may provide for a civil money penalty under subparagraph (B)(ii) for the days on which he finds that the facility was not in compliance with such requirements.

(B) Specified remedies

The Secretary may take the following actions with respect to a finding that a facility has not met an applicable requirement:

(i) Denial of payment

The Secretary may deny any further payments under this subchapter with respect to all individuals entitled to benefits under this subchapter in the facility or with respect to such individuals admitted to the facility after the effective date of the finding.

(ii) Authority with respect to civil money penalties

The Secretary may impose a civil money penalty in an amount not to exceed

$10,000 for each day of noncompliance. The provisions of section 1320a-7aof this title (other than subsections (a) and (b)) shall apply to a civil money penalty under the previous sentence in the same manner as such provisions apply to a penalty or proceeding under section 1320a-7a (a) of this title.

(iii) Appointment of temporary management

In consultation with the State, the Secretary may appoint temporary management to oversee the operation of the facility and to assure the health and safety of the facility's residents, where there is a need for temporary management while -

(I) there is an orderly closure of the facility, or

(II) improvements are made in order to bring the facility into compliance with all the requirements of subsections (b), (c), and (d) of this section. The temporary management under this clause shall not be terminated under subclause (II) until the Secretary has determined that the facility has the management capability to ensure continued compliance with all the requirements of subsections (b), (c), and (d) of this section.

The Secretary shall specify criteria, as to when and how each of such remedies is to be applied, the amounts of any fines, and the severity of each of these remedies, to be used in the imposition of such remedies. Such criteria shall be designed so as to minimize the time between the identification of violations and final imposition of the remedies and shall provide for the imposition of incrementally more severe fines for repeated or uncorrected deficiencies. In addition, the Secretary may provide for other specified remedies, such as directed plans of correction.

Appendix I

Sample Forms

(Source: Centers for Medicare and Medicaid Services)

RESIDENT ADMISSION AGREEMENT
(hereinafter the "Agreement")

_____ (hereinafter the "Facility") and _____ (hereinafter—strike one—the "Resident" / "Resident's Representative"), do hereby agree to the following terms, conditions, and arrangements providing for the nursing and/or personal care of _____ (hereinafter the "Resident"):

1. FINANCIAL AGREEMENT

A. Private Pay Residents

Residents not receiving financial support from either _____ (state Medicaid program), Medicare, or VA, are referred to herein as "Private Pay" residents, and are subject to the following total monthly rate, which includes (strike one—private/semi-private) room, board, included services as set forth in paragraph 2, and therapeutic diets (including tubal feeding if necessary):

Total Monthly Rate$_____

The total monthly rate may be increased upon the giving of 30 days notice. Resident/Resident's Representative agrees to remit payment monthly in advance upon receipt of a billing statement. If the Resident is admitted between the 1st day and the 10th day of the month, the entire monthly rate shall be due for that month. If the Resident is admitted after the 10th day of the month, the Resident shall be responsible for the prorated monthly rate from the date of admission through the end of the month. No refunds shall be given for any days that the Resident is absent from the facility, except in the event of the Resident's death.

B. Medicare Residents

Residents whose care is funded by payments under either Medicare Part A or Part B must meet all eligibility requirements for such payments upon admission and for the duration of this Agreement. All charges not paid by Medicare Part A or Part B are the responsibility of the Resident/Resident's Representative, and shall be payable upon receipt of a billing statement. If Medicare coverage is terminated, the Resident shall be considered a Private Pay Resident and shall be required to execute a new Agreement obligating the Resident to make payment under Private Pay Resident financial agreement provisions.

C. VA Benefits

Residents whose care is funded by benefits received from the Department of Veterans Affairs (hereinafter "VA") agree that all charges not paid by the VA are the responsibility of the Resident/Resident's Representative, and shall be payable upon receipt of a billing statement. If VA coverage is terminated, the Resident shall be considered a Private Pay Resident and shall be required to execute a new Agreement obligating the Resident to make payment under Private Pay Resident financial agreement provisions.

D. Insurance Plans

Residents whose care is funded by benefits received from private or long term care insurance proceeds agree that all charges not paid by such proceeds are the responsibility of the Resident/Resident's Representative, and shall be payable upon receipt of a billing statement.

2. INCLUDED SERVICES

The following services are considered "included services" for purposes of Paragraph 1.A. of this Agreement:

    a. All routine medical and nursing services as needed by the Resident;

    b. Such personal care services as are needed by the Resident, including personal assistance (eating, bathing, dressing, toilet/incontinence services, brushing teeth, shampooing and combing hair, shaving, nail care, laundry);

    c. Such personal care supplies as are needed by the Resident (including soap, shampoo, toothpaste, toothbrush, comb, brush, razor, shaving cream, denture care and adhesive products, deodorant, feminine hygiene products, adult diapers, hand lotion, tissues, cotton swabs);

    d. Bed linens, washcloths and towels;

    e. Laundry service for Resident's clothing; and,

    f. Ordinary safety equipment as needed by the Resident, including bed rails and bath chairs.

3. SERVICES NOT INCLUDED

The following services are not considered "included services" for purposes of Paragraph 1 of this Agreement. These services, however, may be provided by the Facility for the Resident's benefit at the current rate, and shall be billed separately from the total monthly rate:

    a. Medications specifically ordered to be given the Resident by a physician;

    b. Medical equipment as needed by the Resident, including but not limited to walkers, wheelchairs, crutches, oxygen and oxygen delivery equipment, prosthetic devices;

    c. Medical treatment supplies as needed by the Resident, including but not limited to dressings and bandages, catheter supplies, enema supplies, syringes and needles, intravenous administration supplies;

    d Physical, occupational, or speech therapies;

    e. Dental care ;

    f. Eye care; and,

    g. Beautician and barber services.

4. RESIDENT'S/RESIDENT'S REPRESENTATIVE'S AGREEMENT

The Resident/Resident's Representative agrees as follows:

    a. That advance payment for the first month's rate shall be made prior to admission to the Facility;

    b. That Resident/Resident's Representative shall remit payment to the Facility for any additional charges incurred by the resident under Paragraph 3, prior to the end of the month that the charge is billed to the Resident;

    c. That any charges not paid as agreed shall accrue interest at an annual percentage rate of _____%;

    d. That, if all payments are not made as agreed, the Facility may discharge the Resident and, if necessary, provide transportation for the Resident to the Resident's Representative at the Resident's expense;

    e. That, if all payments are not made as agreed, the Resident/Resident's Representative shall be liable for all costs of collection, including court costs and attorneys' fees;

    F. That Resident/Resident's Representative shall provide all items of personal property as needed by the Resident, including but not limited to clothing, and shall suitably label all such property for purposes of identification;

g. That the Resident/Resident's Representative shall provide the Facility with all required information about the Resident, including but not limited to a current physician's report of physical examination, statement of income and assets, and other personal information;

h. That, if Resident is admitted pending approval of eligibility under any private, state or federal insurance or other funding plan, and approval is not obtained by the resident within _____ months after admission, or immediately upon denial of eligibility, the Resident shall be liable for the entire amount of the charges incurred, which charges shall be immediately due and payable by the Resident/Resident's Representative;

i. That the Resident shall be liable for the cost of repair or replacement of any property belonging either to the Facility or to another resident, which has been lost or damaged by the Resident, with the exception of ordinary wear and tear;

j. That the Resident/Resident's Representative shall abide by and be bound by all rules, regulations, policies, and operating procedures set forth by the Facility, including but not limited to those contained in the Facility's official policy manual regarding the following: Resident's rights, Resident assessments, care plans, advance directives, visiting hours, bedhold, the bringing of food or medicine into the Facility, personal property, smoking on the premises, the provision of emergency care, and grievance resolution.

5. FACILITY AGREEMENT

The Facility agrees to provide the Resident with all medical care and treatment required by the Resident's physician, and all nursing care and personal care required under state law.

6. DURATION OF AGREEMENT

This Agreement may be terminated as follows:

A. By the Facility: The Facility may terminate this Agreement, and may transfer or discharge the Resident to the Resident's Representative, at the Resident's expense, upon thirty (30) days notice for any of the following reasons:

(i) The transfer or discharge is necessary for the Resident's welfare and the Resident's needs cannot be met in the facility;

(ii) The transfer or discharge is appropriate because the Resident's health has improved sufficiently so the Resident no longer needs the services provided by the facility;

(iii) The health and safety of the Resident or of other individuals in the facility is endangered; or,

(iv) The Resident has failed, after reasonable and appropriate notice, to pay charges that have become due and owing.

B. By the Resident: The Resident may terminate this Agreement and all obligations under it upon thirty (30) days written notice. The Resident/Resident's Representative shall be responsible for all charges for services performed up to the date of termination.

7. ADMISSION WAIVER

Resident, on Resident's own behalf and on behalf of Resident's heirs, executors, and assigns does hereby agree to waive all claims against, and to indemnify and hold the Facility, its officers, agents, employees, successors and assigns harmless from, any and all liability or claims, against the Facility because of any death, bodily injury, personal injury, or illness, or because of any loss to Resident's property.

_____   _____
(Signature of Resident)   Date

_____   _____
(Signature of Resident's Representative)   Date

_____   _____
(Signature and Title of Agent for Facility)   Date

Numeric Identifier_____

MINIMUM DATA SET (MDS) — *VERSION 2.0*
FOR NURSING HOME RESIDENT ASSESSMENT AND CARE SCREENING

BASIC ASSESSMENT TRACKING FORM

SECTION AA. IDENTIFICATION INFORMATION

1.	RESIDENT NAME⊗				
		a. (First)	b. (Middle Initial)	c. (Last)	d. (Jr/Sr)
2.	GENDER⊗	1. Male		2. Female	
3.	BIRTHDATE⊗	Month — Day — Year			
4.	RACE/ ETHNICITY	1. American Indian/Alaskan Native 2. Asian/Pacific Islander 3. Black, not of Hispanic origin	4. Hispanic 5. White, not of Hispanic origin		
5.	SOCIAL SECURITY⊗ AND MEDICARE NUMBERS⊗ [C in 1st box if non med. no.]	a. Social Security Number — — b. Medicare number (or comparable railroad insurance number)			
6.	FACILITY PROVIDER NO.⊗	a. State No. b. Federal No.			
7.	MEDICAID NO. ["+" if pending, "N" if not a Medicaid recipient] ⊗				
8.	REASONS FOR ASSESS-MENT	[Note—Other codes do not apply to this form] a. Primary reason for assessment 1. Admission assessment (required by day 14) 2. Annual assessment 3. Significant change in status assessment 4. Significant correction of prior full assessment 5. Quarterly review assessment 10. Significant correction of prior quarterly assessment 0. *NONE OF ABOVE* b. *Codes for assessments required for Medicare PPS or the State* *1. Medicare 5 day assessment* *2. Medicare 30 day assessment* *3. Medicare 60 day assessment* *4. Medicare 90 day assessment* *5. Medicare readmission/return assessment* *6. Other state required assessment* *7. Medicare 14 day assessment* *8. Other Medicare required assessment*			

9. Signatures of Persons who Completed a Portion of the Accompanying Assessment or Tracking Form

I certify that the accompanying information accurately reflects resident assessment or tracking information for this resident and that I collected or coordinated collection of this information on the dates specified. To the best of my knowledge, this information was collected in accordance with applicable Medicare and Medicaid requirements. I understand that this information is used as a basis for ensuring that residents receive appropriate and quality care, and as a basis for payment from federal funds. I further understand that payment of such federal funds and continued participation in the government-funded health care programs is conditioned on the accuracy and truthfulness of this information, and that I may be personally subject to or may subject my organization to substantial criminal, civil, and/or administrative penalties for submitting false information. I also certify that I am authorized to submit this information by this facility on its behalf.

Signature and Title	Sections	Date
a.		
b.		
c.		
d.		
e.		
f.		
g.		
h.		
i.		
j.		
k.		
l.		

GENERAL INSTRUCTIONS

Complete this information for submission with all full and quarterly assessments (Admission, Annual, Significant Change, State or Medicare required assessments, or Quarterly Reviews, etc.)

⊗ = Key items for computerized resident tracking

☐ = When box blank, must enter number or letter [a.] = When letter in box, check if condition applies

MDS 2.0 September, 2000

Resident _____   Numeric Identifier_____

MINIMUM DATA SET (MDS) — *VERSION 2.0*
FOR NURSING HOME RESIDENT ASSESSMENT AND CARE SCREENING

BACKGROUND (FACE SHEET) INFORMATION AT ADMISSION

SECTION AB. DEMOGRAPHIC INFORMATION

1.	DATE OF ENTRY	Date the stay began. Note — Does not include readmission if record was closed at time of temporary discharge to hospital, etc. In such cases, use prior admission date

□□ – □□ – □□□□
Month   Day   Year

2.	ADMITTED FROM (AT ENTRY)	1. Private home/apt. with no home health services 2. Private home/apt. with home health services 3. Board and care/assisted living/group home 4. Nursing home 5. Acute care hospital 6. Psychiatric hospital, MR/DD facility 7. Rehabilitation hospital 8. Other
3.	LIVED ALONE (PRIOR TO ENTRY)	0. No 1. Yes 2. In other facility
4.	ZIP CODE OF PRIOR PRIMARY RESIDENCE	□□□□□

5.	RESIDEN-TIAL HISTORY 5 YEARS PRIOR TO ENTRY	(Check all settings resident lived in during 5 years prior to date of entry given in item AB1 above)	
		Prior stay at this nursing home	a.
		Stay in other nursing home	b.
		Other residential facility—board and care home, assisted living, group home	c.
		MH/psychiatric setting	d.
		MR/DD setting	e.
		NONE OF ABOVE	f.

6.	LIFETIME OCCUPA-TION(S) [Put "/" between two occupations]	□□□□□□□□□□□□□□□□

7.	EDUCATION (Highest Level Completed)	1. No schooling 5. Technical or trade school 2. 8th grade/less 6. Some college 3. 9-11 grades 7. Bachelor's degree 4. High school 8. Graduate degree
8.	LANGUAGE	(Code for correct response) a. Primary Language 0. English 1. Spanish 2. French 3. Other b. If other, specify
9.	MENTAL HEALTH HISTORY	Does resident's RECORD indicate any history of mental retardation, mental illness, or developmental disability problem? 0. No 1. Yes

10.	CONDITIONS RELATED TO MR/DD STATUS	(Check all conditions that are related to MR/DD status that were manifested before age 22, and are likely to continue indefinitely)	
		Not applicable—no MR/DD (Skip to AB11)	a.
		MR/DD with organic condition	
		Down's syndrome	b.
		Autism	c.
		Epilepsy	d.
		Other organic condition related to MR/DD	e.
		MR/DD with no organic condition	f.

11.	DATE BACK-GROUND INFORMA-TION COMPLETED	□□ – □□ – □□□□ Month Day Year

SECTION AC. CUSTOMARY ROUTINE

1.	CUSTOMARY ROUTINE (In year prior to DATE OF ENTRY to this nursing home, or year last in community if now being admitted from another nursing home)	(Check all that apply. If all information UNKNOWN, check last box only)	
		CYCLE OF DAILY EVENTS	
		Stays up late at night (e.g., after 9 pm)	a.
		Naps regularly during day (at least 1 hour)	b.
		Goes out 1+ days a week	c.
		Stays busy with hobbies, reading, or fixed daily routine	d.
		Spends most of time alone or watching TV	e.
		Moves independently indoors (with appliances, if used)	f.
		Use of tobacco products at least daily	g.
		NONE OF ABOVE	h.
		EATING PATTERNS	
		Distinct food preferences	i.
		Eats between meals all or most days	j.
		Use of alcoholic beverage(s) at least weekly	k.
		NONE OF ABOVE	l.
		ADL PATTERNS	
		In bedclothes much of day	m.
		Wakens to toilet all or most nights	n.
		Has irregular bowel movement pattern	o.
		Showers for bathing	p.
		Bathing in PM	q.
		NONE OF ABOVE	r.
		INVOLVEMENT PATTERNS	
		Daily contact with relatives/close friends	s.
		Usually attends church, temple, synagogue (etc.)	t.
		Finds strength in faith	u.
		Daily animal companion/presence	v.
		Involved in group activities	w.
		NONE OF ABOVE	x.
		UNKNOWN—Resident/family unable to provide information	y.

SECTION AD. FACE SHEET SIGNATURES

SIGNATURES OF PERSONS COMPLETING FACE SHEET:

a. Signature of RN Assessment Coordinator _____ Date

I certify that the accompanying information accurately reflects resident assessment or tracking information for this resident and that I collected or coordinated collection of this information on the dates specified. To the best of my knowledge, this information was collected in accordance with applicable Medicare and Medicaid requirements. I understand that this information is used as a basis for ensuring that residents receive appropriate and quality care, and as a basis for payment from federal funds. I further understand that payment of such federal funds and continued partici-pation in the government-funded health care programs is conditioned on the accuracy and truthful-ness of this information, and that I may be personally subject to or may subject my organization to substantial criminal, civil, and/or administrative penalties for submitting false information. I also certify that I am authorized to submit this information by this facility on its behalf.

Signature and Title	Sections	Date
b.		
c.		
d.		
e.		
f.		
g.		

□ = When box blank, must enter number or letter   a. = When letter in box, check if condition applies

MDS 2.0 September, 2000

Resident _____ Numeric Identifier _____

MINIMUM DATA SET (MDS) — VERSION 2.0
FOR NURSING HOME RESIDENT ASSESSMENT AND CARE SCREENING
FULL ASSESSMENT FORM
(Status in last 7 days, unless other time frame indicated)

SECTION A. IDENTIFICATION AND BACKGROUND INFORMATION

1.	RESIDENT NAME				
		a. (First)	b. (Middle Initial)	c. (Last)	d. (Jr/Sr)

2.	ROOM NUMBER	

3.	ASSESSMENT REFERENCE DATE	a. Last day of MDS observation period
		Month — Day — Year
		b. Original (0) or corrected copy of form (enter number of correction)

4a.	DATE OF REENTRY	Date of reentry from most recent temporary discharge to a hospital in last 90 days (or since last assessment or admission if less than 90 days)
		Month — Day — Year

5.	MARITAL STATUS	1. Never married 3. Widowed 5. Divorced 2. Married 4. Separated

6.	MEDICAL RECORD NO.	

7.	CURRENT PAYMENT SOURCES FOR N.H. STAY	(Billing Office to indicate; check all that apply in last 30 days)
		Medicaid per diem — a.	VA per diem — f.
		Medicare per diem — b.	Self or family pays for full per diem — g.
		Medicare ancillary part A — c.	Medicaid resident liability or Medicare co-payment — h.
		Medicare ancillary part B — d.	Private insurance per diem (including co-payment) — i.
		CHAMPUS per diem — e.	Other per diem — j.

8.	REASONS FOR ASSESSMENT [Note—If this is a discharge or reentry assessment, only a limited subset of MDS items need be completed]	a. Primary reason for assessment 1. Admission assessment (required by day 14) 2. Annual assessment 3. Significant change in status assessment 4. Significant correction of prior full assessment 5. Quarterly review assessment 6. Discharged—return not anticipated 7. Discharged—return anticipated 8. Discharged prior to completing initial assessment 9. Reentry 10. Significant correction of prior quarterly assessment 0. NONE OF ABOVE
		b. Codes for assessments required for Medicare PPS or the State 1. Medicare 5 day assessment 2. Medicare 30 day assessment 3. Medicare 60 day assessment 4. Medicare 90 day assessment 5. Medicare readmission/return assessment 6. Other state required assessment 7. Medicare 14 day assessment 8. Other Medicare required assessment

9.	RESPONSIBILITY/ LEGAL GUARDIAN	(Check all that apply)
		Legal guardian — a.	Durable power attorney/financial — d.
		Other legal oversight — b.	Family member responsible — e.
		Durable power of attorney/health care — c.	Patient responsible for self — f.
			NONE OF ABOVE — g.

10.	ADVANCED DIRECTIVES	(For those items with supporting documentation in the medical record, check all that apply)
		Living will — a.	Feeding restrictions — f.
		Do not resuscitate — b.	Medication restrictions — g.
		Do not hospitalize — c.	Other treatment restrictions — h.
		Organ donation — d.	NONE OF ABOVE — i.
		Autopsy request — e.	

SECTION B. COGNITIVE PATTERNS

1.	COMATOSE	(Persistent vegetative state/no discernible consciousness) 0. No 1. Yes (If yes, skip to Section G)

2.	MEMORY	(Recall of what was learned or known)
		a. Short-term memory OK—seems/appears to recall after 5 minutes 0. Memory OK 1. Memory problem
		b. Long-term memory OK—seems/appears to recall long past 0. Memory OK 1. Memory problem

3.	MEMORY/ RECALL ABILITY	(Check all that resident was normally able to recall during last 7 days)
		Current season — a.	That he/she is in a nursing home — d.
		Location of own room — b.	
		Staff names/faces — c.	NONE OF ABOVE are recalled — e.

4.	COGNITIVE SKILLS FOR DAILY DECISION-MAKING	(Made decisions regarding tasks of daily life) 0. INDEPENDENT—decisions consistent/reasonable 1. MODIFIED INDEPENDENCE—some difficulty in new situations only 2. MODERATELY IMPAIRED—decisions poor; cues/supervision required 3. SEVERELY IMPAIRED—never/rarely made decisions

5.	INDICATORS OF DELIRIUM— PERIODIC DISORDERED THINKING/ AWARENESS	(Code for behavior in the last 7 days.) [Note: Accurate assessment requires conversations with staff and family who have direct knowledge of resident's behavior over this time]. 0. Behavior not present 1. Behavior present, not of recent onset 2. Behavior present, over last 7 days appears different from resident's usual functioning (e.g., new onset or worsening)
		a. EASILY DISTRACTED—(e.g., difficulty paying attention; gets sidetracked)
		b. PERIODS OF ALTERED PERCEPTION OR AWARENESS OF SURROUNDINGS—(e.g., moves lips or talks to someone not present; believes he/she is somewhere else; confuses night and day)
		c. EPISODES OF DISORGANIZED SPEECH—(e.g., speech is incoherent, nonsensical, irrelevant, or rambling from subject to subject; loses train of thought)
		d. PERIODS OF RESTLESSNESS—(e.g., fidgeting or picking at skin, clothing, napkins, etc; frequent position changes; repetitive physical movements or calling out)
		e. PERIODS OF LETHARGY—(e.g., sluggishness; staring into space; difficult to arouse; little body movement)
		f. MENTAL FUNCTION VARIES OVER THE COURSE OF THE DAY—(e.g., sometimes better, sometimes worse; behaviors sometimes present, sometimes not)

6.	CHANGE IN COGNITIVE STATUS	Resident's cognitive status, skills, or abilities have changed as compared to status of 90 days ago (or since last assessment if less than 90 days) 0. No change 1. Improved 2. Deteriorated

SECTION C. COMMUNICATION/HEARING PATTERNS

1.	HEARING	(With hearing appliance, if used) 0. HEARS ADEQUATELY—normal talk, TV, phone 1. MINIMAL DIFFICULTY when not in quiet setting 2. HEARS IN SPECIAL SITUATIONS ONLY—speaker has to adjust tonal quality and speak distinctly 3. HIGHLY IMPAIRED/absence of useful hearing

2.	COMMUNICATION DEVICES/ TECHNIQUES	(Check all that apply during last 7 days)
		Hearing aid, present and used — a.
		Hearing aid, present and not used regularly — b.
		Other receptive comm. techniques used (e.g., lip reading) — c.
		NONE OF ABOVE — d.

3.	MODES OF EXPRESSION	(Check all used by resident to make needs known)
		Speech — a.	Signs/gestures/sounds — d.
		Writing messages to express or clarify needs — b.	Communication board — e.
		American sign language or Braille — c.	Other — f.
			NONE OF ABOVE — g.

4.	MAKING SELF UNDERSTOOD	(Expressing information content—however able) 0. UNDERSTOOD 1. USUALLY UNDERSTOOD—difficulty finding words or finishing thoughts 2. SOMETIMES UNDERSTOOD—ability is limited to making concrete requests 3. RARELY/NEVER UNDERSTOOD

5.	SPEECH CLARITY	(Code for speech in the last 7 days) 0. CLEAR SPEECH—distinct, intelligible words 1. UNCLEAR SPEECH—slurred, mumbled words 2. NO SPEECH—absence of spoken words

6.	ABILITY TO UNDERSTAND OTHERS	(Understanding verbal information content—however able) 0. UNDERSTANDS 1. USUALLY UNDERSTANDS—may miss some part/intent of message 2. SOMETIMES UNDERSTANDS—responds adequately to simple, direct communication 3. RARELY/NEVER UNDERSTANDS

7.	CHANGE IN COMMUNICATION/ HEARING	Resident's ability to express, understand, or hear information has changed as compared to status of 90 days ago (or since last assessment if less than 90 days) 0. No change 1. Improved 2. Deteriorated

☐ = When box blank, must enter number or letter [a.] = When letter in box, check if condition applies

Resident _____   Numeric Identifier _____

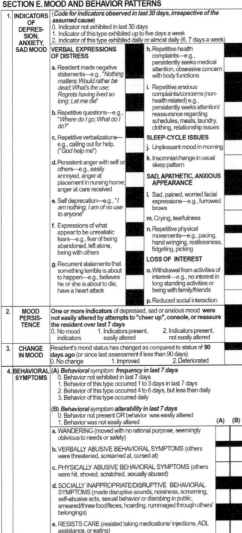

SECTION D. VISION PATTERNS

1.	VISION	(Ability to see in adequate light and with glasses if used) 0. ADEQUATE—sees fine detail, including regular print in newspapers/books 1. IMPAIRED—sees large print, but not regular print in newspapers/books 2. MODERATELY IMPAIRED—limited vision; not able to see newspaper headlines, but can identify objects 3. HIGHLY IMPAIRED—object identification in question, but eyes appear to follow objects 4. SEVERELY IMPAIRED—no vision or sees only light, colors, or shapes; eyes do not appear to follow objects	
2.	VISUAL LIMITATIONS/ DIFFICULTIES	Side vision problems—decreased peripheral vision (e.g., leaves food on one side of tray, difficulty traveling, bumps into people and objects, misjudges placement of chair when seating self)	a.
		Experiences any of following: sees halos or rings around lights; sees flashes of light; sees "curtains" over eyes	b.
		NONE OF ABOVE	c.
3.	VISUAL APPLIANCES	Glasses; contact lenses; magnifying glass 0. No 1. Yes	

SECTION E. MOOD AND BEHAVIOR PATTERNS

1.	INDICATORS OF DEPRES- SION, ANXIETY, SAD MOOD	(Code for indicators observed in last 30 days, irrespective of the assumed cause) 0. Indicator not exhibited in last 30 days 1. Indicator of this type exhibited up to five days a week 2. Indicator of this type exhibited daily or almost daily (6, 7 days a week)		

VERBAL EXPRESSIONS OF DISTRESS

a. Resident made negative statements—e.g., "Nothing matters; Would rather be dead; What's the use; Regrets having lived so long; Let me die"

b. Repetitive questions—e.g., "Where do I go; What do I do?"

c. Repetitive verbalizations—e.g., calling out for help, ("God help me")

d. Persistent anger with self or others—e.g., easily annoyed, anger at placement in nursing home; anger at care received

e. Self deprecation—e.g., "I am nothing; I am of no use to anyone"

f. Expressions of what appear to be unrealistic fears—e.g., fear of being abandoned, left alone, being with others

g. Recurrent statements that something terrible is about to happen—e.g., believes he or she is about to die, have a heart attack

h. Repetitive health complaints—e.g., persistently seeks medical attention, obsessive concern with body functions

i. Repetitive anxious complaints/concerns (non-health related) e.g., persistently seeks attention/reassurance regarding schedules, meals, laundry, clothing, relationship issues

SLEEP-CYCLE ISSUES

j. Unpleasant mood in morning

k. Insomnia/change in usual sleep pattern

SAD, APATHETIC, ANXIOUS APPEARANCE

l. Sad, pained, worried facial expressions—e.g., furrowed brows

m. Crying, tearfulness

n. Repetitive physical movements—e.g., pacing, hand wringing, restlessness, fidgeting, picking

LOSS OF INTEREST

o. Withdrawal from activities of interest—e.g., no interest in long standing activities or being with family/friends

p. Reduced social interaction

2.	MOOD PERSIS- TENCE	One or more indicators of depressed, sad or anxious mood were not easily altered by attempts to "cheer up", console, or reassure the resident over last 7 days 0. No mood indicators 1. Indicators present, easily altered 2. Indicators present, not easily altered	
3.	CHANGE IN MOOD	Resident's mood status has changed as compared to status of 90 days ago (or since last assessment if less than 90 days) 0. No change 1. Improved 2. Deteriorated	

4. BEHAVIORAL SYMPTOMS	(A) Behavioral symptom frequency in last 7 days 0. Behavior not exhibited in last 7 days 1. Behavior of this type occurred 1 to 3 days in last 7 days 2. Behavior of this type occurred 4 to 6 days, but less than daily 3. Behavior of this type occurred daily		
	(B) Behavioral symptom alterability in last 7 days 0. Behavior not present OR behavior was easily altered 1. Behavior was not easily altered	(A)	(B)
a. WANDERING (moved with no rational purpose, seemingly oblivious to needs or safety)			
b. VERBALLY ABUSIVE BEHAVIORAL SYMPTOMS (others were threatened, screamed at, cursed at)			
c. PHYSICALLY ABUSIVE BEHAVIORAL SYMPTOMS (others were hit, shoved, scratched, sexually abused)			
d. SOCIALLY INAPPROPRIATE/DISRUPTIVE BEHAVIORAL SYMPTOMS (made disruptive sounds, noisiness, screaming, self-abusive acts, sexual behavior or disrobing in public, smeared/threw food/feces, hoarding, rummaged through others' belongings)			
e. RESISTS CARE (resisted taking medications/ injections, ADL assistance, or eating)			

5.	CHANGE IN BEHAVIORAL SYMPTOMS	Resident's behavior status has changed as compared to status of 90 days ago (or since last assessment if less than 90 days) 0. No change 1. Improved 2. Deteriorated	

SECTION F. PSYCHOSOCIAL WELL-BEING

1.	SENSE OF INITIATIVE/ INVOLVE- MENT	At ease interacting with others	a.
		At ease doing planned or structured activities	b.
		At ease doing self-initiated activities	c.
		Establishes own goals	d.
		Pursues involvement in life of facility (e.g., makes/keeps friends; involved in group activities; responds positively to new activities; assists at religious services)	e.
		Accepts invitations into most group activities	f.
		NONE OF ABOVE	g.
2.	UNSETTLED RELATION- SHIPS	Covert/open conflict with or repeated criticism of staff	a.
		Unhappy with roommate	b.
		Unhappy with residents other than roommate	c.
		Openly expresses conflict/anger with family/friends	d.
		Absence of personal contact with family/friends	e.
		Recent loss of close family member/friend	f.
		Does not adjust easily to change in routines	g.
		NONE OF ABOVE	h.
3.	PAST ROLES	Strong identification with past roles and life status	a.
		Expresses sadness/anger/empty feeling over lost roles/status	b.
		Resident perceives that daily routine (customary routine, activities) is very different from prior pattern in the community	c.
		NONE OF ABOVE	d.

SECTION G. PHYSICAL FUNCTIONING AND STRUCTURAL PROBLEMS

1.	(A) ADL SELF-PERFORMANCE—(Code for resident's PERFORMANCE OVER ALL SHIFTS during last 7 days—Not including setup) 0. INDEPENDENT—No help or oversight —OR— Help/oversight provided only 1 or 2 times during last 7 days 1. SUPERVISION—Oversight, encouragement or cueing provided 3 or more times during last 7 days —OR— Supervision (3 or more times) plus physical assistance provided only 1 or 2 times during last 7 days 2. LIMITED ASSISTANCE—Resident highly involved in activity; received physical help in guided maneuvering of limbs or other nonweight bearing assistance 3 or more times — OR—More help provided only 1 or 2 times during last 7 days 3. EXTENSIVE ASSISTANCE—While resident performed part of activity, over last 7-day period, help of following type(s) provided 3 or more times: —Weight-bearing support —Full staff performance during part (but not all) of last 7 days 4. TOTAL DEPENDENCE—Full staff performance of activity during entire 7 days 8. ACTIVITY DID NOT OCCUR during entire 7 days

(B) ADL SUPPORT PROVIDED—(Code for MOST SUPPORT PROVIDED OVER ALL SHIFTS during last 7 days; code regardless of resident's self-performance classification) 0. No setup or physical help from staff 1. Setup help only 2. One person physical assist 8. ADL activity itself did not 3. Two+ persons physical assist occur during entire 7 days	(A) SELF-PERF	(B) SUPPORT
a. BED MOBILITY — How resident moves to and from lying position, turns side to side, and positions body while in bed		
b. TRANSFER — How resident moves between surfaces—to/from: bed, chair, wheelchair, standing position (EXCLUDE to/from bath/toilet)		
c. WALK IN ROOM — How resident walks between locations in his/her room		
d. WALK IN CORRIDOR — How resident walks in corridor on unit		
e. LOCOMO- TION ON UNIT — How resident moves between locations in his/her room and adjacent corridor on same floor. If in wheelchair, self-sufficiency once in chair		
f. LOCOMO- TION OFF UNIT — How resident moves to and returns from off unit locations (e.g., areas set aside for dining, activities, or treatments). If facility has only one floor, how resident moves to and from distant areas on the floor. If in wheelchair, self-sufficiency once in chair		
g. DRESSING — How resident puts on, fastens, and takes off all items of street clothing, including donning/removing prosthesis		
h. EATING — How resident eats and drinks (regardless of skill). Includes intake of nourishment by other means (e.g., tube feeding, total parenteral nutrition)		
i. TOILET USE — How resident uses the toilet room (or commode, bedpan, urinal); transfer on/off toilet, cleanses, changes pad, manages ostomy or catheter, adjusts clothes		
j. PERSONAL HYGIENE — How resident maintains personal hygiene, including combing hair, brushing teeth, shaving, applying makeup, washing/drying face, hands, and perineum (EXCLUDE baths and showers)		

Resident _____ Numeric Identifier _____

2.	BATHING	How resident takes full-body bath/shower, sponge bath, and transfers in/out of tub/shower (EXCLUDE washing of back and hair.) *Code for most dependent in self-performance and support.* (A) BATHING SELF-PERFORMANCE codes appear below	(A)	(B)
		0. Independent—No help provided		
		1. Supervision—Oversight help only		
		2. Physical help limited to transfer only		
		3. Physical help in part of bathing activity		
		4. Total dependence		
		8. Activity itself did not occur during entire 7 days		
		(Bathing support codes are as defined in Item 1, code B above)		

3.	TEST FOR BALANCE (see training manual)	*(Code for ability during test in the last 7 days)* 0. Maintained position as required in test 1. Unsteady, but able to rebalance self without physical support 2. Partial physical support during test; or stands (sits) but does not follow directions for test 3. Not able to attempt test without physical help	
		a. Balance while standing	
		b. Balance while sitting—position, trunk control	

4.	FUNCTIONAL LIMITATION IN RANGE OF MOTION (see training manual)	*(Code for limitations during last 7 days that interfered with daily functions or placed resident at risk of injury)* (A) RANGE OF MOTION (B) VOLUNTARY MOVEMENT 0. No limitation 0. No loss 1. Limitation on one side 1. Partial loss 2. Limitation on both sides 2. Full loss	(A)	(B)
		a. Neck		
		b. Arm—Including shoulder or elbow		
		c. Hand—Including wrist or fingers		
		d. Leg—Including hip or knee		
		e. Foot—Including ankle or toes		
		f. Other limitation or loss		

5.	MODES OF LOCOMO-TION	*(Check all that apply during last 7 days)*	
		Cane/walker/crutch	a.	Wheelchair primary mode of locomotion	d.
		Wheeled self	b.		
		Other person wheeled	c.	NONE OF ABOVE	e.

6.	MODES OF TRANSFER	*(Check all that apply during last 7 days)*	
		Bedfast all or most of time	a.	Lifted mechanically	d.
		Bed rails used for bed mobility or transfer	b.	Transfer aid (e.g., slide board, trapeze, cane, walker, brace)	e.
		Lifted manually	c.	NONE OF ABOVE	f.

7.	TASK SEGMENTA-TION	Some or all of ADL activities were broken into subtasks during **last 7 days** so that resident could perform them 0. No 1. Yes	

8.	ADL FUNCTIONAL REHABILITA-TION POTENTIAL	Resident believes he/she is capable of increased independence in at least some ADLs	a.
		Direct care staff believe resident is capable of increased independence in at least some ADLs	b.
		Resident able to perform tasks/activity but is very slow	c.
		Difference in ADL Self-Performance or ADL Support, comparing mornings to evenings	d.
		NONE OF ABOVE	e.

9.	CHANGE IN ADL FUNCTION	Resident's ADL self-performance status has changed as compared to status of **90 days ago** (or since last assessment if less than 90 days) 0. No change 1. Improved 2. Deteriorated	

SECTION H. CONTINENCE IN LAST 14 DAYS

1.	CONTINENCE SELF-CONTROL CATEGORIES *(Code for resident's PERFORMANCE OVER ALL SHIFTS)*
	0. CONTINENT—Complete control *[includes use of indwelling urinary catheter or ostomy device that does not leak urine or stool]*
	1. USUALLY CONTINENT—BLADDER, incontinent episodes once a week or less; BOWEL, less than weekly
	2. OCCASIONALLY INCONTINENT—BLADDER, 2 or more times a week but not daily; BOWEL, once a week
	3. FREQUENTLY INCONTINENT—BLADDER, tended to be incontinent daily, but some control present (e.g., on day shift); BOWEL, 2-3 times a week
	4. INCONTINENT—Had inadequate control BLADDER, multiple daily episodes; BOWEL, all (or almost all) of the time

a.	BOWEL CONTI-NENCE	Control of bowel movement, with appliance or bowel continence programs, if employed	
b.	BLADDER CONTI-NENCE	Control of urinary bladder function (if dribbles, volume insufficient to soak through underpants), with appliances (e.g., foley) or continence programs, if employed	

2.	BOWEL ELIMINATION PATTERN	Bowel elimination pattern regular—at least one movement every three days	a.	Diarrhea	c.
				Fecal impaction	d.
		Constipation	b.	NONE OF ABOVE	e.

3.	APPLIANCES AND PROGRAMS	Any scheduled toileting plan	a.	Did not use toilet room/commode/urinal	f.
		Bladder retraining program	b.	Pads/briefs used	g.
		External (condom) catheter	c.	Enemas/irrigation	h.
		Indwelling catheter	d.	Ostomy present	i.
		Intermittent catheter	e.	NONE OF ABOVE	j.

4.	CHANGE IN URINARY CONTI-NENCE	Resident's urinary continence has changed as compared to status of **90 days ago** (or since last assessment if less than 90 days) 0. No change 1. Improved 2. Deteriorated	

SECTION I. DISEASE DIAGNOSES

Check only those diseases that have a **relationship** to current ADL status, cognitive status, mood and behavior status, medical treatments, nursing monitoring, or risk of death. (Do not list inactive diagnoses.)

1.	DISEASES	*(If none apply, CHECK the NONE OF ABOVE box)*			
		ENDOCRINE/METABOLIC/NUTRITIONAL		Hemiplegia/Hemiparesis	v.
				Multiple sclerosis	w.
		Diabetes mellitus	a.	Paraplegia	x.
		Hyperthyroidism	b.	Parkinson's disease	y.
		Hypothyroidism	c.	Quadriplegia	z.
		HEART/CIRCULATION		Seizure disorder	aa.
		Arteriosclerotic heart disease (ASHD)	d.	Transient ischemic attack (TIA)	bb.
		Cardiac dysrhythmias	e.	Traumatic brain injury	cc.
		Congestive heart failure	f.	**PSYCHIATRIC/MOOD**	
		Deep vein thrombosis	g.	Anxiety disorder	dd.
		Hypertension	h.	Depression	ee.
		Hypotension	i.	Manic depression (bipolar disease)	ff.
		Peripheral vascular disease	j.	Schizophrenia	gg.
		Other cardiovascular disease	k.	**PULMONARY**	
		MUSCULOSKELETAL		Asthma	hh.
		Arthritis	l.	Emphysema/COPD	ii.
		Hip fracture	m.	**SENSORY**	
		Missing limb (e.g., amputation)	n.	Cataracts	jj.
		Osteoporosis	o.	Diabetic retinopathy	kk.
		Pathological bone fracture	p.	Glaucoma	ll.
		NEUROLOGICAL		Macular degeneration	mm.
		Alzheimer's disease	q.	**OTHER**	
		Aphasia	r.	Allergies	nn.
		Cerebral palsy	s.	Anemia	oo.
		Cerebrovascular accident (stroke)	t.	Cancer	pp.
		Dementia other than Alzheimer's disease	u.	Renal failure	qq.
				NONE OF ABOVE	rr.

2.	INFECTIONS	*(If none apply, CHECK the NONE OF ABOVE box)*			
		Antibiotic resistant infection (e.g., Methicillin resistant staph)	a.	Septicemia	g.
				Sexually transmitted diseases	h.
		Clostridium difficile (c. diff.)	b.	Tuberculosis	i.
		Conjunctivitis	c.	Urinary tract infection **in last 30 days**	j.
		HIV infection	d.	Viral hepatitis	k.
		Pneumonia	e.	Wound infection	l.
		Respiratory infection	f.	NONE OF ABOVE	m.

3.	OTHER CURRENT OR MORE DETAILED DIAGNOSES AND ICD-9 CODES	a.				•	
		b.				•	
		c.				•	
		d.				•	
		e.				•	

SECTION J. HEALTH CONDITIONS

1.	PROBLEM CONDITIONS	*(Check all problems present in last 7 days unless other time frame is indicated)*			
		INDICATORS OF FLUID STATUS		Dizziness/Vertigo	f.
				Edema	g.
		Weight gain or loss of 3 or more pounds within a 7 day period	a.	Fever	h.
				Hallucinations	i.
				Internal bleeding	j.
		Inability to lie flat due to shortness of breath	b.	Recurrent lung aspirations in **last 90 days**	k.
		Dehydrated; output exceeds input	c.	Shortness of breath	l.
				Syncope (fainting)	m.
		Insufficient fluid; did NOT consume all/almost all liquids provided during **last 3 days**	d.	Unsteady gait	n.
				Vomiting	o.
		OTHER		NONE OF ABOVE	p.
		Delusions	e.		

Resident _____

Numeric Identifier _____

2.	PAIN SYMPTOMS	(Code the **highest level of pain** present in the **last 7 days**)	
		a. FREQUENCY with which resident complains or shows evidence of pain 0. No pain (**skip to J4**) 1. Pain less than daily 2. Pain daily	**b. INTENSITY** of pain 1. Mild pain 2. Moderate pain 3. Times when pain is horrible or excruciating

3.	PAIN SITE	(If pain present, **check all sites** that apply in **last 7 days**)			
		Back pain	a.	Incisional pain	f.
		Bone pain	b.	Joint pain (other than hip)	g.
		Chest pain while doing usual activities	c.	Soft tissue pain (e.g., lesion, muscle)	h.
		Headache	d.	Stomach pain	i.
		Hip pain	e.	Other	j.

4.	ACCIDENTS	(Check all that apply)			
		Fell in **past 30 days**	a.	Hip fracture in **last 180 days**	c.
		Fell in **past 31-180 days**	b.	Other fracture in **last 180 days**	d.
				NONE OF ABOVE	e.

5.	STABILITY OF CONDITIONS	Conditions/diseases make resident's cognitive, ADL, mood or behavior patterns unstable—(fluctuating, precarious, or deteriorating)	a.
		Resident experiencing an acute episode or a flare-up of a recurrent or chronic problem	b.
		End-stage disease, 6 or fewer months to live	c.
		NONE OF ABOVE	d.

SECTION K. ORAL/NUTRITIONAL STATUS

1.	ORAL PROBLEMS	Chewing problem	a.
		Swallowing problem	b.
		Mouth pain	c.
		NONE OF ABOVE	d.

2.	HEIGHT AND WEIGHT	Record (a.) **height in inches** and (b.) **weight in pounds**. Base weight on most recent measure in **last 30 days**; measure weight consistently in accord with standard facility practice—e.g., in a.m. after voiding, before meal, with shoes off, and in nightclothes
		a. HT (in.) ____ **b.** WT (lb.) ____

3.	WEIGHT CHANGE	a. **Weight loss**—5 % or more in **last 30 days**; or 10 % or more in **last 180 days** 0. No 1. Yes
		b. **Weight gain**—5 % or more in **last 30 days**; or 10 % or more in **last 180 days** 0. No 1. Yes

4.	NUTRI-TIONAL PROBLEMS	Complains about the taste of many foods	a.	Leaves 25% or more of food uneaten at most meals	c.
		Regular or repetitive complaints of hunger	b.	*NONE OF ABOVE*	d.

5.	NUTRI-TIONAL APPROACH-ES	(Check all that apply in **last 7 days**)			
		Parenteral/IV	a.	Dietary supplement between meals	f.
		Feeding tube	b.		
		Mechanically altered diet	c.	Plate guard, stabilized built-up utensil, etc.	g.
		Syringe (oral feeding)	d.	On a planned weight change program	h.
		Therapeutic diet	e.		
				NONE OF ABOVE	i.

6.	PARENTERAL OR ENTERAL INTAKE	(**Skip to Section L** if neither 5a nor 5b is checked)
		a. Code the proportion of **total calories** the resident received through parenteral or tube feedings in the **last 7 days** 0. None 3. 51% to 75% 1. 1% to 25% 4. 76% to 100% 2. 26% to 50%
		b. Code the average **fluid intake** per day by IV or tube in **last 7 days** 0. None 3. 1001 to 1500 cc/day 1. 1 to 500 cc/day 4. 1501 to 2000 cc/day 2. 501 to 1000 cc/day 5. 2001 or more cc/day

SECTION L. ORAL/DENTAL STATUS

1.	ORAL STATUS AND DISEASE PREVENTION	Debris (soft, easily movable substances) present in mouth prior to going to bed at night	a.
		Has dentures or removable bridge	b.
		Some/all natural teeth lost—does not have or does not use dentures (or partial plates)	c.
		Broken, loose, or carious teeth	d.
		Inflamed gums (gingiva); swollen or bleeding gums; oral abcesses; ulcers or rashes	e.
		Daily cleaning of teeth/dentures or daily mouth care—by resident or staff	f.
		NONE OF ABOVE	g.

SECTION M. SKIN CONDITION

1.	ULCERS (Due to any cause)	(Record the number of ulcers at each ulcer stage—regardless of cause. If none present at a stage, record "0" (zero). Code all that apply during **last 7 days**. Code 9 = 9 or more.) **[Requires full body exam.]**	Number at Stage
		a. Stage 1. A persistent area of skin redness (without a break in the skin) that does not disappear when pressure is relieved.	
		b. Stage 2. A partial thickness loss of skin layers that presents clinically as an abrasion, blister, or shallow crater.	
		c. Stage 3. A full thickness of skin is lost, exposing the subcutaneous tissues - presents as a deep crater with or without undermining adjacent tissue.	
		d. Stage 4. A full thickness of skin and subcutaneous tissue is lost, exposing muscle or bone.	

2.	TYPE OF ULCER	(For each type of ulcer, **code for the highest stage in the last 7 days** using scale in item M1—i.e., 0=none; stages 1, 2, 3, 4)	
		a. Pressure ulcer—any lesion caused by pressure resulting in damage of underlying tissue	
		b. Stasis ulcer—open lesion caused by poor circulation in the lower extremities	

3.	HISTORY OF RESOLVED ULCERS	Resident had an ulcer that was resolved or cured in LAST 90 DAYS 0. No 1. Yes	

4.	OTHER SKIN PROBLEMS OR LESIONS PRESENT	(Check all that apply during **last 7 days**)	
		Abrasions, bruises	a.
		Burns (second or third degree)	b.
		Open lesions other than ulcers, rashes, cuts (e.g., cancer lesions)	c.
		Rashes—e.g., intertrigo, eczema, drug rash, heat rash, herpes zoster	d.
		Skin desensitized to pain or pressure	e.
		Skin tears or cuts (other than surgery)	f.
		Surgical wounds	g.
		NONE OF ABOVE	h.

5.	SKIN TREAT-MENTS	(Check all that apply during **last 7 days**)	
		Pressure relieving device(s) for chair	a.
		Pressure relieving device(s) for bed	b.
		Turning/repositioning program	c.
		Nutrition or hydration intervention to manage skin problems	d.
		Ulcer care	e.
		Surgical wound care	f.
		Application of dressings (with or without topical medications) other than to feet	g.
		Application of ointments/medications (other than to feet)	h.
		Other preventative or protective skin care (other than to feet)	i.
		NONE OF ABOVE	j.

6.	FOOT PROBLEMS AND CARE	(Check all that apply during **last 7 days**)	
		Resident has one or more foot problems—e.g., corns, callouses, bunions, hammer toes, overlapping toes, pain, structural problems	a.
		Infection of the foot—e.g., cellulitis, purulent drainage	b.
		Open lesions on the foot	c.
		Nails/calluses trimmed during **last 90 days**	d.
		Received preventative or protective foot care (e.g., used special shoes, inserts, pads, toe separators)	e.
		Application of dressings (with or without topical medications)	f.
		NONE OF ABOVE	g.

SECTION N. ACTIVITY PURSUIT PATTERNS

1.	TIME AWAKE	(Check appropriate time periods over **last 7 days**) Resident awake all or most of time (i.e., naps no more than one hour per time period) in the:			
		Morning	a.	Evening	c.
		Afternoon	b.	*NONE OF ABOVE*	d.

(If resident is comatose, skip to Section O)

2.	AVERAGE TIME INVOLVED IN ACTIVITIES	(When awake and not receiving treatments or ADL care) 0. Most—more than 2/3 of time 2. Little—less than 1/3 of time 1. Some—from 1/3 to 2/3 of time 3. None	

3.	PREFERRED ACTIVITY SETTINGS	(Check all settings in which activities are preferred)			
		Own room	a.		
		Day/activity room	b.	Outside facility	d.
		Inside NH/off unit	c.	*NONE OF ABOVE*	e.

4.	GENERAL ACTIVITY PREFER-ENCES (adapted to resident's current abilities)	(Check all PREFERENCES whether or not activity is currently available to resident)			
		Cards/other games	a.	Trips/shopping	g.
		Crafts/arts	b.	Walking/wheeling outdoors	h.
		Exercise/sports	c.	Watching TV	i.
		Music	d.	Gardening or plants	j.
		Reading/writing	e.	Talking or conversing	k.
		Spiritual/religious activities	f.	Helping others	l.
				NONE OF ABOVE	m.

MDS 2.0 September, 2000

Resident _____   Numeric Identifier _____

5.	PREFERS CHANGE IN DAILY ROUTINE	*Code for resident preferences in daily routines* 0. No change 1. Slight change 2. Major change	
		a. Type of activities in which resident is currently involved	
		b. Extent of resident involvement in activities	

SECTION O. MEDICATIONS

1.	NUMBER OF MEDICA-TIONS	*(Record the number of different medications used in the last 7 days; enter "0" if none used)*	
2.	NEW MEDICA-TIONS	*(Resident currently receiving medications that were initiated during the last 90 days)* 0. No 1. Yes	
3.	INJECTIONS	*(Record the number of DAYS injections of any type received during the last 7 days; enter "0" if none used)*	
4.	DAYS RECEIVED THE FOLLOWING MEDICATION	*(Record the number of DAYS during last 7 days; enter "0" if not used. Note—enter "1" for long-acting meds used less than weekly)*	
		a. Antipsychotic	**d.** Hypnotic
		b. Antianxiety	**e.** Diuretic
		c. Antidepressant	

SECTION P. SPECIAL TREATMENTS AND PROCEDURES

1.	SPECIAL TREAT-MENTS, PROCE-DURES, AND PROGRAMS	**a. SPECIAL CARE**—*Check treatments or programs received during the last 14 days*			
		TREATMENTS		Ventilator or respirator	l.
		Chemotherapy	a.	**PROGRAMS**	
		Dialysis	b.	Alcohol/drug treatment program	m.
		IV medication	c.	Alzheimer's/dementia special care unit	n.
		Intake/output	d.	Hospice care	o.
		Monitoring acute medical condition	e.	Pediatric unit	p.
		Ostomy care	f.	Respite care	q.
		Oxygen therapy	g.	Training in skills required to return to the community (e.g., taking medications, house work, shopping, transportation, ADLs)	r.
		Radiation	h.		
		Suctioning	i.		
		Tracheostomy care	j.		
		Transfusions	k.	*NONE OF ABOVE*	s.

	b. THERAPIES - *Record the number of days and total minutes each of the following therapies was administered (for at least 15 minutes a day) in the last 7 calendar days (Enter 0 if none or less than 15 min. daily) [Note—count only post admission therapies]*		
	(A) = # of days administered for 15 minutes or more **(B)** = total # of minutes provided in last 7 days	**DAYS (A)**	**MIN (B)**
	a. Speech - language pathology and audiology services		
	b. Occupational therapy		
	c. Physical therapy		
	d. Respiratory therapy		
	e. Psychological therapy (by any licensed mental health professional)		

2.	INTERVEN-TION PROGRAMS FOR MOOD, BEHAVIOR, COGNITIVE LOSS	*(Check all interventions or strategies used in last 7 days—no matter where received)*	
		Special behavior symptom evaluation program	a.
		Evaluation by a licensed mental health specialist in **last 90 days**	b.
		Group therapy	c.
		Resident-specific deliberate changes in the environment to address mood/behavior patterns—e.g., providing bureau in which to rummage	d.
		Reorientation—e.g., cueing	e.
		NONE OF ABOVE	f.

3.	NURSING REHABILITA-TION/ RESTOR-ATIVE CARE	*Record the NUMBER OF DAYS each of the following rehabilitation or restorative techniques or practices was provided to the resident for more than or equal to 15 minutes per day in the last 7 days (Enter 0 if none or less than 15 min. daily.)*		
		a. Range of motion (passive)	**f.** Walking	
		b. Range of motion (active)	**g.** Dressing or grooming	
		c. Splint or brace assistance	**h.** Eating or swallowing	
		TRAINING AND SKILL PRACTICE IN:	**i.** Amputation/prosthesis care	
		d. Bed mobility	**j.** Communication	
		e. Transfer	**k.** Other	

4.	DEVICES AND RESTRAINTS	*(Use the following codes for last 7 days:)* 0. Not used 1. Used less than daily 2. Used daily	
		Bed rails	
		a. — Full bed rails on all open sides of bed	
		b. — Other types of side rails used (e.g., half rail, one side)	
		c. Trunk restraint	
		d. Limb restraint	
		e. Chair prevents rising	
5.	HOSPITAL STAY(S)	Record number of times resident was admitted to hospital with an overnight stay **in last 90 days** (or since last assessment if less than 90 days). (*Enter 0 if no hospital admissions*)	
6.	EMERGENCY ROOM (ER) VISIT(S)	Record number of times resident visited ER without an overnight stay **in last 90 days** (or since last assessment if less than 90 days). (*Enter 0 if no ER visits*)	
7.	PHYSICIAN VISITS	In the **LAST 14 DAYS** (or since admission if less than 14 days in facility) how many days has the physician (or authorized assistant or practitioner) examined the resident? (*Enter 0 if none*)	
8.	PHYSICIAN ORDERS	In the **LAST 14 DAYS** (or since admission if less than 14 days in facility) how many days has the physician (or authorized assistant or practitioner) changed the resident's orders? *Do not include order renewals without change.* (*Enter 0 if none*)	
9.	ABNORMAL LAB VALUES	Has the resident had any abnormal lab values during the **last 90 days** (or since admission)? 0. No 1. Yes	

SECTION Q. DISCHARGE POTENTIAL AND OVERALL STATUS

1.	DISCHARGE POTENTIAL	**a.** Resident expresses/indicates preference to return to the community 0. No 1. Yes	
		b. Resident has a support person who is positive towards discharge 0. No 1. Yes	
		c. Stay projected to be of a short duration— discharge projected **within 90 days** (do not include expected discharge due to death) 0. No 2. Within 31-90 days 1. Within 30 days 3. Discharge status uncertain	
2.	OVERALL CHANGE IN CARE NEEDS	Resident's overall self sufficiency has changed significantly as compared to status of **90 days ago** (or since last assessment if less than 90 days) 0. No change 1. Improved—receives fewer 2. Deteriorated—receives supports, needs less more support restrictive level of care	

SECTION R. ASSESSMENT INFORMATION

1.	PARTICIPA-TION IN ASSESS-MENT	**a.** Resident:	0. No	1. Yes	
		b. Family:	0. No	1. Yes	2. No family
		c. Significant other:	0. No	1. Yes	2. None

2. SIGNATURE OF PERSON COORDINATING THE ASSESSMENT:

a. Signature of RN Assessment Coordinator (sign on above line)

b. Date RN Assessment Coordinator signed as complete							
	Month		Day		Year		

Resident _____

SECTION T. THERAPY SUPPLEMENT FOR MEDICARE PPS

1.	SPECIAL TREAT-MENTS AND PROCE-DURES	**a. RECREATION THERAPY**—*Enter number of days and total minutes of recreation therapy administered (**for at least 15 minutes a day**) in the last 7 days* (Enter 0 if none)

DAYS   MIN

(A)   (B)

(A) = **# of days** administered for 15 minutes or more

(B) = **total # of minutes** provided in last 7 days

Skip unless this is a Medicare 5 day or Medicare readmission/return assessment.

b. ORDERED THERAPIES—*Has physician ordered any of following therapies to begin in FIRST 14 days of stay—physical therapy, occupational therapy, or speech pathology service?*
0. No   1. Yes

If not ordered, skip to item 2

c. Through day 15, provide an estimate of the number of days when at least 1 therapy service can be expected to have been delivered.

d. Through day 15, provide an estimate of the number of therapy minutes (across the therapies) that can be expected to be delivered?

2.	WALKING WHEN MOST SELF SUFFICIENT	*Complete item 2 if ADL self-performance score for TRANSFER (G.1.b.A) is 0,1,2, or 3 AND at least one of the following are present:*

    • Resident received physical therapy involving gait training (P.1.b.c)
    • Physical therapy was ordered for the resident involving gait training (T.1.b)
    • Resident received nursing rehabilitation for walking (P.3.f)
    • Physical therapy involving walking has been discontinued within the past 180 days

Skip to item 3 if resident did not walk in last 7 days

(FOR FOLLOWING FIVE ITEMS, BASE CODING ON THE EPISODE WHEN THE RESIDENT WALKED THE FARTHEST WITHOUT SITTING DOWN. INCLUDE WALKING DURING REHABILITATION SESSIONS.)

a. Furthest distance walked without sitting down during this episode.

0. 150+ feet   3. 10-25 feet
1. 51-149 feet   4. Less than 10 feet
2. 26-50 feet

b. Time walked without sitting down during this episode.

0. 1-2 minutes   3. 11-15 minutes
1. 3-4 minutes   4. 16-30 minutes
2. 5-10 minutes   5. 31+ minutes

c. Self-Performance in walking during this episode.

0. *INDEPENDENT*—No help or oversight
1. *SUPERVISION*—Oversight, encouragement or cueing provided
2. *LIMITED ASSISTANCE*—Resident highly involved in walking; received physical help in guided maneuvering of limbs or other nonweight bearing assistance
3. *EXTENSIVE ASSISTANCE*—Resident received weight bearing assistance while walking

d. Walking support provided associated with this episode (code regardless of resident's self-performance classification).

0. No setup or physical help from staff
1. Setup help only
2. One person physical assist
3. Two+ persons physical assist

e. Parallel bars used by resident in association with this episode.

0. No   1. Yes

3.	CASE MIX GROUP	Medicare [ ][ ][ ][ ] State [ ][ ][ ][ ]

SECTION V. RESIDENT ASSESSMENT PROTOCOL SUMMARY   Numeric Identifier _____

Resident's Name:	Medical Record No.:

1. Check if RAP is triggered.

2. For each triggered RAP, use the RAP guidelines to identify areas needing further assessment. Document relevant assessment information regarding the resident's status.

   • Describe:
   — Nature of the condition (may include presence or lack of objective data and subjective complaints).
   — Complications and risk factors that affect your decision to proceed to care planning.
   — Factors that must be considered in developing individualized care plan interventions.
   — Need for referrals/further evaluation by appropriate health professionals.

   • Documentation should support your decision-making regarding whether to proceed with a care plan for a triggered RAP and the type(s) of care plan interventions that are appropriate for a particular resident.

   • Documentation may appear anywhere in the clinical record (e.g., progress notes, consults, flowsheets, etc.).

3. Indicate under the <u>Location of RAP Assessment Documentation</u> column where information related to the RAP assessment can be found.

4. For each triggered RAP, indicate whether a new care plan, care plan revision, or continuation of current care plan is necessary to address the problem(s) identified in your assessment. The Care Planning Decision column must be completed within 7 days of completing the RAI (MDS and RAPs).

A. RAP PROBLEM AREA	(a) Check if triggered	Location and Date of RAP Assessment Documentation	(b) Care Planning Decision—check if addressed in care plan
1. DELIRIUM			
2. COGNITIVE LOSS			
3. VISUAL FUNCTION			
4. COMMUNICATION			
5. ADL FUNCTIONAL/ REHABILITATION POTENTIAL			
6. URINARY INCONTINENCE AND INDWELLING CATHETER			
7. PSYCHOSOCIAL WELL-BEING			
8. MOOD STATE			
9. BEHAVIORAL SYMPTOMS			
10. ACTIVITIES			
11. FALLS			
12. NUTRITIONAL STATUS			
13. FEEDING TUBES			
14. DEHYDRATION/FLUID MAINTENANCE			
15. DENTAL CARE			
16. PRESSURE ULCERS			
17. PSYCHOTROPIC DRUG USE			
18. PHYSICAL RESTRAINTS			

B.

1. Signature of RN Coordinator for RAP Assessment Process _____   2. ☐☐ — ☐☐ — ☐☐☐☐
   Month   Day   Year

3. Signature of Person Completing Care Planning Decision _____   4. ☐☐ — ☐☐ — ☐☐☐☐
   Month   Day   Year

MDS 2.0 September, 2000

Numeric Identifier _____

MDS QUARTERLY ASSESSMENT FORM

A1.	**RESIDENT NAME**	
		a. (First) b. (Middle Initial) c. (Last) d. (Jr/Sr)
A2.	**ROOM NUMBER**	
A3.	**ASSESS-MENT REFERENCE DATE**	a. Last day of MDS observation period
		☐☐ — ☐☐ — ☐☐☐☐ Month Day Year
		b. Original (0) or corrected copy of form (enter number of correction)
A4a	**DATE OF REENTRY**	Date of reentry from most recent temporary discharge to a hospital in last 90 days (or since last assessment or admission if less than 90 days)
		☐☐ — ☐☐ — ☐☐☐☐ Month Day Year
A6.	**MEDICAL RECORD NO.**	

B1.	**COMATOSE**	(Persistent vegetative state/no discernible consciousness) 0. No 1. Yes **(Skip to Section G)**
B2.	**MEMORY**	(Recall of what was learned or known) **a.** Short-term memory OK—seems/appears to recall after 5 minutes 0. Memory OK 1. Memory problem **b.** Long-term memory OK—seems/appears to recall long past 0. Memory OK 1. Memory problem
B4.	**COGNITIVE SKILLS FOR DAILY DECISION-MAKING**	(Made decisions regarding tasks of daily life) 0. INDEPENDENT—decisions consistent/reasonable 1. MODIFIED INDEPENDENCE—some difficulty in new situations only 2. MODERATELY IMPAIRED—decisions poor; cues/supervision required 3. SEVERELY IMPAIRED—never/rarely made decisions
B5.	**INDICATORS OF DELIRIUM—PERIODIC DISORDERED THINKING/ AWARENESS**	(Code for behavior in the last 7 days.) [Note: Accurate assessment requires conversations with staff and family who have direct knowledge of resident's behavior over this time]. 0. Behavior not present 1. Behavior present, not of recent onset 2. Behavior present, over last 7 days appears different from resident's usual functioning (e.g., new onset or worsening) **a.** EASILY DISTRACTED—(e.g., difficulty paying attention; gets sidetracked) **b.** PERIODS OF ALTERED PERCEPTION OR AWARENESS OF SURROUNDINGS—(e.g., moves lips or talks to someone not present; believes he/she is somewhere else; confuses night and day) **c.** EPISODES OF DISORGANIZED SPEECH—(e.g., speech is incoherent, nonsensical, irrelevant, or rambling from subject to subject; loses train of thought) **d.** PERIODS OF RESTLESSNESS—(e.g., fidgeting or picking at skin, clothing, napkins, etc; frequent position changes; repetitive physical movements or calling out) **e.** PERIODS OF LETHARGY—(e.g., sluggishness; staring into space; difficult to arouse; little body movement) **f.** MENTAL FUNCTION VARIES OVER THE COURSE OF THE DAY—(e.g., sometimes better, sometimes worse; behaviors sometimes present, sometimes not)
C4.	**MAKING SELF UNDER-STOOD**	(Expressing information content—however able) 0. UNDERSTOOD 1. USUALLY UNDERSTOOD—difficulty finding words or finishing thoughts 2. SOMETIMES UNDERSTOOD—ability is limited to making concrete requests 3. RARELY/NEVER UNDERSTOOD
C6.	**ABILITY TO UNDER-STAND OTHERS**	(Understanding verbal information content—however able) 0. UNDERSTANDS 1. USUALLY UNDERSTANDS—may miss some part/intent of message 2. SOMETIMES UNDERSTANDS—responds adequately to simple, direct communication 3. RARELY/NEVER UNDERSTANDS
E1.	**INDICATORS OF DEPRES-SION, ANXIETY, SAD MOOD**	(Code for indicators observed in last 30 days, irrespective of the assumed cause) 0. Indicator not exhibited in last 30 days 1. Indicator of this type exhibited up to five days a week 2. Indicator of this type exhibited daily or almost daily (6, 7 days a week) **VERBAL EXPRESSIONS OF DISTRESS** **a.** Resident made negative statements—e.g., "Nothing matters; Would rather be dead; What's the use; Regrets having lived so long; Let me die" **b.** Repetitive questions—e.g., "Where do I go; What do I do?" **c.** Repetitive verbalizations—e.g., calling out for help, ("God help me") **d.** Persistent anger with self or others—e.g., easily annoyed, anger at placement in nursing home; anger at care received **e.** Self deprecation—e.g., "I am nothing; I am of no use to anyone"

E1.	**INDICATORS OF DEPRES-SION, ANXIETY, SAD MOOD (cont.)**	**VERBAL EXPRESSIONS OF DISTRESS** **f.** Expressions of what appear to be unrealistic fears—e.g., fear of being abandoned, left alone, being with others **g.** Recurrent statements that something terrible is about to happen—e.g., believes he or she is about to die, have a heart attack **h.** Repetitive health complaints—e.g., persistently seeks medical attention, obsessive concern with body functions **i.** Repetitive anxious complaints/concerns (non-health related) e.g., persistently seeks attention/reassurance regarding schedules, meals, laundry, clothing, relationship issues **SLEEP-CYCLE ISSUES** **j.** Unpleasant mood in morning **k.** Insomnia/change in usual sleep pattern **SAD, APATHETIC, ANXIOUS APPEARANCE** **l.** Sad, pained, worried facial expressions—e.g., furrowed brows **m.** Crying, tearfulness **n.** Repetitive physical movements—e.g., pacing, hand wringing, restlessness, fidgeting, picking **LOSS OF INTEREST** **o.** Withdrawal from activities of interest—e.g., no interest in long standing activities or being with family/friends **p.** Reduced social interaction
E2.	**MOOD PERSIS-TENCE**	One or more indicators of depressed, sad or anxious mood were not easily altered by attempts to "cheer up", console, or reassure the resident over last 7 days 0. No mood indicators 1. Indicators present, easily altered 2. Indicators present, not easily altered
E4.	**BEHAVIORAL SYMPTOMS**	**(A) Behavioral symptom frequency in last 7 days** 0. Behavior not exhibited in last 7 days 1. Behavior of this type occurred 1 to 3 days in last 7 days 2. Behavior of this type occurred 4 to 6 days, but less than daily 3. Behavior of this type occurred daily **(B) Behavioral symptom alterability in last 7 days** 0. Behavior not present OR behavior was easily altered 1. Behavior was not easily altered (A) (B) **a.** WANDERING (moved with no rational purpose, seemingly oblivious to needs or safety) **b.** VERBALLY ABUSIVE BEHAVIORAL SYMPTOMS (others were threatened, screamed at, cursed at) **c.** PHYSICALLY ABUSIVE BEHAVIORAL SYMPTOMS (others were hit, shoved, scratched, sexually abused) **d.** SOCIALLY INAPPROPRIATE/DISRUPTIVE BEHAVIORAL SYMPTOMS (made disruptive sounds, noisiness, screaming, self-abusive acts, sexual behavior or disrobing in public, smeared/threw food/feces, hoarding, rummaged through others' belongings) **e.** RESISTS CARE (resisted taking medications/ injections, ADL assistance, or eating)
G1.	**(A) ADL SELF-PERFORMANCE**—(Code for resident's **PERFORMANCE OVER ALL SHIFTS during last 7 days**—Not including setup)	0. INDEPENDENT—No help or oversight —OR— Help/oversight provided only 1 or 2 times during last 7 days 1. SUPERVISION—Oversight, encouragement or cueing provided 3 or more times during last 7 days —OR— Supervision (3 or more times) plus physical assistance provided only 1 or 2 times during last 7 days 2. LIMITED ASSISTANCE—Resident highly involved in activity; received physical help in guided maneuvering of limbs or other nonweight bearing assistance 3 or more times — OR—More help provided only 1 or 2 times during last 7 days 3. EXTENSIVE ASSISTANCE—While resident performed part of activity, over last 7-day period, help of following type(s) provided 3 or more times: —Weight-bearing support —Full staff performance during part (but not all) of last 7 days 4. TOTAL DEPENDENCE—Full staff performance of activity during entire 7 days 8. ACTIVITY DID NOT OCCUR during entire 7 days (A)
	a. BED MOBILITY	How resident moves to and from lying position, turns side to side, and positions body while in bed
	b. TRANSFER	How resident moves between surfaces—to/from: bed, chair, wheelchair, standing position (EXCLUDE to/from bath/toilet)
	c. WALK IN ROOM	How resident walks between locations in his/her room.
	d. WALK IN CORRIDOR	How resident walks in corridor on unit.
	e. LOCOMO-TION ON UNIT	How resident moves between locations in his/her room and adjacent corridor on same floor. If in wheelchair, self-sufficiency once in chair
	f. LOCOMO-TION OFF UNIT	How resident moves to and returns from off unit locations (e.g., areas set aside for dining, activities, or treatments). If facility has only one floor, how resident moves to and from distant areas on the floor. If in wheelchair, self-sufficiency once in chair
	g. DRESSING	How resident puts on, fastens, and takes off all items of **street clothing,** including donning/removing prosthesis
	h. EATING	How resident eats and drinks (regardless of skill). Includes intake of nourishment by other means (e.g., tube feeding, total parenteral nutrition).

MDS 2.0 September, 2000

Resident_____   Numeric Identifier _____

i.	TOILET USE	How resident uses the toilet room (or commode, bedpan, urinal); transfer on/off toilet, cleanses, changes pad, manages ostomy or catheter, adjusts clothes
j.	PERSONAL HYGIENE	How resident maintains personal hygiene, including combing hair, brushing teeth, shaving, applying makeup, washing/drying face, hands, and perineum (EXCLUDE baths and showers)

G2.	BATHING	How resident takes full-body bath/shower, sponge bath, and transfers in/out of tub/shower (EXCLUDE washing of back and hair.) **Code for most dependent** in self-performance. **(A)** BATHING SELF-PERFORMANCE codes appear below **(A)** 0. Independent—No help provided 1. Supervision—Oversight help only 2. Physical help limited to transfer only 3. Physical help in part of bathing activity 4. Total dependence 8. Activity itself did not occur during entire 7 days

G4.	FUNCTIONAL LIMITATION IN RANGE OF MOTION	*(Code for limitations during **last 7 days** that interfered with daily functions or placed residents at risk of injury)* **(A)** RANGE OF MOTION **(B)** VOLUNTARY MOVEMENT 0. No limitation 0. No loss 1. Limitation on one side 1. Partial loss 2. Limitation on both sides 2. Full loss **(A) (B)** a. Neck b. Arm—Including shoulder or elbow c. Hand—Including wrist or fingers d. Leg—Including hip or knee e. Foot—Including ankle or toes f. Other limitation or loss

G6.	MODES OF TRANSFER	*(Check that apply during **last 7 days**)* Bedfast all or most of time a. NONE OF ABOVE f. Bed rails used for bed mobility or transfer b.

H1.	CONTINENCE SELF-CONTROL CATEGORIES **(Code for resident's PERFORMANCE OVER ALL SHIFTS)** 0. CONTINENT—Complete control *[includes use of indwelling urinary catheter or ostomy device that does not leak urine or stool]* 1. USUALLY CONTINENT—BLADDER, incontinent episodes once a week or less; BOWEL, less than weekly 2. OCCASIONALLY INCONTINENT—BLADDER, 2 or more times a week but not daily; BOWEL, once a week 3. FREQUENTLY INCONTINENT—BLADDER, tended to be incontinent daily, but some control present (e.g., on day shift); BOWEL, 2-3 times a week 4. INCONTINENT—Had inadequate control BLADDER, multiple daily episodes; BOWEL, all (or almost all) of the time

a.	BOWEL CONTI-NENCE	Control of bowel movement, with appliance or bowel continence programs, if employed
b.	BLADDER CONTI-NENCE	Control of urinary bladder function (if dribbles, volume insufficient to soak through underpants), with appliances (e.g., foley) or continence programs, if employed

H2.	BOWEL ELIMINATION PATTERN	Fecal impaction d. NONE OF ABOVE e.
H3.	APPLIANCES AND PROGRAMS	Any scheduled toileting plan a. Indwelling catheter d. Bladder retraining program b. Ostomy present i. External (condom) catheter c. NONE OF ABOVE j.
I2.	INFECTIONS	Urinary tract infection in **last 30 days** NONE OF ABOVE m.
I3.	OTHER CURRENT DIAGNOSES AND ICD-9 CODES	*(Include **only** those diseases diagnosed in the **last 90 days** that have a relationship to current ADL status, cognitive status, mood or behavior status, medical treatments, nursing monitoring, or risk of death)* a. _____ ||| • || b. _____ ||| • ||

J1.	PROBLEM CONDITIONS	*(Check all problems present in **last 7 days**)* Dehydrated; output exceeds input c. Hallucinations i. NONE OF ABOVE p.

J2.	PAIN SYMPTOMS	*(Code the **highest level** of pain present in the **last 7 days**)* **a. FREQUENCY** with which resident complains or shows evidence of pain 0. No pain *(**skip to** J4)* 1. Pain less than daily 2. Pain daily **b. INTENSITY** of pain 1. Mild pain 2. Moderate pain 3. Times when pain is horrible or excruciating

J4.	ACCIDENTS	*(Check all that apply)* Fell in **past 30 days** a. Hip fracture in **last 180 days** c. Fell in **past 31-180 days** b. Other fracture in **last 180 days** d. NONE OF ABOVE e.

J5.	STABILITY OF CONDITIONS	Conditions/diseases make resident's cognitive, ADL, mood or behavior status unstable—(fluctuating, precarious, or deteriorating) a. Resident experiencing an acute episode or a flare-up of a recurrent or chronic problem b. End-stage disease, 6 or fewer months to live c. NONE OF ABOVE d.

K3.	WEIGHT CHANGE	**a. Weight loss**—5 % or more in **last 30 days**; or 10 % or more in **last 180 days** 0. No 1. Yes **b. Weight gain**—5 % or more in **last 30 days**; or 10 % or more in **last 180 days** 0. No 1. Yes

K5.	NUTRI-TIONAL APPROACH-ES	Feeding tube b. On a planned weight change program h. NONE OF ABOVE i.

M1.	ULCERS (Due to any cause)	*(Record the number of ulcers at each ulcer stage—regardless of cause. If none present at a stage, record "0" (zero). Code all that apply during **last 7 days**. Code 9 = 9 or more.) [**Requires full body exam.**]* Number at Stage a. Stage 1. A persistent area of skin redness (without a break in the skin) that does not disappear when pressure is relieved. b. Stage 2. A partial thickness loss of skin layers that presents clinically as an abrasion, blister, or shallow crater. c. Stage 3. A full thickness of skin is lost, exposing the subcutaneous tissues - presents as a deep crater with or without undermining adjacent tissue. d. Stage 4. A full thickness of skin and subcutaneous tissue is lost, exposing muscle or bone.

M2.	TYPE OF ULCER	*(For each type of ulcer, **code for the highest stage in the last 7 days** using scale in item M1—i.e., 0=none; stages 1, 2, 3, 4)* a. Pressure ulcer—any lesion caused by pressure resulting in damage of underlying tissue b. Stasis ulcer—open lesion caused by poor circulation in the lower extremities

N1.	TIME AWAKE	*(Check appropriate time periods over **last 7 days**)* Resident awake all or most of time (i.e., naps no more than one hour per time period) in the: Morning a. Evening c. Afternoon b. NONE OF ABOVE d.

(If resident is comatose, skip to Section O)

N2.	AVERAGE TIME INVOLVED IN ACTIVITIES	**(When awake and not receiving treatments or ADL care)** 0. Most—more than 2/3 of time 2. Little—less than 1/3 of time 1. Some—from 1/3 to 2/3 of time 3. None
O1.	NUMBER OF MEDICA-TIONS	*(Record the number of **different** medications used in the **last 7 days**; enter "0" if none used)*
O4.	DAYS RECEIVED THE FOLLOWING MEDICATION	*(Record the number of DAYS during **last 7 days**; enter "0" if not used. Note—enter "1" for long-acting meds used less than weekly)* a. Antipsychotic d. Hypnotic b. Antianxiety e. Diuretic c. Antidepressant

P4.	DEVICES AND RESTRAINTS	Use the following codes for **last 7 days**: 0. Not used 1. Used less than daily 2. Used daily Bed rails a. — Full bed rails on all open sides of bed b. — Other types of side rails used (e.g., half rail, one side) c. Trunk restraint d. Limb restraint e. Chair prevents rising

Q2.	OVERALL CHANGE IN CARE NEEDS	Resident's overall level of self sufficiency has changed significantly as compared to status of **90 days ago** (or since last assessment if less than 90 days) 0. No change 1. Improved—receives fewer 2. Deteriorated—receives supports, needs less more support restrictive level of care

R2.	SIGNATURE OF PERSON COORDINATING THE ASSESSMENT:

a. Signature of RN Assessment Coordinator (sign on above line)

b. Date RN Assessment Coordinator signed as complete   \|\|\| — \|\| — \|\|\|\|
                                                   Month   Day   Year

Index

About the Author

Linda Connell received her undergraduate degree in psychology from the University of Illinois at Urbana, and her law degree from Notre Dame Law School. After law school, she worked as a municipal attorney, first in-house with the City of Joliet, and then in private practice in Chicago's western suburbs.

She eventually decided that she preferred legal research and writing to litigation, and an opportunity opened up on the editorial staff at a legal study aide organization. She worked there until shortly after she started her family, when she decided to go into business for herself as a freelance writer and editor.

Ms. Connell worked her way through school both as an activities assistant and as an administrative assistant at several Chicago area skilled care facilities. During this experience, Ms. Connell learned that life is not over for a person just because he or she lives in a nursing home. It fueled her desire to write a book about this subject. Ms. Connell has always wanted to write, and this was the perfect opportunity to combine her legal background with the career she wanted to pursue.

She currently lives with her family in the Chicago suburbs. *Nursing Homes and Assisted Living Facilities* is Ms. Connell's second book.

Your #1 Source for Real World Legal Information...

Sphinx® Publishing
An Imprint of Sourcebooks, Inc.®

- Written by lawyers • Simple English explanation of the law
  - Forms and instructions included

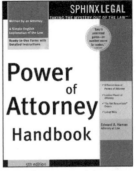

HOW TO WRITE YOUR OWN
LIVING WILL, 4E

POWER OF ATTORNEY HANDBOOK, 5E

Without a living will, doctors and hospitals may give you medical treatment you would not want at a time when you are unable to make your own choices known. This indispensible guide contains ready-to-use forms that are applicable in every state.

One out of every two Americans will suffer some type of long-term disability. *Power of Attorney Handbook* details what you need to know in a variety of power of attorney situations, including appropriate laws for all 50 states.

248 pages; $18.95;
ISBN 1-57248-233-8

344 pages; $22.95;
ISBN 1-57248-388-1

What our customers say about our books:

"It couldn't be more clear for the layperson." —R.D.

"I want you to know I really appreciate your book. It has saved me a lot of time and money." —L.T.

"Your real estate contracts book has saved me nearly $12,000.00 in closing costs over the past year." —A.B.

"...many of the legal questions that I have had over the years were answered clearly and concisely through your plain English interpretation of the law." —C.E.H.

"If there weren't people out there like you I'd be lost. You have the best books of this type out there." —S.B.

"...your forms and directions are easy to follow." —C.V.M.

Sphinx Publishing's Legal Survival Guides are directly available from Sourcebooks, Inc., or from your local bookstores.

*For credit card orders call 1–800–432-7444,
write P.O. Box 4410, Naperville, IL 60567-4410, or fax 630-961-2168*

SPHINX® PUBLISHING'S STATE TITLES
Up-to-Date for Your State

California Titles

CA Power of Attorney Handbook (2E)	$18.95
How to File for Divorce in CA (4E)	$26.95
How to Probate & Settle an Estate in CA	$26.95
How to Start a Business in CA (2E)	$21.95
How to Win in Small Claims Court in CA (2E)	$18.95
The Landlord's Legal Guide in CA (2E)	$24.95
Make Your Own CA Will	$18.95
Tenants' Rights in CA	$21.95

Florida Titles

Child Custody, Visitation and Support in FL	$26.95
How to File for Divorce in FL (8E)	$28.95
How to Form a Corporation in FL (6E)	$24.95
How to Form a Limited Liability Co. in FL (2E)	$24.95
How to Form a Partnership in FL	$22.95
How to Make a FL Will (6E)	$16.95
How to Probate and Settle an Estate in FL (5E)	$26.95
How to Start a Business in FL (7E)	$21.95
How to Win in Small Claims Court in FL (7E)	$18.95
Land Trusts in Florida (6E)	$29.95
Landlords' Rights and Duties in FL (9E)	$22.95

Georgia Titles

How to File for Divorce in GA (5E)	$21.95
How to Make a GA Will (4E)	$16.95
How to Start a Business in Georgia (3E)	$21.95

Illinois Titles

Child Custody, Visitation and Support in IL	$24.95
How to File for Divorce in IL (3E)	$24.95
How to Make an IL Will (3E)	$16.95
How to Start a Business in IL (3E)	$21.95
The Landlord's Legal Guide in IL	$24.95

Maryland, Virginia and the District of Columbia Titles

How to File for Divorce in MD, VA and DC	$28.95
How to Start a Business in MD, VA or DC	$21.95

Massachusetts Titles

How to Form a Corporation in MA	$24.95
How to Make a MA Will (2E)	$16.95
How to Start a Business in MA (3E)	$21.95
The Landlord's Legal Guide in MA (2E)	$24.95

Michigan Titles

How to File for Divorce in MI (3E)	$24.95
How to Make a MI Will (3E)	$16.95
How to Start a Business in MI (3E)	$18.95

Minnesota Titles

How to File for Divorce in MN $21.95
How to Form a Corporation in MN $24.95
How to Make a MN Will (2E) $16.95

New Jersey Titles

How to File for Divorce in NJ $24.95
How to Start a Business in NJ $21.95

New York Titles

Child Custody, Visitation and Support in NY $26.95
File for Divorce in NY $26.95
How to Form a Corporation in NY (2E) $24.95
How to Make a NY Will (3E) $16.95
How to Start a Business in NY (2E) $18.95
How to Win in Small Claims Court in NY (2E) $18.95
Landlords' Legal Guide in NY $24.95
New York Power of Attorney Handbook $19.95
Tenants' Rights in NY $21.95

North Carolina and South Carolina Titles

How to File for Divorce in NC (3E) $22.95
How to Make a NC Will (3E) $16.95
How to Start a Business in NC or SC $24.95
Landlords' Rights & Duties in NC $21.95

Ohio Titles

How to File for Divorce in OH (2E) $24.95
How to Form a Corporation in OH $24.95
How to Make an OH Will $16.95

Pennsylvania Titles

Child Custody, Visitation and Support in PA $26.95
How to File for Divorce in PA (3E) $26.95
How to Form a Corporation in PA $24.95
How to Make a PA Will (2E) $16.95
How to Start a Business in PA (3E) $21.95
The Landlord's Legal Guide in PA $24.95

Texas Titles

Child Custody, Visitation and Support in TX $22.95
How to File for Divorce in TX (4E) $24.95
How to Form a Corporation in TX (2E) $24.95
How to Make a TX Will (3E) $16.95
How to Probate and Settle an Estate in TX (3E) $26.95
How to Start a Business in TX (3E) $18.95
How to Win in Small Claims Court in TX (2E) $16.95
The Landlord's Legal Guide in TX $24.95

SPHINX® PUBLISHING'S NATIONAL TITLES
Valid in All 50 States

LEGAL SURVIVAL IN BUSINESS

The Complete Book of Corporate Forms	$24.95
The Complete Partnership Book	$24.95
The Complete Patent Book	$26.95
Employees' Rights	$18.95
Employer's Rights	$24.95
The Entrepreneur's Internet Handbook	$21.95
The Entrepreneur's Legal Guide	$26.95
How to Form a Limited Liability Company (2E)	$24.95
How to Form a Nonprofit Corporation (2E)	$24.95
How to Form Your Own Corporation (4E)	$26.95
How to Register Your Own Copyright (5E)	$24.95
How to Register Your Own Trademark (3E)	$21.95
Incorporate in Delaware from Any State	$26.95
Incorporate in Nevada from Any State	$24.95
The Law (In Plain English)® for Small Business	$19.95
Most Valuable Business Legal Forms You'll Ever Need (3E)	$21.95
Profit from Intellectual Property	$28.95
Protect Your Patent	$24.95
The Small Business Owner's Guide to Bankruptcy	$21.95
Tax Smarts for Small Business	$21.95

LEGAL SURVIVAL IN COURT

Attorney Responsibilities & Client Rights	$19.95
Crime Victim's Guide to Justice (2E)	$21.95
Grandparents' Rights (3E)	$24.95
Help Your Lawyer Win Your Case (2E)	$14.95
Legal Research Made Easy (3E)	$21.95
Winning Your Personal Injury Claim (2E)	$24.95

LEGAL SURVIVAL IN REAL ESTATE

The Complete Kit to Selling Your Own Home	$18.95
Essential Guide to Real Estate Contracts (2E)	$18.95
Essential Guide to Real Estate Leases	$18.95
Homeowner's Rights	$19.95
How to Buy a Condominium or Townhome (2E)	$19.95
How to Buy Your First Home	$18.95
Working with Your Homeowners Association	$19.95

LEGAL SURVIVAL IN SPANISH

Cómo Hacer su Propio Testamento	$16.95
Cómo Restablecer su propio Crédito y Renegociar sus Deudas	$21.95
Cómo Solicitar su Propio Divorcio	$24.95
Guía de Inmigración a Estados Unidos (3E)	$24.95
Guía de Justicia para Víctimas del Crimen	$21.95
Guía Esencial para los Contratos de Arrendamiento de Bienes Raices	$22.95
Inmigración y Ciudadanía en los EE. UU. Preguntas y Respuestas	$16.95
Inmigración a los EE. UU. Paso a Paso	$22.95
Manual de Beneficios para el Seguro Social	$18.95
El Seguro Social Preguntas y Respuestas	$16.95

LEGAL SURVIVAL IN PERSONAL AFFAIRS

101 Complaint Letters That Get Results	$18.95
The 529 College Savings Plan (2E)	$18.95
The Antique and Art Collector's Legal Guide	$24.95
The Complete Legal Guide to Senior Care	$21.95
Credit Smart	$18.95
Family Limited Partnership	$26.95
Gay & Lesbian Rights	$26.95
How to File Your Own Bankruptcy (5E)	$21.95
How to File Your Own Divorce (5E)	$26.95
How to Make Your Own Simple Will (3E)	$18.95
How to Write Your Own Living Will (4E)	$18.95
How to Write Your Own Premarital Agreement (3E)	$24.95
Law School 101	$16.95
Living Trusts and Other Ways to Avoid Probate (3E)	$24.95
Mastering the MBE	$16.95
Most Valuable Personal Legal Forms You'll Ever Need (2E)	$26.95
The Power of Attorney Handbook (5E)	$22.95
Repair Your Own Credit and Deal with Debt (2E)	$18.95
Quick Cash	$14.95
Sexual Harassment:Your Guide to Legal Action	$18.95
The Social Security Benefits Handbook (3E)	$18.95
Social Security Q&A	$12.95
Teen Rights	$22.95
Traveler's Rights	$21.95
Unmarried Parents' Rights (2E)	$19.95
U.S. Immigration and Citizenship Q&A	$18.95
U.S. Immigration Step by Step (2E)	$24.95
U.S.A. Immigration Guide (5E)	$26.95
The Visitation Handbook	$18.95
The Wills, Estate Planning and Trusts Legal Kit	&26.95
Win Your Unemployment Compensation Claim (2E)	$21.95
Your Right to Child Custody, Visitation and Support (3E)	$24.95

SPHINX® PUBLISHING ORDER FORM

BILL TO:				SHIP TO:		

Phone #		Terms	F.O.B.	Chicago, IL	Ship Date

Charge my: ☐ VISA ☐ MasterCard ☐ American Express   ☐ **Money Order or Personal Check**

Credit Card Number   Expiration Date

Qty	ISBN	Title	Retail	Qty	ISBN	Title	Retail
	SPHINX PUBLISHING NATIONAL TITLES				1-57248-158-7	Incorporate in Nevada from Any State	$24.95
	1-57248-363-6	101 Complaint Letters That Get Results	$18.95		1-57248-250-8	Inmigración a los EE.UU. Paso a Paso	$22.95
	1-57248-361-X	The 529 College Savings Plan (2E)	$18.95		1-57248-400-4	Inmigración y Ciudadanía en los EE. UU.	$16.95
	1-57248-349-0	The Antique and Art Collector's Legal Guide	$24.95			Preguntas y Respuestas	
	1-57248-347-4	Attorney Responsibilities & Client Rights	$19.95		1-57248-377-6	The Law (In Plain English)® for Small Business	$19.95
	1-57248-148-X	Cómo Hacer su Propio Testamento	$16.95		1-57248-374-1	Law School 101	$16.95
	1-57248-226-5	Cómo Restablecer su propio Crédito y	$21.95		1-57248-223-0	Legal Research Made Easy (3E)	$21.95
		Renegociar sus Deudas			1-57248-165-X	Living Trusts and Other Ways to	$24.95
	1-57248-147-1	Cómo Solicitar su Propio Divorcio	$24.95			Avoid Probate (3E)	
	1-57248-166-8	The Complete Book of Corporate Forms	$24.95		1-57248-186-2	Manual de Beneficios para el Seguro Social	$18.95
	1-57248-353-9	The Complete Kit to Selling Your Own Home	$18.95		1-57248-220-6	Mastering the MBE	$16.95
	1-57248-229-X	The Complete Legal Guide to Senior Care	$21.95		1-57248-167-6	Most Val. Business Legal Forms	$21.95
	1-57248-391-1	The Complete Partnership Book	$24.95			You'll Ever Need (3E)	
	1-57248-201-X	The Complete Patent Book	$26.95		1-57248-360-1	Most Val. Personal Legal Forms	$26.95
	1-57248-369-5	Credit Smart	$18.95			You'll Ever Need (2E)	
	1-57248-163-3	Crime Victim's Guide to Justice (2E)	$21.95		1-57248-388-1	The Power of Attorney Handbook (5E)	$22.95
	1-57248-367-9	Employees' Rights	$18.95		1-57248-332-6	Profit from Intellectual Property	$28.95
	1-57248-365-2	Employer's Rights	$24.95		1-57248-329-6	Protect Your Patent	$24.95
	1-57248-251-6	The Entrepreneur's Internet Handbook	$21.95		1-57248-385-7	Quick Cash	$14.95
	1-57248-235-4	The Entrepreneur's Legal Guide	$26.95		1-57248-344-X	Repair Your Own Credit and Deal with Debt (2E)	$18.95
	1-57248-346-6	Essential Guide to Real Estate Contracts (2E)	$18.95		1-57248-350-4	El Seguro Social Preguntas y Respuestas	$16.95
	1-57248-160-9	Essential Guide to Real Estate Leases	$18.95		1-57248-217-6	Sexual Harassment: Your Guide to Legal Action	$18.95
	1-57248-254-0	Family Limited Partnership	$26.95		1-57248-219-2	The Small Business Owner's Guide to Bankruptcy	$21.95
	1-57248-331-8	Gay & Lesbian Rights	$26.95		1-57248-168-4	The Social Security Benefits Handbook (3E)	$18.95
	1-57248-139-0	Grandparents' Rights (3E)	$24.95		1-57248-216-8	Social Security Q&A	$12.95
	1-57248-188-9	Guía de Inmigración a Estados Unidos (3E)	$24.95		1-57248-221-4	Teen Rights	$22.95
	1-57248-187-0	Guía de Justicia para Víctimas del Crimen	$21.95		1-57248-366-0	Tax Smarts for Small Business	$21.95
	1-57248-253-2	Guía Esencial para los Contratos de	$22.95		1-57248-335-0	Traveler's Rights	$21.95
		Arrendamiento de Bienes Raíces			1-57248-236-2	Unmarried Parents' Rights (2E)	$19.95
	1-57248-103-X	Help Your Lawyer Win Your Case (2E)	$14.95		1-57248-362-8	U.S. Immigration and Citizenship Q&A	$18.95
	1-57248-334-2	Homeowner's Rights	$19.95		1-57248-387-3	U.S. Immigration Step by Step (2E)	$24.95
	1-57248-164-1	How to Buy a Condominium or Townhome (2E)	$19.95		1-57248-392-X	U.S.A. Immigration Guide (5E)	$26.95
	1-57248-328-8	How to Buy Your First Home	$18.95		1-57248-192-7	The Visitation Handbook	$18.95
	1-57248-191-9	How to File Your Own Bankruptcy (5E)	$21.95		1-57248-225-7	Win Your Unemployment	$21.95
	1-57248-343-1	How to File Your Own Divorce (5E)	$26.95			Compensation Claim (2E)	
	1-57248-222-2	How to Form a Limited Liability Company (2E)	$24.95		1-57248-330-X	The Wills, Estate Planning and Trusts Legal Kit	$26.95
	1-57248-231-1	How to Form a Nonprofit Corporation (2E)	$24.95		1-57248-138-2	Winning Your Personal Injury Claim (2E)	$24.95
	1-57248-345-8	How to Form Your Own Corporation (4E)	$26.95		1-57248-333-4	Working with Your Homeowners Association	$19.95
	1-57248-232-X	How to Make Your Own Simple Will (3E)	$18.95		1-57248-380-6	Your Right to Child Custody,	$24.95
	1-57248-379-2	How to Register Your Own Copyright (5E)	$24.95			Visitation and Support (3E)	
	1-57248-104-8	How to Register Your Own Trademark (3E)	$21.95				
	1-57248-394-6	How to Write Your Own Living Will (4E)	$18.95			**Form Continued on Following Page** **SubTotal_____**	
	1-57248-156-0	How to Write Your Own	$24.95				
		Premarital Agreement (3E)					
	1-57248-230-3	Incorporate in Delaware from Any State	$26.95				

Qty	ISBN	Title	Retail
		CALIFORNIA TITLES	
____	1-57248-150-1	CA Power of Attorney Handbook (2E)	$18.95
____	1-57248-337-7	How to File for Divorce in CA (4E)	$26.95
____	1-57248-145-5	How to Probate and Settle an Estate in CA	$26.95
____	1-57248-336-9	How to Start a Business in CA (2E)	$21.95
____	1-57248-194-3	How to Win in Small Claims Court in CA (2E)	$18.95
____	1-57248-246-X	Make Your Own CA Will	$18.95
____	1-57248-397-0	The Landlord's Legal Guide in CA (2E)	$24.95
____	1-57248-241-9	Tenants' Rights in CA	$21.95
		FLORIDA TITLES	
____	1-57071-363-4	Florida Power of Attorney Handbook (2E)	$16.95
____	1-57248-396-2	How to File for Divorce in FL (8E)	$28.95
____	1-57248-356-3	How to Form a Corporation in FL (6E)	$24.95
____	1-57248-203-6	How to Form a Limited Liability Co. in FL (2E)	$24.95
____	1-57071-401-0	How to Form a Partnership in FL	$22.95
____	1-57248-113-7	How to Make a FL Will (6E)	$16.95
____	1-57248-088-2	How to Modify Your FL Divorce Judgment (4E)	$24.95
____	1-57248-354-7	How to Probate and Settle an Estate in FL (5E)	$26.95
____	1-57248-339-3	How to Start a Business in FL (7E)	$21.95
____	1-57248-204-4	How to Win in Small Claims Court in FL (7E)	$18.95
____	1-57248-381-4	Land Trusts in Florida (7E)	$29.95
____	1-57248-338-5	Landlords' Rights and Duties in FL (9E)	$22.95
		GEORGIA TITLES	
____	1-57248-340-7	How to File for Divorce in GA (5E)	$21.95
____	1-57248-180-3	How to Make a GA Will (4E)	$16.95
____	1-57248-341-5	How to Start a Business in Georgia (3E)	$21.95
		ILLINOIS TITLES	
____	1-57248-244-3	Child Custody, Visitation, and Support in IL	$24.95
____	1-57248-206-0	How to File for Divorce in IL (3E)	$24.95
____	1-57248-170-6	How to Make an IL Will (3E)	$16.95
____	1-57248-247-8	How to Start a Business in IL (3E)	$21.95
____	1-57248-252-4	The Landlord's Legal Guide in IL	$24.95
		MARYLAND, VIRGINIA AND THE DISTRICT OF COLUMBIA	
____	1-57248-240-0	How to File for Divorce in MD, VA and DC	$28.95
____	1-57248-359-8	How to Start a Business in MD, VA or DC	$21.95
		MASSACHUSETTS TITLES	
____	1-57248-128-5	How to File for Divorce in MA (3E)	$24.95
____	1-57248-115-3	How to Form a Corporation in MA	$24.95
____	1-57248-108-0	How to Make a MA Will (2E)	$16.95
____	1-57248-248-6	How to Start a Business in MA (3E)	$21.95
____	1-57248-398-9	The Landlord's Legal Guide in MA (2E)	$24.95
		MICHIGAN TITLES	
____	1-57248-215-X	How to File for Divorce in MI (3E)	$24.95
____	1-57248-182-X	How to Make a MI Will (3E)	$16.95
____	1-57248-183-8	How to Start a Business in MI (3E)	$18.95
		MINNESOTA TITLES	
____	1-57248-142-0	How to File for Divorce in MN	$21.95
____	1-57248-179-X	How to Form a Corporation in MN	$24.95
____	1-57248-178-1	How to Make a MN Will (2E)	$16.95
		NEW JERSEY TITLES	
____	1-57248-239-7	How to File for Divorce in NJ	$24.95
____	1-57248-448-9	How to Start a Business in NJ	$21.95

Qty	ISBN	Title	Retail
		NEW YORK TITLES	
____	1-57248-193-5	Child Custody, Visitation and Support in NY	$26.95
____	1-57248-351-2	File for Divorce in NY	$26.95
____	1-57248-249-4	How to Form a Corporation in NY (2E)	$24.95
____	1-57248-401-2	How to Make a NY Will (3E)	$16.95
____	1-57248-199-4	How to Start a Business in NY (2E)	$18.95
____	1-57248-198-6	How to Win in Small Claims Court in NY (2E)	$18.95
____	1-57248-197-8	Landlords' Legal Guide in NY	$24.95
____	1-57071-188-7	New York Power of Attorney Handbook	$19.95
____	1-57248-122-6	Tenants' Rights in NY	$21.95
		NORTH CAROLINA AND SOUTH CAROLINA TITLES	
____	1-57248-185-4	How to File for Divorce in NC (3E)	$22.95
____	1-57248-129-3	How to Make a NC Will (3E)	$16.95
____	1-57248-371-7	How to Start a Business in NC or SC	$24.95
____	1-57248-091-2	Landlords' Rights & Duties in NC	$21.95
		OHIO TITLES	
____	1-57248-190-0	How to File for Divorce in OH (2E)	$24.95
____	1-57248-174-9	How to Form a Corporation in OH	$24.95
____	1-57248-173-0	How to Make an OH Will	$16.95
		PENNSYLVANIA TITLES	
____	1-57248-242-7	Child Custody, Visitation and Support in PA	$26.95
____	1-57248-211-7	How to File for Divorce in PA (3E)	$26.95
____	1-57248-358-X	How to Form a Corporation in PA	$24.95
____	1-57248-094-7	How to Make a PA Will (2E)	$16.95
____	1-57248-357-1	How to Start a Business in PA (3E)	$21.95
____	1-57248-245-1	The Landlord's Legal Guide in PA	$24.95
		TEXAS TITLES	
____	1-57248-171-4	Child Custody, Visitation, and Support in TX	$22.95
____	1-57248-399-7	How to File for Divorce in TX (4E)	$24.95
____	1-57248-114-5	How to Form a Corporation in TX (2E)	$24.95
____	1-57248-255-9	How to Make a TX Will (3E)	$16.95
____	1-57248-214-1	How to Probate and Settle an Estate in TX (3E)	$26.95
____	1-57248-228-1	How to Start a Business in TX (3E)	$18.95
____	1-57248-111-0	How to Win in Small Claims Court in TX (2E)	$16.95
____	1-57248-355-5	The Landlord's Legal Guide in TX	$24.95

SubTotal This page _____

SubTotal previous page _____

Shipping— $5.00 for 1st book, $1.00 each additional _____

Illinois residents add 6.75% sales tax _____

Connecticut residents add 6.00% sales tax _____

Total _____